when

the state

kills

when

CAPITAL PUNISHMENT AND

the state

THE AMERICAN CONDITION

kills

by Austin Sarat

PRINCETON UNIVERSITY PRESS · PRINCETON AND OXFORD

Copyright © 2001 by Princeton University Press
Published by Princeton University Press, 41 William Street,
Princeton, New Jersey 08540
In the United Kingdom: Princeton University Press,
3 Market Place, Woodstock, Oxfordshire OX20 1SY

Library of Congress Cataloging-in-Publication Data

Sarat, Austin.
When the state kills : capital punishment and the American
condition / Austin Sarat.
p. cm.
Includes bibliographical references and index.
ISBN 0-691-00726-8 (alk. paper)
1. Capital punishment—United States. I. Title.
HV8699.U5 S27 2001
364.66′0973—dc21   00-059862

This book has been composed in Trump and American Type-
writer Typefaces

The paper used in this publication meets the minimum
requirements of ANSI/NISO Z39.48-1992 (R1997)
(*Permanence of Paper*)

www.pup.princeton.edu

Printed in the United States of America

10   9   8   7   6   5   4   3   2   1

TO MY SON,

BENJAMIN,

WITH JOY,

GRATITUDE,

AND HOPE

CONTENTS

ACKNOWLEDGMENTS

My writing has been nurtured by political commitment and the hope that scholarship of the kind represented here can help make a difference in changing the way Americans think about the death penalty. I am deeply grateful to those whose words are recorded in these pages, especially the death penalty lawyers and capital jurors who shared their experiences and perspectives with me. Among them, I would like to extend a special thanks to Stephen Bright, Steve Hawkins, David Bruck, and Bryan Stevenson. Their efforts to end state killing deserve our deepest admiration.

This book also reflects my belief that the time is now right for students of state killing to take advantage of insights available in various forms of interdisciplinary legal scholarship, in particular the cultural analysis of law, and that such scholarship is enriched when it encounters the harsh realities of capital punishment in the United States. I have been fortunate to work in environments where that belief has been encouraged, namely Amherst College's Department of Law, Jurisprudence, and Social Thought and the Law and Society Association.

I am grateful to many friends, colleagues, and collaborators for their generous help. Thomas Dumm has been a constant and inspiring intellectual companion. His energy and imagination enrich my work. George Kateb, a great teacher, scholar, and friend, shared with me his passion and clarity in thinking about state killing. Martha Umphrey's excellence as reader and critic as well as the keen intelligence and high standards of Marianne Constable did much to strengthen the argument of this book. Stuart

Scheingold's innovative work on the politics of crime and justice has been influential in shaping my understanding of capital punishment while Patricia Ewick's insightful analysis highlighted possibilities I would otherwise have neglected. Nasser Hussain, always generous with his praise, asked hard but helpful questions.

Others read and provided valuable suggestions on drafts of individual chapters or of the entire manuscript: Amrita Basu, Bill Bowers, Robert Burt, Carol Clover, Lawrence Douglas, Carol Greenhouse, Joel Handler, Sally Merry, Richard Moran, Frank Munger, Lauren Sarat, and Susan Silbey. I am grateful to each of them. My work has also benefited greatly from the scholarship of, and conversations with, Jennifer Culbert, Peter Fitzpatrick, Mona Lynch, Martha Minow, Jonathan Simon, and Alison Young.

I am grateful to the Capital Jury Project and to a former student, Aaron Schuster, my coauthor on an earlier version of what is now chapter 8 in this book. Three other former students, Roger Berkowitz, Cliff Rosky, and Shannon Selden, were helpful interlocutors as I worked on this project. Over several years, I tried out my arguments in different venues, including Queen Mary and Westfield College; the Harry Frank Guggenheim Conference on Revenge, Madrid, Spain; the School of Justice Studies at Arizona State University; the Faculty Workshop on Social and Political Thought at Columbia University; the National Conference on Juries and the Death Penalty at the Indiana University School of Law; the conference on Political Lawyering: Conversations on Progressive Social Change at Harvard Law School; and at various annual meetings of the Law and Society Association. Late in the project I organized a conference entitled Capital Punishment in Law and Culture, which eventuated in an edited collection: *The Killing State: Capital Punishment in Law, Politics, and Culture* (1999). That conference reaffirmed my belief in the importance of exploring the cultural life of capital punishment. I appreciate the responses, criticism, and inspiration received from the participants in all these events.

I want to thank my editors at Princeton, Malcolm Litchfield and Ian Malcolm, for their interest and support. Malcolm signed the book and believed in what I was doing from the very beginning. When he left PUP, Ian took over, providing incisive and helpful comments, skillfully combining encouraging praise and thoughtful criticism with wonderful editorial judgment.

Financial support for my work has been provided by the Amherst College Faculty Research Award Program and, for the research discussed in chapter 5, the Law and Social Sciences Program of the National Science Foundation, grant NSF SES-9013252. I want to thank the Dean of the Faculty at Amherst, Lisa Raskin, for her support and generosity.

My greatest debt is to my family for its unfailing love and loyalty. Let me say here, in but a few words, what I hope they all already know. Thanks to my aunts Irene Cohen and Rose Sock for combining lively minds and loving hearts. Thanks to my daughters, Lauren and Emily, for being two of my most important teachers and to my son Benjamin, who has brought so much happiness into my life. And thanks, most of all, to Stephanie Sandler, who sustains me and gives me hope.

Parts of this book have previously appeared in different forms elsewhere and are used here with permission. Chapter 2 is a revised version of "Vengeance, Victims and the Identities of Law." *Social & Legal Studies: An Interdisciplinary Journal* 6 (1997): 163–90 (© by Sage Publications, Ltd.). Chapter 3 was previously published as "Killing Me Softly: On the Technologies of Taking Life," in Desmond Manderson, ed., *Courting Death: The Legal Constitution of Mortality* (© 1999 by Pluto Press). Chapter 4 first appeared as "Speaking of Death: Narratives of Violence in Capital Trials," *Law & Society Review* 27 (1993): 19–58 (© by Law and Society Association). Chapter 5 includes portions of "Violence, Representation, and Responsibility in Capital Trials: The View from the Jury," *Indiana Law Journal* 70 (1995): 1103–36 (© by *Indiana Law Journal*) and of "Folk Knowledge as Legal Action: Death Penalty Judgments and the Tenet of Early Release in a Culture of Mistrust and Punitiveness," *Law & Society Review* 33 (1999): 461–506, with Benjamin Steiner and William Bowers (© by Law and Society Association). Chapter 6 was published as

"Narrative Strategy and Death Penalty Advocacy," *Harvard Civil Rights–Civil Liberties Law Review* 31 (1996): 353–82 (© by *Harvard Civil Rights–Civil Liberties Law Review*). Chapter 7 originally appeared as "To See or Not to See: Television, Capital Punishment, and Law's Violence," *Yale Journal of Law & the Humanities* 7 (1995): 397–432, with Aaron Schuster (© *Yale Journal of Law & the Humanities*). Chapter 8 is a revised version of "The Cultural Life of Capital Punishment: Responsibility and Representation in *Dead Man Walking* and *Last Dance*," *Yale Journal of Law & the Humanities* 11 (1999): 153–90 (© by *Yale Journal of Law & the Humanities*). Chapter 9 is taken from "Recapturing the Spirit of *Furman*: The American Bar Association and the New Abolitionist Politics," *Law and Contemporary Problems* 61 (1998): 5–24 (© by *Law and Contemporary Problems*).

Photo of firefighter with baby courtesy Charles Porter/Corbis Sygma. Photo of Timothy McVeigh courtesy AP/Wide World Photos.

when

the state

kills

1

INTRODUCTION:

"IF TIMOTHY MCVEIGH DOESN'T DESERVE

TO DIE, WHO DOES?"

> *Political power . . . I take to be the right of making*
> *laws with the penalty of death.*
> —JOHN LOCKE, *Second Treatise of Government*

Monstrous Deeds, Cold-Blooded Killers, and the
Politics of Capital Punishment

April 19, 1995, was a bright, clear, spring day in Oklahoma City, the kind that refreshes and uplifts and makes doing the mundane tasks of daily life seem almost effortless. Early that morning Sharon and Claude Medearis woke up to their normal routine. Over coffee, they talked about Claude's plans for the day: a trip to El Paso after a stop at the office downtown, where he worked for the United States Customs Service. After breakfast, Sharon gave him a kiss good-bye and saw him off to work. Elsewhere in town, Bob Westberry and his wife Mathilda started the morning more sadly, remembering that the next day would mark the seventh anniversary of their oldest daughter's death. With that somber thought in the background, Bob went to work at the Defense Investigative Service downtown. About the same time, Linda Florence, mother of eighteen-month-old son Tray, left for her job as a secretary at the Oklahoma City office of the Department of Housing and Urban Development. At roughly the time she arrived, one-year-old Erin Langer was dropped off by her father at the America's Kids day care center.

Bob Westberry, Claude Medearis, Linda Florence, and Erin Langer never returned to their homes or loved ones. At 9:02 A.M. on that April morning they and 164 others were killed by a massive explosion that gutted the Alfred Murrah Federal Building. Investigators quickly determined that the explosion was caused by a powerful bomb. Suspicion first focused on overseas groups. Was the bombing the work of Arab terrorists, striking deep in America's heartland? As the *New York Times* reported, "So far no conclusive evidence has emerged that Arabs played any role in the bombing. Indeed, Federal officials have described the two known suspects as 'white,' a racial designation that seems to leave open their ethnic origin. Yet the speculation of Muslim involvement continues, fed by some news reports that have not been confirmed."[1] That speculation proved unfounded when, three days after the bombing, Timothy McVeigh was arrested and charged with murder in the worst act of domestic terrorism in the history of the United States.

Two images, broadcast widely and repeatedly to the nation and the world, provided the frame within which many came to think about the bombing and its perpetrator. The first, a photograph of a firefighter tenderly carrying the lifeless body of one-year-old Baylee Almon from the charred ruins of the Murrah building, captured the depth of McVeigh's monstrous deed. This act took lives indiscriminately, killing innocent children. The photograph invited the question, "What kind of person could commit such a crime?" (see Figure 1).

The second photograph gave us an answer. The initial glimpse of McVeigh came as he was being escorted out of the Noble

County Courthouse in Perry, Oklahoma, where he was held prior to his arraignment in Oklahoma City. We saw McVeigh, dressed in an orange prison jumpsuit, in handcuffs and leg irons, surrounded by people wearing FBI jackets. Confronted by a crowd of angry citizens, McVeigh, his demeanor steely stern, showed no emotion (see Figure 2). He quickly became the personification of the cold-blooded killer, a living, breathing endorsement of capital punishment.

No sooner had the dust settled at the site of the bombing than the politics of capital punishment began. Newspapers across the country reported President Clinton's first comments, "Let there be no room for doubt. We will find the people who did this. When we do, justice will be swift, certain and severe. These people are killers, and they must be treated like killers."[2] Joining the president, Attorney General Janet Reno added, "We cannot tell how long it will be before we can say with certainty what occurred and who is responsible, but we will find the perpetrators and bring them to justice." Without waiting for the detailed internal case-by-case review mandated by Justice Department procedures, Reno made clear her view of what justice required. She told the press "Eighteen U.S.C., Section 844, relates to those who maliciously damage or destroy a Federal building. If there is a death, if death occurs, the death penalty is available, and we will seek it."[3] A day later the attorney general said of the then still unknown perpetrators, "We will find them, we will convict them, and we will seek the death penalty against them."[4]

Ordinary citizens also took up this equation of justice with state killing. "His children should be shot," someone shouted from a crowd of several hundred who had gathered outside the Noble County Courthouse to see McVeigh. As one man who witnessed this scene later explained to a reporter, "They should give him a taste of his own medicine and put him inside a bomb and blow it up."[5] Two years later, as McVeigh's trial unfolded, a *USA Today*/CNN/Gallup poll reported that 61 percent of Americans thought that McVeigh should get the death penalty.[6] Yet commentators also noted that "an overwhelming percentage of

Americans feel that executing McVeigh is simply not enough. The law's prescribed punishment satisfies neither our sense of justice nor does it requite our desire for vengeance." [7]

McVeigh on Trial

Not surprisingly, the McVeigh trial was extraordinary. In response to the anticipated difficulty of finding an unbiased jury in Oklahoma, it was moved to Denver. Coming in the wake of other sensational trials, including the O. J. Simpson case, the presiding judge, Richard Matsch, refused to allow this trial to be televised and imposed a gag order limiting what participants in the case could say to the press. Nevertheless, in a move indicative of the increasing power of the victims' rights movement in the United States, the judge made special arrangements for a closed-circuit broadcast of the trial to victims and survivors in Oklahoma City.

A team of experienced and respected federal prosecutors was assembled to handle the case against McVeigh, who was charged in an eleven-count indictment for murder and conspiracy. An equally talented and respected group of six attorneys—headed by Stephen Jones—defended him. Jury selection began on March 31, 1997, and took nearly a month. Yet the trial itself was conducted expeditiously.

As the government's case proceeded, prosecutors called people close to McVeigh to testify against him. Witnesses revealed that he had divulged detailed plans to bomb the Murrah Building months before the attack and had devoured the antigovernment novel, *The Turner Diaries*, which describes the destruction of a federal building as a way to spark a civil war. The government also produced rental documents, phone records, and witnesses who identified him as the man who rented the Ryder truck used in the bombing under the alias Robert Kling. Other evidence pointed to McVeigh's efforts to buy and steal bomb-making supplies. The defense countered by trying to show that McVeigh was swept up in a rush to judgment and that the government's case was based on the testimony of lying, opportunist witnesses, and scientific evidence tainted by FBI mishandling and lab contamination.

The jury deliberated for more than twenty-three hours over four days before finding McVeigh guilty on all counts of the original indictment. President Clinton, again signaling the importance of victims in the politics of crime and punishment, immediately hailed the verdict as a "long overdue day for the survivors and the families of those who died in Oklahoma City."[8] Many of those survivors and families remained focused on ensuring that McVeigh was sentenced to death. "Jannie Coverdale, who lost two young grandsons in the bombing, confessed that she felt mixed emotions.'This is bittersweet,' she said. 'After all, this is a young man who has wasted his life. I'm glad they found him guilty, but I'm sad for him, too. I feel sorry for him. He had so much to offer his country.' She added, 'I want him to get the death penalty, but not out of revenge. It's necessary. I haven't seen any remorse from Timothy McVeigh. If he ever walked the streets, he would murder again. I don't want to see that.'"[9] Others who were less ambivalent also focused on the issue of capital punishment. "'He's not human,' said Charles Tomlin, who lost a grown son in the bombing. 'This is a monster that blew up a building.' Peggy Broxterman, who listened to the verdict in an auxiliary courtroom, called it an 'absolute thrill,' but said vindication for the death of her 43-year-old son and others wasn't complete.'It's not over until he's dead,' she said."[10]

After McVeigh's conviction, his trial entered the so-called penalty phase in which the jury that had convicted him was asked to decide on his sentence. In the federal system, during the penalty phase the jury is presented with aggravating and mitigating factors on the question of execution. If it decides on the death penalty, the judge cannot overrule its decision. As the trial entered the penalty phase the key question was what role the survivors and the families of those killed would play. How much of their stories would they be allowed to tell and with what level of detail?

Responding to defense motions, Judge Matsch barred prosecutors from presenting victims' wedding photos, a poem by a victim's father, and testimony on funeral arrangements. He also ex-

cluded testimony about how relatives identified victims, a video
of a routine day at a credit union office in the Alfred P. Murrah
Federal Building, and testimony about a mourning ceremony outside the building by one family. "We have to guard this hearing
to ensure that the ultimate result and the jury's decision is truly
a moral response to appropriate information rather than an emotional response," said Matsch.[11] While acknowledging that it is
natural to feel anger at such a horrible crime and empathy with
its victims, he reminded jurors that the purpose of the sentencing
trial was not to "seek revenge against Timothy McVeigh."[12] This
admonition did not sit well with some of the victims. For example, Roy Sells, whose wife was killed in the explosion, explained
"It's revenge for me. It's very simple. Look at what he's done.
Could anyone deserve to die more?"[13]

The judge did allow the testimony of a ten-year-old boy whose
mother died and a rescuer who held a hand buried in the rubble,
only to feel the pulse stop. Matsch also admitted photos of
maimed survivors; pictures of victims being wheeled into hospi-
tals; and testimony from the coroner about the various causes of
death, including that of a man who died slowly, as the presence
of gravel in his lungs revealed. "We can't sanitize this scene,"
Matsch noted. But "the penalty phase hearing here cannot be
turned into some type of a lynching."[14]

In fact, prosecutors called thirty-eight witnesses, twenty-six
relatives of those who were killed, three injured survivors, one
employee of the day care center, and eight rescue or medical
workers, each of whom described how the bombing physically
and emotionally devastated their lives. The penalty phase of the
trial was dominated by this victim impact testimony.[15] The prosecution urged that jurors not think of what happened in Oklahoma
City as "mass murder. . . . There are 168 people, all unique, all
individual. . . . All had families, all had friends, and they're different."[16] The prosecution claimed that McVeigh "knew exactly
what the effects of this bomb were going to be," and that he "intended to see blood flow in the streets."[17]

The prosecution closed its case by calling one last family member of a victim of the bombing. Glenn A. Seidl testified about the

death of his wife, Kathy, who was an investigative assistant at the Secret Service Office in the Murrah Building, and the impact it had on him and his nine-year-old son, Clint. "I deal with Clint's hurt all the time," he said.

> I mean, it's—I mean, he's a normal boy. We try to live a normal life, but I'm always reminded this isn't a normal situation. Clint's eighth birthday, we had a big birthday party, Grandma and Grandpa, aunts and uncles. And after everybody left, Clint climbed up on my lap and started crying. And he asked me—he said, "Do you think my mom loved me?" And I said, "Well, your mom loves you more than anything in the world." And he said, "Why isn't she here."[18]

Seidl ended his testimony by reading a letter from Clint. "I miss my Mom, we used to go for walks," the nine-year-old's letter said. "She would read to me. We would go to Wal-Mart. . . . Sometimes at school around the holidays I will still make my Mother's Day and Valentine's Day cards like the other kids."[19]

McVeigh's defense sought to turn the penalty phase into a trial of the government's handling of the siege at the Branch Davidian compound near Waco, Texas, in 1992, some five years earlier. Eschewing the usual strategy that focuses on distinctive personal circumstances in the defendant's background—physical abuse and neglect, for example—McVeigh's defense portrayed him as an average American child, a patriotic war veteran whose life was radically changed by the fiery climax of the standoff at Waco. "You'll see how the fire of Waco continued to burn in Mr. McVeigh," said Richard Burr, one of the nation's foremost death penalty lawyers and leader of the defense in the penalty phase.[20]

In his opening statement he argued that the case was rooted in McVeigh's beliefs that the eighty cultists who died at the Branch Davidian compound were murdered by the federal government. "He is at the middle of this," Burr said. "There is violence at both ends, there is much death, there is tremendous suffering, but there is also a person at the center who you will not be able to dismiss easily as a monster or a demon, who could be your son, who could be your brother, who could be your grandson."

To ensure that the jury could not dismiss or demonize McVeigh, the defense called more than twenty witnesses from McVeigh's past, including family, friends, neighbors, teachers, co-workers, and a woman who "loved him like a brother." Four officers who knew McVeigh in the Army testified that the convicted terrorist had been an exemplary soldier who stood far above his peers. Jurors also were shown an hour-long videotape titled *Day 51: The True Story of Waco.* It depicted the Davidians as an innocent Bible study group purposely slaughtered by government agents after a fifty-one-day standoff. Reminiscent of the video jurors saw earlier of the building McVeigh destroyed, the tape showed the Davidian compound in flames, panning to a doll left in the rubble.

The defense concluded its effort to save McVeigh's life by presenting testimony from his parents. The defendant's father showed a twelve-minute video he made about his son's life, including footage from old home movies and photographs of a young, happy Timothy McVeigh and his family. Calling him "Timmy," the elder McVeigh recounted his son's life in the small towns of Lockport and Pendleton, New York. The tape included footage from Halloweens and Christmases of Timothy McVeigh's childhood, and typical fatherly remarks, such as a comment by the elder McVeigh that his son "was a good student, although he never got the grades I thought he was capable of."

He told the jury that after a stint in the military including meritorious service in the Persian Gulf War, Timothy McVeigh returned home in 1991. "He seemed to be happy." The defense then showed jurors a photo of the father and son, smiling, their arms wrapped around one another. "To me, it's a happy Tim. It's the Tim I remember most in my life," William McVeigh noted. The father concluded his testimony by saying he loved "the Tim in this courtroom" and wanted him to stay alive.

McVeigh's mother testified that she "still can't believe to this very day he could have caused this devastation." Too many unanswered questions remain in the case, she said, adding: "He is not the monster he has been portrayed as." She remembered her son as "a loving son and a happy child. . . . He was a child any mother could be proud of." She told the jurors that despite his conviction, the twenty-nine-year-old military veteran is still a son, a brother, and a cousin to those who care about him. "I am pleading for my son's life. He is a human being as we all are."

Despite the emotional pleas of his parents, the jury sentenced Timothy McVeigh to death. Today McVeigh's case is still on appeal, the Supreme Court having recently refused to hear the claim that his conviction was tainted by pretrial publicity and juror prejudice. Whether or not he is executed, McVeigh already has become a poster boy for capital punishment, the cold-blooded, mass-murderer.

From Timothy McVeigh to the Killing State

Today McVeigh's name is regularly brought up in arguments about the place of capital punishment in America. It is used as the ultimate trump card, the living, breathing embodiment of the necessity and justice of the death penalty. Even people normally opposed to, or indifferent about, capital punishment find themselves drawn to it in McVeigh's case. Typical is the reaction of one newspaperman who wrote, "Capital punishment has never been one of my hot button issues. Still, when asked my opinion or moved to write about it, I for years have come out against the government's killing someone after that person no longer represented a threat to society. . . . To my surprise, the Timothy McVeigh trial has convinced me that I could support the death penalty."[21] Or, as another editorial writer put it, "We cannot undo his [McVeigh's] action, but we can deny him what is left of his life. . . . I agree with the jury that he deserves to die. But this decision did not come easily for me."[22]

For many McVeigh has joined the pantheon of notorious killers—Adolf Hitler, John Paul Gacey, Jeffrey Dahmer—whose names do much of the argumentative work in the national debate about capital punishment. Yet neither McVeigh, his crime, nor his case typifies the killers, the crimes, or the cases in the capital punishment system. Most of the more than 3,600 persons now on death row are there because they committed crimes of passion or lost their head and killed someone in the course of a robbery gone bad; few had adequate defense lawyers or elaborate trials; more than one-half are nonwhites; many come from economically disadvantaged backgrounds.[23] Unlike McVeigh's, their cases receive little or no national publicity.

Nevertheless, McVeigh's case makes vivid many of the themes surrounding the debate about the death penalty in the United States—its importance to political elites as both a political issue and a technique for governing; the increased salience of victims; the appeal of revenge as a foundation for legal punishment; the strains and conflicts that capital punishment imposes on, and exposes in, our legal system; and the iconography through which we come to know crime and punishment. Seen through the lens of the McVeigh case, as well as the hundreds of more "mundane" death penalty cases that are decided every year, Americans today live in a killing state in which violence is met with violence, and the measure of our sovereignty as a people is found in our ability both to make laws carrying the penalty of death and to translate those laws into a calm, bureaucratic bloodletting.

At the turn of the century, capital punishment is alive and well as one of the most prominent manifestations of our killing state, defying the predictions of many scholars[24] who thought it would fade away long ago. Despite the recent reawakening of some abolitionist activity[25] and a modest decline in public support for the death penalty, today more than two-thirds of Americans say they favor capital punishment for persons convicted of murder.[26] Scholars report that vengeance, retribution, and the simple justice of an "eye for an eye" sort provide the basis for much of this support.[27] This may reflect "a growing sense that capital punishment no longer needs to be defended in terms of its social utility. . . . The current invocation of vengeance reflects . . . a sense of entitlement to the death penalty as a satisfying personal experience for victims and a satisfying gesture for the rest of the community."[28]

Yet, as the legal historian Stuart Banner rightly observes,

> Capital punishment . . . presents several puzzles. It gets more attention than any other issue of criminal justice, yet it is a minus-

cule part of our criminal justice system. It is very popular despite well-known shortcomings—it does not deter crime, it is inflicted in a systematically biased manner, it is sometimes imposed on the innocent, and it is quite expensive to administer. . . . It is often justified in simple retributive terms, as the worst punishment for the worst crime, but it is not hard to conceive of worse punishments, such as torture. . . . While capital punishment is intended to deter others, we inflict it in private, and allow prospective criminals to learn very little about it.[29]

If all this were not puzzling enough, we remain committed to state killing in the face of increasing doubts about the reliability and fairness of the capital punishment system,[30] criticism in the international arena and long after almost all other democratic nations have abandoned it.[31] Moreover, we are becoming freer in its use. For a brief period after the Supreme Court reinstated capital punishment in 1976,[32] it tightly supervised the death penalty and imposed great restraint on its use, but that period is now long gone.[33] Despite domestic doubts and international criticism, the pressure is on to move from merely sentencing people to death and then warehousing them to carrying out executions by reducing procedural protections and expediting the death penalty process.[34]

We live in a state in which killing is an increasingly important part of criminal justice policy and a powerful symbol of political power. Every year many of those on death row are actually put to death.[35] Capital punishment has been routinized. Indeed executions have become so commonplace that in some states, such as Texas and Virginia, it is difficult for abolitionist groups to mount a visible presence every time the state kills.[36] So great is the momentum in favor of executions that they sometimes proceed in cases where serious issues of innocence remain unresolved.[37] It now appears that the killing state will be a regular feature of the landscape of American politics for a long time to come.

What does the persistence of capital punishment mean for our law, politics, and culture? What impulses does state killing nurture in our responses to grievous wrongs? What demands does it place on our legal institutions? How is the death penalty represented in our culture? In addressing these questions, *When the State Kills* is animated by the belief that capital punishment has played, and continues to play, a major, and dangerous, role in the modern economy of power. If we are to understand this role, our thinking about the death penalty has to go beyond treating it as simply a matter of moral argument and policy debate. We must examine the connections between capital punishment and certain fundamental issues facing our legal, political, and cultural systems. We must ask what the death penalty does *to* us, not just what it does *for* us.

State killing exacerbates some of the most troubling aspects of the American condition. Capital punishment provides a seemingly simple solution to complex problems, encouraging our society to focus compulsively on fixing individual responsibility and apportioning blame, as if the evil deeds of the McVeighs of the world could be wished away by repeating "evil people do evil things." Moreover, part of what is at stake in the contemporary politics of the death penalty is a contest to claim the status of victim. Today this label is widely appropriated, used by persons accused of capital crimes to explain what they did and why they did it as well as by the so-called victims' rights movement to claim that the only *real* victims are those innocent citizens whose lives are tragically ended by capital crimes.[38]

Instead of the difficult, often frustrating work of understanding what in our society breeds such heinous acts of violence, state killing offers all of us a way out. Those acts are "their" fault, not our problem. The world can and should be understood in a set of clear typologies of good and evil, victim and villain. State killing depends on flattened narratives of criminal or personal responsibility of the type found in melodrama and responds to insistent demands that we use punishment to restore clarity to the moral order.[39] As Harvard law professor Martha Minow argues, the struggle over "blame . . . obscures the complex interactions of individual choice, social structures, and the historical obstacles within which both individuals and institutions operate. As a result, public debate, legal solutions, and political talk neglect the complex solutions needed to sustain and equip victimized individuals to choose differently while also restricting the individuals and social forces that oppress them."[40] This is not to say that responsibility and blame should not be assigned; but state killing, by responding to and encouraging a yearning for a world without moral ambiguity, does not make us safer or our society healthier.

Capital punishment is caught up in, and sustained by, a series of contradictions in our social and political attitudes. The power of the victims' rights movement in the United States arises, in part, from increasing distrust of governmental and legal institutions, yet it is to those very institutions that the families of victims must turn as they seek to ensure an adequate response to capital crimes. This same contradiction sometimes is revealed when jurors decide to impose the death penalty. Some jurors do so because they doubt that a life sentence will actually mean life. They express this doubt by imposing a death sentence because they believe that appellate courts will ensure that state killing is used with great scrupulousness. Moreover, our society's continued support for capital punishment is fueled by both a deep awareness of the complexities of life at the dawn of the twenty-first century and, at the same time, a willed blindness to these complexities and their implications.[41]

State killing distracts. It encourages the quest for revenge rather than efforts at reconciliation and social reconstruction. Who after all could forgive McVeigh or seek some common meaning with him? But does state killing make our society any less violent than it would otherwise be? Ask McVeigh. The prospect of a death sentence did not keep him from blowing up the Murrah Building. And, in the quest to kill the killers do we exacerbate the racial divide that continues to plague the American condition? Does race continue to be a shadow presence when the state kills? The answer, I fear, is yes.

State killing damages us all, calling into question the extent of the difference between the killing done in our name and the killing that all of us would like to stop and, in the process, weakening, not strengthening, democratic political institutions. It leaves America angrier, less compassionate, more intolerant, more divided, further from, not closer to, solutions to our most pressing problems. While ending state killing would not be a cure for our ills, doing so would allow us to focus more clearly on dealing with those issues.

When the State Kills brings a broadened perspective to the study of the death penalty. It addresses the powerful symbolic politics of state killing, the way capital punishment pushes to, and beyond, the limits of law's capacity to do justice justly, and the place of the politics of state killing in contemporary "culture wars." It points the way toward a new abolitionist politics in which the focus is not on the immorality or injustice of the death penalty as a response to killing, but is, instead, on the ways that the persistence of capital punishment affects our politics, law, and culture.

State Killing and Democratic Politics

What is the political meaning of state killing in a democracy? Does it express or frustrate popular sovereignty, strengthen or weaken the values on which democratic deliberation depends? Or, we might ask more directly, is capital punishment compatible with democratic values? Surely there must be serious doubts that it is.[42] Capital punishment is the ultimate assertion of righteous indignation, of power pretending to its own infallibility. By definition it leaves no room for reversibility.[43] It expresses either a "we don't care" anger or an unjustified confidence in our capacity to recognize and respond to evil with wisdom and propriety. Democracy cannot well coexist with either such anger or such confidence. For it to thrive it demands a different context, one marked by a spirit of openness, of reversibility, of revision quite at odds with the confidence and commitment necessary to dispose of human life in a cold and deliberate way.[44] Moreover, democratically administered capital punishment, that is, punishment in which citizens act in an official capacity to approve the deliberate killing of other citizens, contradicts and diminishes the respect for the worth or dignity of all persons that is the enlivening value of democratic politics.[45] A death penalty democratically administered implicates us all as agents of state killing.

"Capital punishments," Benjamin Rush once observed, "are the natural offspring of monarchical governments. . . . An execution in a republic is like a human sacrifice in a religion."[46] Along with the right to make war, the death penalty is the ultimate measure of sovereignty and the ultimate test of political power.[47] With the transition from monarchical to democratic regimes, one might have thought that such a vestige of monarchical power would have no place and, as a result, would wither away. Yet, at least in the United States, which purports to be the most democratic of democratic nations, it persists with a vengeance. How are we to explain this?

It may be that our attachment to state killing is paradoxically a result of our deep attachment to popular sovereignty. Where sovereignty is most fragile, as it always is where its locus is in "the people," dramatic symbols of its presence, like capital punishment, may be most important. Capital punishment may be necessary to demonstrate that sovereignty can reside in the people. In this view, if the sovereignty of the people is to be genuine, it has to mimic the power and prerogatives of the monarchical forms it displaced and about whose sovereignty there could be few doubts. Yet while state killing does this for us, what it does to us is to violate or impede the achievement of the more capacious ideas of democracy associated with what I labeled the tentativeness and scrupulousness of democratic politics and democratic respect for persons.

As any American who lived through the 1970s, 1980s, and 1990s surely knows, the politics of law and order have been at center stage for a long time. From Richard Nixon's "law and order" rhetoric to Bill Clinton's pledge to represent people who "work hard and play by the rules," crime has been such an important issue that some now argue that we are being "governed through crime."[48] In the hurry to show that one is tough on crime the symbolism of capital punishment has been crucial.[49] Thus former speaker of the United States House of Representatives Newt Gingrich once explained that the key to building a new conservative majority in the United States rests with "low taxes and the death penalty."[50]

Capital punishment also has been crucial in the processes of demonizing young, black males and using them in the pantheon of public enemies to replace the Soviet "evil empire."[51] The death penalty is directed disproportionately not only against racial minorities, but also against those who kill white victims.[52] In some jurisdictions blacks receive the death penalty at a rate 38 percent higher than all others; since 1976, 35 percent of those executed have been African Americans.[53] State killing is thus but one part of the intense criminalization of African American populations that occurred during the 1990s. "Governing through crime," law professor and criminologist Jonathan Simon contends, "is a way of reviving the traditional appeal of white supremacy that African-Americans be governed in a distinct and degrading set of institutions."[54]

Moreover, the politics of capital punishment is crucial in an era when government action in other areas of our social and political life is under suspicion. When, as President Bill Clinton announced, "the era of big government is over," emphasis is increasingly placed on freedom and responsibility as a prevailing cultural ethos. Yet this era also is associated with a hardening of attitudes toward crime and a dramatic escalation of state investment in the apparatus of punishment. As a result, no American politician today wants to be caught on the wrong side of the death penalty debate.

At a time when citizens are skeptical that government activism is appropriate or effective, the death penalty provides one arena in which the state can redeem itself by taking action with clear and popular results. This helps explain why the immediate response to the bombing in Oklahoma City was the promise that someone would be sentenced to death, and it also helps explain the energy behind recently successful efforts to limit habeas corpus and speed up the time from death sentences to state killings.[55] A state unable to execute those it condemns to die would seem too impotent to carry out almost any policy whatsoever.

At the same time we have been witnessing a push for more executions, we have also seen an increased emphasis on victims and victimization as the touchstone of crime policy in general and death penalty politics specifically. In this one sense the McVeigh case was by no means exceptional. In even the least celebrated cases the death penalty reinforces public anxieties about violence at the same time as it seeks to satisfy public desires for revenge. "The centrality of crime to governing, especially in a democratic state," Simon explains, "requires citizens who imagine themselves to be potential victims or those responsible for the care of such victims. . . . The death penalty remains the ultimate form of public victim recognition."[56]

Our politics increasingly emphasizes the special place of victims as carriers of civic virtues; what unites us as citizens is our vulnerability and our dependence on the state to prevent and respond to our pain.[57] "I draw most of my strength from victims," Attorney General Reno recently said, "for they represent America to me: people who will not be put down, people who will not be defeated, people who will rise again and stand again for what is right. . . . You are my heros and heroines. You are but little lower than the angels."[58]

State Violence and Legal Legitimacy

If it is true that capital punishment plays an increasingly powerful role in our politics and governance, it is equally true that its importance is growing in our legal institutions. To be legitimate at all, state killing must appear to be different from the violence to which it is opposed and to which it is seen as a response. A crucial part of this difference is in the way law deals with those accused of capital crimes and those who are sentenced to death. In these cases does law respect or reject its own basic values? Does it treat capital defendants with respect and bend over backward to ensure fairness for those sentenced to death?

Given the political importance of capital punishment and the pressure to turn death sentences into executions, the answer to these questions may be no. It is precisely this hydraulic political pressure that threatens to undermine important legal values, such as due process and equal protection. The much-publicized execution of Robert Alton Harris is one of the most striking examples of how this can happen. The first execution in California after the Supreme Court reinstated the death penalty in 1976, the case is a sobering reminder of the pressure on law to compromise its highest values and aspirations in the rush toward execution.[59] During the twelve-hour period immediately preceding Harris's execution, no less than four separate stays were issued by the Ninth Circuit Court of Appeals.[60] Ultimately, in an exasperated and dramatic expression of Justice Rehnquist's blunt aphoristic response to the seemingly endless appeals in capital cases—"Let's get on with it"—the Supreme Court took the unprecedented, and illegal, step of ordering that "no further stays shall be entered . . . except upon order of this court."[61] In so doing it displaced Harris as the soon-to-be victim of law, and portrayed law itself as the victim of Harris and his manipulative lawyers. To defend the virtue of law required an assertion of the Court's supremacy against both the vexatious sympathies of other courts and the efforts of Harris and his lawyers to keep alive a dialogue about death. With this order, the Court stopped the talk and took upon itself the responsibility for Harris's execution.

In so doing it took an enormous risk. What kind of law is it that would do something illegal to ensure the death of one man? The Court's action in the Harris case was symptomatic of a state of affairs in which impatience to facilitate state killing arouses anxiety and fear; it suggests that state violence bears substantial traces of the violence it is designed to deter and punish. The bloodletting that the Court enables strains against and ultimately disrupts all efforts to normalize or routinize state killing as just another legally justifiable and legally controlled act. It may be that law is controlled by, rather than controls, the imperatives of the killing state.

Numerous recent decisions of the Supreme Court have eroded, not enhanced, the procedural integrity of the death sentencing process.[62] Moreover, in 1996 Congress delivered a one-two punch directed against those who have tried to stop state killing. First it enacted Title I of the Anti-Terrorism and Effective Death Penalty Act, which severely limited the reach of federal habeas corpus protections for those on death row by barring federal courts from reviewing state court judgments unless the state proceeding "resulted in a decision that was contrary to, or involved an unreasonable application of, clearly established federal law as determined by the United States Supreme Court."[63] It then defunded Post-Conviction Defender Organizations, which provided legal representation for many of those contesting their death sentences.[64]

Even as evidence emerges that innocent persons have, with some frequency, been sentenced to death, American society seems ever more impatient with the procedural niceties and delays attendant to what many now seem as excessive scrupulousness in the handling of capital cases. What good is having the death penalty, so the refrain goes, if there are so few executions? Blood must be let; lives must be turned into corpses; the "charade" of repeated appeals prolonging the lives of those on death row must be brought to an end.

And yet, if legitimacy is to be preserved, the state's violence must, in the daily operations of the death penalty system, seem different from lawless violence. For many, this need seems to answer itself. State violence is after all legal. What more is there to say? But for those who confront state violence at the end of a police baton, in the vivid images of the tape-recorded beating of Rodney King, or in the increasingly frequent reports of the death of yet another victim of America's attachment to capital punishment, those questions will be direct, immediate, and painful. For them, some answer must be given.

In our current political situation there is, and must be, an uneasy linkage between law and violence. Law cannot work its lethal will and ally itself with the killing state while remaining aloof and unstained by the deeds themselves. As pervasive and threatening as this alliance is, it is, nonetheless, difficult to understand that relationship or even to define clearly what it might be. This difficulty arises because law is violent in many ways.[65]

Violence, as both a linguistic and physical phenomena, as fact and metaphor, is integral to the constitution of modern law. A thoroughly nonviolent legality is inconceivable in a society like this one.

Yet to say that law is a creature of both a literal, life-threatening, body-crushing violence, and of imaginings and threats of force, disorder, and pain, is not to say that it must embrace all kinds of violence under all conditions. If law cannot adequately define the boundary between life and death, guilty killing and justifiable execution, then what is left of law? If law cannot adequately effect a reconciliation between violence and reason, then how can law itself survive?

Only in and through its claims to legitimacy is state killing privileged and distinguished from "the violence that one always deems unjust."[66] Legitimacy is thus one way of charting the boundaries of state violence. It is also the minimal answer to skeptical questions about the ways that state violence differs from the turmoil and disorder the state is allegedly brought into being to conquer. But the need to legitimate this violence is nagging and continuing, never fully resolved in any single gesture. When law, as in the Harris case, goes too far in facilitating state killing, it undermines its own claims to legitimacy and thus casts doubt on all its violent acts.

The Cultural Life of Capital Punishment

The impact of state killing is, however, not limited to our political and legal lives but has a pervasive effect in our culture as well. *When the State Kills* seeks to trace those cultural effects. It takes up law professor David Garland's argument, namely that we should attend to the "cultural role" of legal practices, to their ability to "create social meaning and thus shape social worlds," and that among those practices none is more important than how we punish.[67] This book extends that argument to the domain of the death penalty.

Punishment, Garland tells us, "helps shape the overarching culture and contribute to the generation and regeneration of its terms"; it is a set of signifying practices that "teaches, clarifies, dramatizes and authoritatively enacts some of the most basic moral-political categories and distinctions which help shape our symbolic universe."[68] Punishment lives in culture through its pedagogical effects. It teaches us how to think about categories like intention, responsibility, and injury, and it models the socially appropriate ways of responding to injuries done to us.

But crime and punishment also live as a set of images, like the compelling photographs in the McVeigh case, and as a pervasive aspect of our popular culture.[69] We are surrounded by reminders of crime and punishment, not just in the architecture of the prison, or the speech made by a judge as he sends someone to prison, but in novels, television, and film. Punishment has traditionally been one of the great subjects of cultural production, suggesting the powerful allure of humankind's fall from grace and of our prospects for redemption.

What is true of punishment in general is certainly true of those instances in which the punishment is death. Traditionally the public execution was one of the great spectacles of power and instructions in the mysteries of responsibilities and retribution. Yet making execution private has not ended the pedagogy of the scaffold.[70] Execution itself, the moment of state killing, is even now an occasion for the production of public images of evil or of an unruly freedom that must be contained by a state-imposed death, and for fictive recreations of the scene of death in popular culture.

Traditionally, the cultural politics of state killing has focused on shoring up of status distinctions and distinguishing particular ways of life from others.[71] Thus it is not surprising that the death penalty marks an important fault line in our contemporary culture wars. To be for capital punishment is to be a defender of traditional morality against permissivism and of the rights of the innocent over the rights of the guilty. To oppose it is to carry the burden of explaining why the state should not kill people like Timothy McVeigh, of producing a new theory of responsibility and of responsible punishment, and of humanizing inhuman deeds.

Yet all of this may miss the deepest cultural significance of state killing. To understand state killing and the American condition, then, we have to move from the drama and spectacle of cases like McVeigh's, to the grim, day-to-day realities of the capital punishment system, from the hypervisibility of the celebrated case to the often unnoticed workings of the execution system. When we do, we will see that state killing is today carried on against the background of cultural divides that are becoming ever more intense as they become more complex and unpredictable.

Overview of the Book

The next two chapters begin my exploration of capital punishment and the American condition by taking up the question of why the state kills and kills as it does. State killing, I contend, both expresses sovereign prerogative and, as in the McVeigh case, satisfies public desires for vengeance by responding to the pain of the victims of crime. However, responding to those desires reveals both the weakness of the state and its strength, its dependence and its power. State killing co-opts the call for vengeance and the politics of resentment as much as it seems, at first, to express them.

Chapter 2 illuminates this duality by connecting the political popularity of capital punishment with the search for simple solutions to complex problems and a politics of "demonization." We kill those who murder because we have lost faith in our ability to figure out other ways to prevent killing. Politicians embrace the death penalty to show their toughness and to provide symbolic satisfaction to constituencies searching for recognition at a time of deep and deepening cynicism about our political process.[72]

To develop this argument I concentrate on the contemporary victims' rights movement and, in particular, on its mobilization in capital cases. Victim politics looks like vengeance pure and simple. Yet it is also a symptom of frustration and cynicism with our public institutions. While the goals of the victims' rights movement are complex, emphasizing crime prevention and pressing for policy changes in addition to expressive, punitive responses, it is "more expedient for politicians to respond to the victims' punitive than their preventive impulses."[73] Calls for victims' rights are taken to be indicators of dissatisfaction with the state and its criminal justice policies, and, to some extent, they are. Yet by looking at the controversy surrounding calls to allow the survivors of murder victims to play a larger role in capital cases we see a slightly more complex and revealing picture.

Bringing the families of murder victims into the capital punishment system both amplifies and co-opts their voices. Ceding a place to victims exemplifies a legitimacy crisis felt in neoliberal regimes as public confidence in political and legal institutions wanes. It is also a deft way of giving those aggrieved by crime voice without giving them control. In this way state killing walks a dangerous and uncertain line, fueling, while also trying to manage, anger, resentment, and the desire for revenge.

One of the deep contradictions of state killing in the United States is that even as the death penalty responds to and stirs up the passion for "an eye for an eye," the recent history of execution is marked by repeated efforts to find ever more "humane" technologies for taking life. Chapter 3 suggests that the movement from hanging to electrocution, from electrocution to the gas chamber, from gas to lethal injection reads like a macabre version of the triumph of progress, with each new technique enthusiastically embraced as the latest and best way to kill without imposing pain. Yet, if bringing victims into the capital punishment process is meant to give voice to their anger, the practice of killing painlessly may force questions from those who see in state killing a way to satisfy the calls of vengeance.

In chapter 3 I discuss various court cases dealing with the ways the state kills: hanging, electrocution, lethal gas, lethal injection. In most of them the key question is, Do these methods kill painlessly? Yet one might quite reasonably ask whether the state should be concerned about the suffering of those it puts to death. In addition, what does it tell us about the condition of America that we seek to kill, but yet to kill gently? It is not, as some in the victims' rights movement have argued, that we are moved by misplaced sympathy. The quest to kill painlessly, I contend, is better understood as an act of grace or, better yet, as itself part of a strategy of political legitimation.

The next three chapters move from broad themes about why the state kills and kills as it does to examine the legal process through which judgments are made about who will be sentenced to death, describing that process through the words of the legal professionals and ordinary citizens who help make those judgments. In addition, these chapters analyze the cultural significance of the legal strategies and arguments used in capital cases.

The fragile accommodation that marks state killing in the United States is on display in every capital case, from the most dramatic to the most common. Chapter 4 presents the story of a single, uncelebrated capital case that I traveled to a small Georgia town to observe, hoping to understand, as much as an outsider could, the pain that surrounds every so-called ordinary murder and the challenges that law faces in attempting to respond to that pain. This case drew me into the excruciatingly sad story of the rape and murder of a white woman, Jeannine Galloway, by a young, African-American man, William Brooks.

In this case, as in almost every other, three narratives compete for primacy. First, of course, is the story of the victim and the crime. Typically it has a simple structure, an evil person, so we are told, unjustifiably takes the life of an innocent citizen. Violence is a matter of monstrous deeds done by individuals who must be held responsible for those deeds. This story deliberately ignores the social conditions that some say give rise to crime. The second narrative is one of denial or doubt designed to exculpate the accused, which often becomes one of excuse or mitigation, a story used to explain why the evil act was committed. It recounts the life of the defendant and incorporates precisely those elements—poverty, neglect, social decay—that the first story excludes. The third story is of punishment. In this tale prosecution and defense produce different versions of the appropriateness of the death penalty for this crime and this criminal.

These three stories highlight many of the most important aspects of contemporary America. They illustrate the pervasiveness and power of ideas of victimization as well as the way decisions about punishment may come to depend on our ability to recognize who in our society are the "real" victims. These stories depend on an appeal to sentimentality, asking listeners to identify with the alleged victim, engaging emotion, and promising moral clarity.[74] Moreover, the stories told in cases like that of William Brooks feature central themes in today's politics and culture, in particular the sexualization and racialization of danger and of our responses to it. These cases show how deep a cultural divide there is over responsibility and its limits. I show in chapter 4 how all these complexities and others were played out before a jury asked to decide this one man's fate.

Chapter 5 considers the remarkable role of the jury in capital cases. At almost no other time does a group of citizens calmly and rationally contemplate taking the life of another, all the while acting under the color of law. This kind of democratically administered death penalty is a reminder of an enduring puzzle in social life, namely the question of how otherwise decent people come to participate in projects of violence and how cultural inhibitions against the infliction of pain can be turned into legal support for such action. In the jury's decision to condemn someone to death, or to allow him to live, we see an affirmation of the kind of sovereign prerogative I mentioned earlier, only now carefully circumscribed and transferred to the people.

This chapter addresses the controversy surrounding the role of the jury in capital cases by again examining the kind of case that is on court dockets everyday throughout the United States, this time the senseless killing of a clerk during a convenience store robbery by a young man, John Henry Connors. I use interviews to allow the Connors jurors to describe their experience in their own words. Those interviews reveal a deep sense of responsibility in judging both his guilt and whether he should be executed as well as the ambivalent reaction many Americans have to the "sad stories" of troubled lives that lead to criminal violence. Jurors were torn between a sympathetic understanding of the defendant and a powerful insistence that just because someone has had a difficult life that can be no excuse for killing. Another part of the story that this chapter tells is how both mistrust of government and the legal system itself, of the kind that today is so prevalent, led the Connors jurors to vote for death.

After a death verdict is rendered, the effort to prevent state killing often does not end. At the center of the continuing effort to stop state killing in the United States stands a small group of lawyers who dedicate their professional lives to saving those condemned from being killed by the state. As do the lawyers in the cases discussed in chapters 4 and 5, they take on the burden of representing some of the most hated persons in America. Unlike trial lawyers, who defend a legally innocent person against the most serious criminal charges, these lawyers seek to save the lives of those already found guilty and sentenced to death. They are widely blamed for unfairly complicating the process of moving from executions to state killings. They are said, by conservative leaders in the culture wars, to exemplify elitist indifference to the lives and pains of ordinary people. Death penalty proponents as well as the grieving relatives of murder victims regularly ask, What kind of people are these who would give aid and comfort to murderers?

Chapter 6 tries to answer this question. It is based on interviews I conducted with more than forty death penalty lawyers from across the United States. In these meetings I heard the story of state killing as it is lived and told by those on the firing line in the daily struggle to prevent that killing. This version, not popular in the current pro–death penalty climate, is one that must be heard if we are to understand the killing state. It shows how the practices of state killing increasingly rub up against the legal protections that, not a generation ago, were thought essential to guaranteeing fairness in capital cases. Today, death penalty lawyers carry on a rearguard action to vindicate those guarantees of fairness, to ensure that law is not stampeded in the service of political expediency.

In the chapters that constitute part three I move from the legal process in which judgments about life and death are made to consider the cultural representations and resonances of capital punishment, the connection between what we see and what we believe about state killing and the American condition.

Modern executions are no longer public. Nevertheless, newspaper accounts and television news reports, as well as courtroom narratives, all attempt to capture the act of execution. Still the question persists of how widely shared the privilege of witnessing and viewing should be and what, if any, limits should be placed on the media's representation. Chapter 7 discusses whether executions should be televised and asks what it would mean for us and for our culture if citizens could choose to become viewers of capital punishment?

While executions are not televised, they are frequently portrayed in popular culture. From such cinema classics as *Angels with Dirty Faces* and *I Want to Live* to contemporary hits like *Dead Man Walking*, there is now a substantial body of film dealing with state killing. Chapter 8 examines the presentation of state killing in death penalty films as well as their cultural politics.

The appearance of capital punishment in film, I suggest, typically distracts from an adequate assessment of the impact of state killing on the American condition. I develop this argument through an extended analysis of three recent films: *Dead Man Walking*, *Last Dance*, and *The Green Mile*. These and other death penalty films get their dramatic force by focusing narrowly on the question of whether a particular person really deserves to die rather than on broader questions about state killing or about the social conditions that produce violence in America. As a result, such films highlight the issue of individual character and responsibility and rely frequently on categories of thought that are key weapons of the most conservative elements in today's culture wars. Moreover, they silently acquiesce in the bureaucratization and privatization of capital punishment through their "You are there" representations of execution itself, seeking, through such representations, to inspire confidence that their viewers can "know" the truth about the death penalty even as they raise doubts about its appropriateness in particular cases.

The conclusion of *When the State Kills* summarizes the main arguments, namely that state killing contributes to some of the most dangerous features of contemporary America. Among them are the substitution of a politics of revenge and resentment for sustained attention to the social problems responsible for so much violence today; the use of crime to pit various social groups against one another and to generate political capital; what has been called an effort to "govern through crime"; the racializing of danger and, in so doing, the perpetuation of racial fear and antagonism; the erosion of basic legal protections and legal values in favor of short-term political expediency; the turning of state killing into an invisible, bureaucratic act, which can divorce citizens from the responsibility for the killing that the state does in their name. In response I argue for what I call a "new abolitionism." This view suggests that the time may be at hand to condemn state killing for what it does *to*, not *for*, America and what Americans most cherish.

part

one

STATE KILLING AND THE

POLITICS OF VENGEANCE

2

THE RETURN OF REVENGE:

HEARING THE VOICE OF THE VICTIM

IN CAPITAL TRIALS

Just as the legislature legitimately may conclude that capital punishment deters crime, so it may conclude that capital punishment serves a vital social function as society's expression of moral outrage.—ROBERT BORK, Brief for the United States, submitted in *Gregg v. Georgia*

Revenge is a kind of wild justice, which the more man's nature runs to, the more ought law to weed it out.
—FRANCIS BACON, "Of Revenge"

No authority more useful and necessary can be granted to those appointed to look after the liberties of a state than that of being able to indict before the people . . . such citizens as have committed any offense prejudicial to the freedom of the state. . . . An outlet is provided for that ill feeling which is apt to grow up in cities against some particular citizen . . . ; and when for such ill feeling there is no normal outlet, recourse is had to abnormal methods likely to bring disaster on the republic as a whole.—MACHIAVELLI, *The Disourses*

The call to revenge forms the least discussed and most pervasive

force in the desire to punish.

—WILLIAM CONNOLLY, *The Ethos of Pluralization*

From the beginning, Timothy McVeigh's trial for the bombing in Oklahoma City was dominated by extreme solicitude for the victims and their families. Much of the concern, of course, was right and appropriate. However, it gradually became clear that the main measure of justice in the trial and the politics surrounding it was simply whether the outcome satisfied the victims' need for closure and their sense of what an appropriate punishment would be. It was unusual for victims to have this sort of power. But what was true in the McVeigh case is increasingly true whenever there is a prospect of capital punishment.

Legal systems in the United States and Europe recently have been confronted by stern challenges in the name of victims' rights.[1] Here and elsewhere a tide of resentment is rising against a system of justice that traditionally has tried to substitute structured public processes for unpredictable private action and, in so doing, to justify punishment as a response to injuries to public order rather than to particular individuals.[2] The tendency of criminal justice systems in Western democracies has been to displace the victim, to shut the door on those with the greatest interest in responding to a crime. In response, victims are demanding that their voices be heard throughout the criminal process. As in the McVeigh trial and in Attorney General Janet Reno's description of victims as the true heroes and heroines of America, their demands are being met.[3]

Yet the idea that victims need rights or that the victim has been superseded in modern law is somewhat odd. Victims are always present.[4] Almost every criminal trial centers around the reconstruction of the victim's injury. The suffering of the victim measures, in substantial part, the guilt of the offender. Nonetheless, the victims' rights movement wants more. It seeks participation and power by making the victim the symbolic heart of modern legality. It contests the attempted appropriation of the role of the victim by offenders and what it sees as the promiscuous use of the language of victimization throughout our culture. The movement draws on standard stories and mobilizes around incidents that are "horrifying and aberrational,"[5] generating sentimental narratives of lives lost, families ruined, evil done. In addition, it partly represents, bubbling just beneath the surface, growing pressure for the return of revenge.

The victims' rights movement contests the fairness of legal procedures that are distant and unresponsive to crime victims' grief and rage.[6] By transforming courts into sites for the rituals of grieving, that movement seeks to make private experiences part of public discourse. Prosecutors encourage this development, while politicians manipulate victim politics, marginalizing the pragmatic interest of victims in more effective crime prevention and fanning their anger and desire for punishment.

Moreover, when victims speak in the political or legal process, public scrutiny invades some of the most personal aspects of their lives—the ways they suffer and grieve. The victims' rights movement points to the difficulty of "reconciling grief and rage and vengefulness with practicable moral enforcements of civil association [and] of reconciling a cultural preoccupation with vengeance and . . . forms of legal punishment which deny it."[7] Legal norms no longer, if they ever did, adequately express common moral commitments. Instead, we seem to be bound together by our shared recognition of, and aversion to, pain, suffering, and grief.

Although it is "counter-intuitive to think of a subjective experience like pain as establishing a publicly valid authority," this is precisely what the victims' rights movement seeks to do.[8] By allowing victims to use legal processes to express their grief and rage as they, or their surrogates, seek to enlist the loyalty of judges and juries in a quest for revenge, it turns the quest for justice into a quest of voice, where the absence of voice is treated as an absence of justice.[9]

In the United States the high tide of the victims' rights movement occurred in *Payne v. Tennessee*,[10] a murder case in which
the Supreme Court allowed the use of victim impact testimony
during sentencing. In cases like *Payne* the voice of the most obvious victim has been permanently silenced. Because the victim is
dead there is in one sense no victim impact beyond that fact. Yet
those who secured the opportunity to use victim impact statements in capital trials did so to extend the idea of the victim to
include survivors, those left behind to bear the burden of suffering
and grief. As in the McVeigh case, relatives of murder victims
describe for the jury, during the sentencing phase of the trial, the
effects of the death of a loved one, and they present first-person
accounts of emotional trauma and continuing personal distress.[11]

Earlier, in *Booth v. Maryland*, another murder case arising from
the killing of two elderly residents of Baltimore, the Supreme
Court had drawn the line against the victims' rights movement
by barring victim impact statements in capital cases.[12] *Payne*'s
reversal of *Booth*, however, was not only an unusual departure
from precedent but also provided a vivid indication of the status
of vengeance in modern law. *Payne* ended the repression of revenge and gave it constitutional legitimacy in a way that no other
decision of the United States Supreme Court ever had. Constitutional scrupulousness would no longer be a barrier to hearing the
voice of the victim. In *Payne* a central fact of contemporary legality came to light, namely its inability to rid itself of vengeance.
Vengeance may be a threatening evil, but it is also indispensable
to legal justice itself. Moreover, vengeance is the ultimate measure of loyalty to those who cannot avenge themselves. It is the
supreme test of social bonds. Played out in an address to a jury,
the claims of revenge are subject to judgment in accordance with
rules whose substance is not fully encompassed by the imperatives of loyalty or kinship.

Payne's legitimation of revenge is a response to but also an expression of several factors. First is the discrediting of traditional
ideas about rehabilitation. Second is the increased importance of
crime as a political issue and of crime fighting as a way of express-

ing commitment to particular moral values. Third is anxiety about our capacity to defend and sustain those very values.

Revenge presumes that we know who the criminals and the victims are, and that we know the difference between them. Brutality, the vengeful voice utters, must be met with brutality. It is a simple philosophy. Yet the return of revenge foretells a complex crisis in the ideological apparatus of modern legality. It reveals the unstable, fragile boundaries separating private and public justice, passion, and reason. Indeed if revenge succeeds in making itself a force in legal justice, it does so by tearing down these boundaries and rearranging these categories. It blurs the line between public and private justice, between the justice of the state acting against those who defy its order and the justice of the victim calling for vengeance against those who are responsible for private pain and suffering. Victim politics, in addition, is based on a critique of the state but also a desire for a stronger, more powerful state.[13] Because revenge now must enlist the very state apparatus of which it has been so suspicious, a symbiotic relationship of private motive and public processes emerges.[14]

Not surprisingly, the return of revenge has figured as a central theme in arguments over the death penalty.[15] When the repercussions of public justice are most grave, as they are in capital trials, law has sought the most thorough repression of vengeance. Consequently, from the decision in *Furman v. Georgia* that struck down the death penalty[16] until its decision in *Payne*, the Supreme Court constructed a system of "super due process" through which capital defendants could be assured an extra measure of protection from arbitrariness, caprice, or emotionalism.[17] In the sentencing phase of capital trials, the jury's attention was directed exclusively to the task of ascertaining the precise, personal culpability of the defendant. Did this particular murderer, given the full circumstances of his or her life, deserve to die at the hands of the state? Here the courts carried out the most exacting calculus of retribution.

Precision in calculating and responding to particular motives and circumstances is said, in the legitimating story of law, to have no place in systems of vengeance. In such systems the focus is on damage done and harm inflicted. Yet, as we will see, just such an exclusive focus on harm provided the key rationale in *Payne*. So it might be said that *Payne* changed everything. Or did it?

In the remainder of this chapter I describe the enormous theoretical energy that has been put into the effort to distinguish revenge from retribution. I then show how victim impact statements work to prompt a return of revenge. I also consider the ways *Payne* both uncloaked and legitimated vengeance and, at the same time, revealed the instability of the revenge-retribution distinction. I conclude by assessing the significance of the return of revenge for an understanding of the politics of state killing and the American condition.

Ideology in Action: Retribution against Revenge

> COALHOUSE WALKER: *I tried every legal means to get satisfaction, and I was humiliated at every turn.*
>
> BOOKER T. WASHINGTON: *And you think this revenge will restore your damaged pride? You are wrong to the depths of your soul. Vengeance does nothing but perpetuate more vengeance and on and on until some race can find the strength to say "No, I will not avenge. I shall stand with dignity until my enemies are won over because they honor and respect me," and only when that happens will we have our pride back.*
>
> COALHOUSE WALKER: *You speak like an angel, Mr. Washington. It's too bad we're living on the earth.*—From the film *Ragtime*

The effort to distinguish revenge from retribution and, in so doing, to discourage the former while legitimating the latter has an illustrious history in political and legal thought.[18] Philosophers such as Kant and Hegel are well known for their embrace of retributive punishment and their critiques of vengeance.[19] Modern legality itself is founded on the belief that revenge must and can be repressed, that legal punishment can be founded on reason, that due process can discipline passion, and that these categories are knowable *and* distinct.[20]

Contemporary, Western legal systems have sought to weed out revenge and silence vengeance in the search for a supposedly superior and more rational form of justice. Churches and cemeteries, and even therapists' offices, are the approved sites for mourning and outrage, not courtrooms. By constructing boundaries between courts and those sites, legal justice could be retributive without being vengeful.[21]

Retribution, with its advertised virtues of measured proportionality, cool detachment, and consistency, is contrasted with vengeance—the voice of the other, the primitive, the savage call of unreason, a "wildness" inside the house of law, which, by nature, will not succumb to rational forms of justice. Vengeance must be kept at bay, so the argument goes, because it represents an unwarranted concession to an anger and passion that knows no limits. Akin to such vindictive punishment is hatred, a defiant and "sinful" unwillingness to forgive those who injure us.[22] Vengeance, in this view, is "crazed, uncontrolled, subjective, individual, admitting no reason, no rule of limitation. . . . Conventional wisdom conceives of vengeance cultures as barely cultured at all, all id and no superego: big dumb brutes looking for excuses to kill."[23]

In their unceasing efforts to overcome id with superego and to construct a legitimating ideology, Western legal orders substitute the calm calculation of deterrence, the disciplining logic of rehabilitation, and the stern but controlled authority of retribution for the emotionalism of revenge. Justice becomes public and the passionate voice of the victim, or the vengeful anger of the victim's kin or champion, is merged with the detached state bureaucracy, which speaks for "the people" against whom all offenses to the criminal law are said to be directed. "It is sometimes the custom," criminologist Cesare Beccaria wrote more than two hundred years ago, "to release a man from the punishment of a slight crime when the injured pardons him: an act, indeed, which is in accordance with mercy and humanity but contrary to public

policy; as if a private citizen could by his remission do away with
the necessity of the example in the same way that he can excuse
the reparation due for an offense. The right of punishing does not
rest with an individual, but with the community as a whole, or
the sovereign."[24]

The contrast between revenge and retribution reflects a tension
between passion and reason that structures American political
thought generally and our legal system in particular. Despite
prominent efforts to portray revenge[25] as rational and to reveal its
normative content,[26] this opposition still persists in philosophical treatments of the subject. Thus, for example, political theorist
Judith Shklar contends that revenge is "uniquely subjective, not
measurable, and probably an unquenchable urge of the provoked
heart. It is the very opposite of justice, in every respect, and inher-
ently incompatible with it. . . . Revenge is not detached, impersonal, proportionate or rule bound."[27]

Not being "detached, impersonal, proportionate, or rule
bound" are the defining defects of revenge, which are juxtaposed
to the "advantages" legal punishment (at least in theory) provides. But Shklar herself admits that vengeance is never effectively and fully purged from a system of justice: "If effective justice preempts, neutralizes, dilutes, and all but replaces revenge,
it cannot abolish it, either as an emotion or as an active response
available to us, especially in personal relations. For most people
retributive justice is justice, but it remains a frustrating substitute for revenge, neither eliminating nor satisfying its urging."[28]
The stubborn pull of revenge explains the persistent efforts to
identify how it differs from retribution.

The philosopher Robert Nozick makes one of the most influential and important of these efforts.[29] According to Nozick there
are five ways to distinguish retribution from revenge. First, retribution is only done for a "wrong," whereas revenge "may be done
for an injury or harm or slight and need not be for a wrong."[30]
The wrong to which he refers is an action officially and formally
prohibited by law. Doing a wrong requires a consciousness of
wrongdoing combined with a desire to do that wrong. Injury,

harm, or slight need have no such official prohibition nor need they derive from a conscious will to injure. What counts in the realm of injury, harm, or slight is the pain of the victim and not the intent of the person whose action caused that pain. Revenge in this case is closely linked to the "idea of reciprocity and the notion of debt. You owe someone for the harms they inflict on you."[31] Retribution, in contrast, is a response to action for which someone might be said to be morally blameworthy. Harm without blameworthiness is not sufficient to merit a retributive response.

Next, whereas retribution "sets an internal limit to the amount of punishment, according to the seriousness of the wrong, . . . revenge internally need set no limit to what is inflicted."[32] What Nozick means is that retributive punishment must be proportional to the wrong committed. Yet retribution in itself can set no threshold or level of punitive response; it simply enjoins to "punish proportionally." The level of retributive punishment depends on prevailing cultural standards. As a result, no guarantee exists that the punishment exacted for any offense will be any less severe under a retributive rationale than it would have been had it been motivated simply by revenge. Moreover, the continuing attraction of revenge is in part a function of this problem of setting levels of punishment. Where the level of legal punishment is too low, revenge insists on a kind of fairness. In this sense vengeance is "not without normative constraints. . . . The avenger functions in equity. He does not deny law, he improves it. And he does not improve it by some standardless set of rules."[33]

Nozick's third point is crucial for understanding victim impact statements and the return of revenge. Revenge, Nozick tells us, is "personal," whereas the "agent of retribution need have no special or personal tie to the victim."[34] It is, of course, just this element of impersonality in retribution that causes discomfort and concern in the victims' rights movement. The goal of victims and those who take up their cause is to repersonalize criminal justice so that the sentencer has to declare an alliance with either the victim or the offender. Criminal sentencing thus becomes a test of loyalty.

Yet, what Nozick does not see is that at another level, revenge always entails exposure of the personal to public norms. Vengeance does not simply involve a movement of the private into the public, but also entails public scrutiny and surveillance of the self whose injuries call for our attention. This was vividly apparent in prosecutor Marcia Clark's summation in the O. J. Simpson criminal case, and is always in play when a judge or a jury is presented with a victim impact statement. Private pain and grief are heard but are also subject to public judgment. In response, the sentence imposed becomes a way of saying "this is because of what you did to [self, father, group, and so on]."[35] The victim impact statement ensures that the criminal knows that his punishment is an expression of personal loyalty and connection between state and victim.

Because of its personal quality, vengeance "involves a particular tone, pleasure, in the suffering of another";[36] retribution involves no "emotional tone." Here Nozick restates the distinction between revenge and retribution as that between passion and reason. The desire to experience a direct, immediate, passionate connection to the suffering of the criminal fuels the victims' rights movement. When the victim's voice is silent, punishment cannot restore the victim's sense of being in control or being able to exert power. Only when victims become agents in the suffering of the people responsible for their own suffering can they achieve a kind of social equilibrium.

Finally, Nozick writes that revenge is different from retribution in that "there need be no generality in revenge." Exacting vengeance in one specific case does not commit the avenger to similar action in any other case. Retribution, in contrast, is based on "general principles . . . mandating punishment in other similar circumstances." Here again an opposition is set up in which revenge is associated with the savage, the primitive, the undeveloped. And lest there be any doubt about this, Nozick confidently asserts that retribution can be distinguished from revenge because it is, "on its surface at least, less primitive."[37]

Nevertheless, despite the best efforts of legal systems to purge themselves of vengeful motives, revenge almost always is just below the surface of criminal punishment. Its banishment can never be complete. Revenge, Shklar argues, "is an insatiable urge of the human heart."[38] It is an urge lurking in the shadows, whose presence provides one reason for the founding of the modern state, and whose continuing force fuels the apparatus of punishment itself. Revenge can be renamed but not contained. It can be repressed but neither denied nor forgotten.

Most efforts to distinguish between revenge and retribution can only be understood if we accept these oppositions: public versus private, impersonal versus personal, general versus specific. Yet the categories necessary to sustain Nozick's understanding are all being called into question by the conditions of modern life. Today neither side of the id-superego divide seems to mean what it once did.[39] The personal becomes the political, and even sovereignty itself is no longer secure.[40] In such a condition, the stable distinctions between criminal and victim that have structured our understanding of crime, justice, and punishment are no longer satisfactory. At issue in the return of revenge is the very constitution of our law as well as conventional understandings of identity, action, and response.

While the victims' rights movement demands that the legal justice of the modern state be rendered more personal, more emotional, and more specific, it and the use of victim impact statements that it advocates do not leave the dichotomies undisturbed. Private becomes public and public becomes private; passion is introduced into the temple of reason, and yet passion itself is subject to the discipline of reason. Every effort to distinguish revenge and retribution nevertheless reveals that "vengeance arrives among us in a judicious disguise . . . vengeance always cloaks itself in the most current styles of 'justice.' "[41] The demand for victims' rights and the insistence that we hear the voices of the victims are just the latest "style" in which vengeance has disguised itself.

Vengeance Uncloaked: Victim Impact Statements
and the Death Penalty

> *The instinct for retribution is part of the nature of man, and*
> *channeling that instinct in the administration of criminal*
> *justice serves an important purpose in promoting the stability*
> *of a society governed by law. When people begin to believe*
> *that organized society is unwilling or unable to impose upon*
> *criminal offenders the punishment they "deserve," then there*
> *are sown the seeds of anarchy—of self-help, vigilante justice,*
> *and lynch law.*—JUSTICE STEWART, *Furman v. Georgia*

The critique of prevailing ideologies is generally thought to be a
staple of academic labor. Scholars strive to uncloak the hidden
residues of meaning through which social processes work to identify the dangers and possibilities suppressed in conventional or
dominant ways of thinking. For the Supreme Court of the United
States, often considered a pillar of the status quo, to be engaged in
such work would be surprising enough. That it has been actively
questioning the dominant ideology in the context of one of the
most contentious legal issues, the death penalty, is thus all the
more remarkable.

Uncloaking the hidden layers of vengeance and moving them
from the margins to the center of legal justice is precisely the
work of *Payne v. Tennessee*. *Payne* allowed the use of victim impact statements in capital trials. The case gave a voice to victims
by expanding the legal recognition of victimhood to include the
collateral suffering of those left behind and insisting on vengeful justice for the survivors. *Payne* constituted an admission
that "the State does not adequately represent the interest of
the people in whose name it pursues its cases. It is necessary for
these people to represent themselves and personally address the
court in order for their point of view to be brought to bear on the
proceedings."[42]

Payne brought revenge out of the shadows and accorded it an honored place in the jurisprudence of capital punishment by overruling an earlier case, *Booth v. Maryland*, which had done the traditional ideological work of resisting revenge, of denying a place for victims in capital sentencing.[43] *Booth* was the case of two men, John Booth and William Reid, who in 1983 entered the West Baltimore home of Irvin and Rose Bronstein, Booth's neighbors, with the intent to steal money. Finding the Bronsteins at home, Booth and Reid bound, gagged, and stabbed them several times in the chest with a kitchen knife. The killers were subsequently arrested and convicted on two counts of first-degree murder, two counts of robbery, and one count of conspiracy to commit robbery.

As in the McVeigh case, jurors were presented with victim impact statements, during the sentencing phase of the trial, this time in the form of a third-person account of interviews with the Bronsteins's son, daughter, son-in-law, and granddaughter.[44] Although the victim impact statement in this case contained an elaborate description of the reaction of each of those people to the death of the Bronsteins, it concentrated on the daughter and the son. The jury was told that "The victims' daughter . . . states that she doesn't sleep through a single night and thinks a part of her died too when her parents were killed. She reports that she doesn't find much joy in anything and her powers of concentration aren't good. She feels as if her brain is on overload. . . . The victims' daughter states that wherever she goes she sees and hears her parents."[45]

This statement, presented as the clinical narrative of a public official, nonetheless conveys the pain, grief, and torment of the daughter left behind. She is a kind of corpse, yet she is haunted by uncontrollable memories. It is as if her parents are not entirely dead; they live on in visions and voices known only to her. Such haunting visions and voices stir the vengeful desires of all survivors. Moreover, they create empathetic bonds between speaker and listener seeking to evoke compassion by presenting an artificial and incomplete portrait of a formerly blissful family life, ruined by villainous acts.

Similarly eerie suggestions concerning visions of the dead are found in the statement of the Bronsteins's son.

> The victims' son states that he can only think of his parents in the context of how he found them that day, and he can feel their fear and horror. It was 4:00 P.M. when he discovered their bodies and this stands out in his mind. He is always aware of when 4:00 P.M. comes each day, even when he is not near a clock. . . . He is unable to drive on the streets that pass near his parents' home. . . . He is constantly reminded of his parents. He sees his father coming out of synagogues, sees his parents' car, and feels very sad whenever he sees old people.

Murdered parents discovered in a grisly scene live on as ghosts. For this victim, memory is the true source of pain. He lives in a present in which the past refuses to die. This unendurable past constitutes true victimization. The call of the victim is to rectify the past, to placate memory by silencing the ghosts whose constant call is for vengeance.

The voice of the victim is an urgent call both to remember and to obliterate memory, to attend to the past and to forge a different recollection of it. One hope is that bloodletting punishment can eradicate the memory of the crime. Vengeance expresses "a wish to change the world and right the past, to be seen and counted in a private and ultimately a public conversion of memory, to reassign guilt and to end that unending memory of horror that is, says Aeschylus, 'a relentless anguish gnawing at the heart.' "[46]

This desire to replace an unendurable past with a new image of the suffering of the criminal is also apparent in the victim impact statements of the Bronstein children. Thus the son contended that "his parents were not killed, but were butchered like animals. He doesn't think anyone should be able to do something like that and get away with it. He is very angry. . . . He states that he is frightened by his own reaction of what he would do if someone hurt him or a family member." And the daughter noted that

> her parents were stabbed repeatedly with viciousness and she could never forgive anyone for killing them that way. She can't

believe that anyone could do that to someone. The victims' daughter states that animals wouldn't do this. They didn't have to kill because there was no one to stop them from looting. . . . The murders show the viciousness of the killers' anger. She doesn't feel that the people who did this could ever be rehabilitated and she doesn't want them to be able to do this again or put another family through this.[47]

In both these statements we can see how a dynamic of responsibility and monstrosity works in the urge to punish. "They didn't have to kill" suggests beings capable of calculating, of knowing what has to be done, and of making decisions about how to act. The killers are, at the same time, presented as inferior to "animals." In addition, while the daughter's words contain the element of generality that Nozick insists is properly part of retribution, her statement, as well as that of her brother, is cast in the kind of personal, emotional tone that Nozick would attribute to vengeance. Finally, the son's self-described anxiety about his own reaction suggests just the kind of uncontrollable response to injury that public justice hopes to displace, if not fully satisfy. That anxiety contains a kind of threat, or a reminder of the possibility of a more dangerous violence lurking just below the surface of civil society.

The legal question presented to the Supreme Court in *Booth* was whether such victim impact evidence rendered the death sentences of Booth and Reid unconstitutional under the Eighth Amendment's ban on "cruel and unusual punishment." The Court, with Justice Powell writing for the majority, held that it did. In Powell's judgment, because the victim impact statement presented the jury with emotionally compelling testimony, it created a substantial risk of prejudice. The power of the victim's voice represents its greatest danger. The victim impact statement, despite its obvious rhetorical force, was "irrelevant" to the capital sentencing decision because it did not and could not contribute to an assessment of the "blameworthiness" of the defendants.[48]

For such a person to be blameworthy, Powell contended, he would have had to have known about and contemplated the dam-

aging impact on the victims' family that the murder of the
Bronsteins would have. A wrong is different from a harm, and
while Powell had no doubt about the harm done to the family, he
insisted that it was irrelevant in a proceeding in which the focus
should be on whether the wrong committed was sufficiently egre-
gious as to warrant the death penalty. To allow the jury to hear the
Bronsteins' victim impact statement would focus its attention on
factors of which the defendants were "unaware" and would "divert the jury's concern from the defendant's background and
record, and the circumstances of the crime."[49]

Moreover, the use of victim impact statements, in Powell's
view, turns capital sentencing into a test of the rhetorical profi-
ciency of surviving relatives.[50] Rather than skill at arms, verbal
acumen would become the tool for exacting revenge. The use of
the victim impact statement placed the family in the position of
seeking a champion, using language to persuade the jury to do
what the law forbids the family from doing directly. "Articulate"
and "persuasive" family members would be able to secure a result
unavailable to those who were less well able to express their
"grief."[51] Retributive punishment is general in its reach; revenge
is particular, specific, personalistic, and contingent upon individual ability.

Finally, Powell rejected victim impact statements because they
introduce passion and emotion, and threaten to overwhelm the
"reasoned decision making we require in capital cases." The
voice of the victim breaches the delicate boundary between passion and reason, serving to "inflame the jury and divert it from
deciding the case on the relevant evidence. . . . As we have noted,
any decision to impose the death sentence must 'be, and appear
to be, based on reason rather than caprice or emotion.'"[52] Here
the construction and policing of a boundary between retribution
and revenge is fully on display. The dichotomies that animate
Nozick's analytic philosophy are threatened by the demand to
hear the voice of the victim in capital trials, and yet they live on
in Powell's judicial opinion. What Powell refuses to see is that
victim impact evidence, were it admitted in capital trials, would
unsettle the very distinctions that he so confidently asserts.

However, Powell's was not the only voice in *Booth*, nor the only one to respond to the call to hear the victim in terms of the revenge-retribution distinction and its associated binary oppositions. Justices White and Scalia both produced dissenting opinions, which would provide the basis for *Payne*'s reversal of this case just four years later. White asserted that the proper focus of sentencing in capital cases was not only the "internal disposition" of the murderer but "the full extent of the harm he caused." Echoing Nozick's definition of revenge, White said that it was not "unfair to confront a defendant with an account of the loss his . . . act has caused the victim's family." In this view, punishment could and should be based on a calculus of harms and injuries as well as of wrongs. Punishment might properly be enhanced, White said, "on the basis of harm caused, irrespective of the offender's specific intention to cause such harm."[53]

White saw victim impact statements in capital cases as essential in counteracting the "mitigating evidence which the defendant is entitled to put in." Victim impact evidence reminds the sentencer, White noted, that the "victim is an individual whose death represents a unique loss to . . . his family."[54] But who would need to receive such a reminder and hear such an assertion? By providing both, White indicts the legal order, and by insisting that punishment should be aimed at responding to the family's loss, he seems to privatize public processes.

Yet his suggestion that the jury should be invited to hear the voice of the victim does more than turn a public process into a vehicle for private vengeance. It facilitates the breakdown of the categories of public and private on which the debate about revenge and retribution has traditionally depended. Justice that is removed, abstract, and impersonal is no justice at all; instead the immediate, concrete, and personal reality of pain and grief must be made comprehensible to an audience of strangers through a complicated semiotic process.

Scalia too believes that harm is separate from moral guilt and that it provides an equally valid reason for imposing the death penalty. As he puts it, harm and moral guilt are "distinct justifications that operate independently of each other."[55] In addition,

Scalia insists that the Court should acknowledge "an outpouring of popular concern for what has come to be known as 'victims' rights'." The victim impact statement lays before the jury "the full reality of human suffering the defendant has produced," which Scalia contends is "one of the reasons society deems his act worthy of the prescribed penalty."[56] Scalia's references to an "outpouring of popular concern" and what society "deems" necessary in the way of punishment suggest that legal values are too far removed from social values. His reaction to this problem was to ensure that punishment would be, and would appear to be, responsive to suffering and that law itself will heed the "outpouring of popular concern" as well as what society "deems" appropriate.

Scalia's efforts—first, to distinguish between the defendant's moral guilt and the victim's harm and, second, to emphasize the assertion of a generalized public sense of justice through the criminal justice process—are both deeply inconsistent with the retributivist tradition. Revenge returns and the ideological construction of a boundary between a system of public justice based in retribution and its vengeance-based alternative is unraveled.

Vengeance cannot and does not simply replace retribution. As it transforms the terrain of law, it is itself transformed. In *Booth*, "Justice Scalia implies that the potential for injustice regarding a particular capital defendant is outweighed by society's need to use capital trials to purge its collective anger and moral outrage at violent crime."[57] Yet Scalia's view cannot prevail. Revenge is blunted as anger and moral outrage encounter the impersonal solemnity of public justice. And, just as surely as revenge and retribution clash, public justice is forced to become less solemn.

From *Booth* to *Payne*

The White-Scalia view, a minority position in *Booth*, four years later became the majority position in *Payne*. In that case the Supreme Court heard the appeal of Pervis Payne, who, in June 1987, attacked twenty-eight-year-old Charisse Christopher and her two children when she resisted Payne's sexual advances. Hearing "blood curdling" screams from the Christophers' apartment, a neighbor called the police who arrived a few minutes later to find the bodies of Charisse and Lacie, Charisse's two-year-old daughter, dead on the kitchen floor each having received multiple stab wounds. They also found Charisse's son Nicholas laying barely alive beside his mother and sister, himself the recipient of similar wounds. Payne was later apprehended and convicted of two counts of first-degree murder and one count of assault with intent to murder.

During the sentencing phase of Payne's trial the State presented testimony by Charisse's mother who was Nicholas's legal guardian. When the prosecutor asked her what impact the crime had had on her grandson, she replied, "He cries for his mom. He doesn't seem to understand why she doesn't come home. And he cries for Lacie. He comes to me many times during the week and asks me 'Grandmama, do you miss my Lacie?' And I tell him yes. He says, 'I'm worried about my Lacie.'"[58] In his closing argument the prosecutor observed:

> There is nothing you can do to ease the pain of any of the families in this case . . . there is obviously nothing you can do for Charisse and Lacey Jo. But there is something that you can do for Nicholas. Somewhere down the road Nicholas is going to grow up, hopefully. He's going to want to know what happened. And he is going to know what happened to his baby sister and his mother. He is going to want to know what type of justice was done. He is going to want to know what happened. Your verdict, you will provide the answer.

Payne was sentenced to death.

When he appealed his death sentence, the Supreme Court again confronted the constitutionality of victim impact statements in capital cases. This time, however, the Court found their use constitutional. Justice Rehnquist, following White and Scalia's lead in *Booth* and embodying Nozick's understanding of revenge, contended that punishment need not be limited to wrongs but could and should be meted out differently depending on the harm that is actually done. "Victim impact evidence," Rehnquist argued, "is simply another form or method of informing the sentencing authority about the specific harm caused by the crime in question."[59]

Moreover, Rehnquist argued that the state should be allowed to introduce victim impact evidence to provide a " 'a quick glimpse of the life' that the defendant 'chose to extinguish.' " Doing so would ensure that the victim is not a " 'faceless stranger at the penalty phase of the trial,' " and would redress what Rehnquist saw as the "unfairness" that occurred when criminal sentencing focused solely on the life and circumstances of the offender. From anonymity to embodiment, from absence to presence, victim impact evidence becomes a vehicle for resurrecting the dead and allowing them to speak as their killers are being judged. Giving voice to victims moves them to the center of the judicial process, even as it expands the notion of who qualifies as a victim. In Rehnquist's view it presents the jury a fuller picture of the "human cost of the crime of which the defendant stands convicted."[60]

Focusing on that cost by hearing the voice of the victim personalizes death sentencing in just the way revenge personalizes all punishment. In this understanding "the body in pain is the source of a unique . . . authority. . . . The body in pain provides a basis for assuming the authority to assert that a particular action not only did happen, but that the person who did it should be condemned for it and punished."[61] The victim impact statement seeks to move the jury from strangeness to familiarity, overcome distance, and establish identification. And identification, in turn, becomes the basis for vengeful action.

Justice O'Connor, in whose opinion White joined, reiterated Scalia's position in *Booth* by noting the existence of a "strong societal consensus" in favor of victim impact statements. Like Scalia, O'Connor wanted the criminal justice system to bend to that consensus and thus turn away from the traditional social contract view in which law resists the clamor of a vengeful public. Moreover, the possibility that passion might triumph over reason need not, in itself, preclude the use of the victim impact

statement. That such statements might be "unduly inflammatory" does not mean they should be constitutionally barred.[62]

Murder, O'Connor declared, replaying Rehnquist's theme of
death and resurrection, "transforms a living person with hopes,
dreams, and fears into a corpse. . . . The Constitution does not
preclude the State from deciding to give some of that back."[63]
Victim impact evidence is valuable precisely because it is not
abstract and impersonal. It insists that punishment respond to
real pain. The jury is asked to hear that pain and to avenge it, to
repay death with death to end the victimization. The unmasking
of the retribution-revenge distinction, as well as the return of revenge, is now complete as the victim is given both a voice and a
champion.

Scalia's brief concurrence in *Payne* fully underlines the unveil-
ing of revenge and its newfound status as a legitimate motive in
capital sentencing. Focusing solely on mitigating evidence while
excluding evidence about victim impact would be, in Scalia's
view, an "injustice." "*Booth*'s stunning *ipse dixit*," Scalia argued,
"that a crime's unanticipated consequences must be deemed 'irrelevant' to the sentence conflicts with a public sense of justice
keen enough that it has found voice in a nationwide 'victim's
rights' movement."[64]

Scalia's opinion works to establish a series of rhetorical link-
ages. What is unjust is what conflicts with the public's sense of
justice. In this instance Scalia positions himself as the spokes-
man for the victims' rights movement, and he defines justice by
a political rather than an ethical standard. Finding "voice" is exactly what is at stake in *Payne*, or, more precisely, what is at stake
is the question of whose voice will determine the public's sense
of justice.

Scalia would not only allow victim impact evidence but would
also place limits on the mitigation evidence that is allowed in
capital trials. He would direct attention away from the moral
blameworthiness of the defendant to the harm done to the victims, unintentionally transforming the juridical subject into one

whose inner life counts for less than his outer actions. "A system arranged in this way," law professor Steven Gey rightly notes,

> would permit sentencers in capital trials to ignore the defendant's character altogether and react solely to the bare facts of the crime and its ancillary consequences. The defendant is viewed in one-dimensional fashion as nothing more than the agent of harm. Instead of meting out justice in retributive fashion, according to the defendant's moral deserts, Scalia's system avenges a harm by killing the agent of harm. Society's anger is assuaged, even if in traditional retributive terms the punishment is disproportionate to the offense.[65]

While Rehnquist, O'Connor, and Scalia unveiled and legitimated the vengeful side of legal justice, one justice in *Payne* tried, albeit in a strained and convoluted manner, to reconcile the use of victim impact statements in capital cases with the maintenance of the revenge-retribution dichotomy. Justice Souter alone recognized the scrambling of categories that the victims' rights movement inspires. He did so by insisting that the harms which a victim impact statement would bring to the attention of the jury would, in fact, be "foreseeable" by an offender. They would be wrongs of the kind that Nozick said provided the basis for retributive punishment, yet they would not be done with an individualized consciousness of wrongdoing. "While a defendant's anticipation of specific consequences to the victims of his intended act is relevant to sentencing," Souter contended,

> such *detailed* foreknowledge does not exhaust the category of morally relevant fact. . . . Murder has foreseeable consequences. When it happens, it is always to distinct individuals, and after it happens other victims are left. Every defendant knows . . . that the life he will take by his homicidal behavior is that of a unique person . . . and that the person killed probably has close associates . . . who will suffer harms and deprivations from the victim's death. . . . That foreseeability of the killing's consequences imbues them with direct moral relevance.[66] (emphasis added)

Souter seeks to personalize the victim by turning the offender into an impersonal repository of stipulated knowledge. Thus for him the harm to the victim's family is a culpable wrong because it is *always* foreseeable. That wrong is as blameworthy as the wrong done to the person murdered.

But Souter's effort to provide a retributive rationale for victim impact evidence proves too much. If every murderer knows, or can foresee, damage to surviving relatives resulting from his act, then there is no need to inform the jury about the nature of such damage because it would not help differentiate murderers who deserve to die from those who deserve life in prison. If Souter is right, victim impact statements personalize the suffering of the survivors and undermine the very distinction between revenge and retribution that his opinion seeks to preserve.

Justice Stevens's *Payne* dissent points out this consequence of Souter's reasoning. For him the only way to preserve the retributive basis for capital punishment is to prohibit the use of victim impact statements. Not surprisingly, throughout his opinion Stevens distinguishes reason from passion, a distinction that, he suggests, the use of victim impact evidence erodes. He argues that, though the majority opinion will have "strong political appeal," it has "no proper place in a reasoned judicial opinion." Moreover he insists that unless it can be shown that collateral harm associated with a murder was known in its particularity to the murderer, then it is of no consequence or relevance in determining his blameworthiness or in calculating an appropriate response to the wrong of his act. The use of a victim impact statement is, in his view, unacceptable because it "allows a jury to hold a defendant responsible for a whole array of harms that he could not foresee and for which he is therefore not blameworthy."[67]

Stevens suggests that, even in the face of the "political strength of the 'victims' rights' movement," law should not give in.[68] At stake is the viability of what he calls the "retribution rationale" for criminal punishment. Allowing the use of a victim impact statement in capital sentencing will, he warns, be "greeted with enthusiasm by a large number of . . . citizens," yet it "serves no purpose other than to encourage jurors to decide in favor of death rather than life on the basis of their emotions rather than their reason"[69] and, in so doing, undermines the very basis of legal legitimacy.

Yet the *Payne* decision did, in fact, open up the legal process and the process through which punishment is imposed to satisfy "a public sense of justice," which is equated with the movement for victims' rights.[70] The case did, despite the efforts of the justices on both sides, destabilize the revenge-retribution dichotomy even as it seemed to proclaim the return of revenge. With the exception of Souter, the justices did not acknowledge the potentially disruptive impact of the urgent call to hear the voice of the victim, even as they acted it out in their rhetoric.[71] They responded to the challenge posed by the victims' rights movement by reiterating categories whose very meaning was up for grabs.

As it was in the McVeigh case, hearing the voice of the victim may be a political imperative and *Payne* may be a political concession to a desire for vengeance, yet neither can be contained within the traditional revenge-retribution framework.[72] The case is thus not simply a triumph for vengeance. Rather it is an opportunity for vengeful victims to participate in an unfamiliar medium of discourse in which grief and rage are joined to rational argument and complex rules of evidence. *Payne* shatters the very opposition that the return of revenge seems to reassert.

This development is what Justice Marshall identified, in his opinion in *Payne*, as the ultimate significance of the case. In his judgment, what was really at stake was the ominous suggestion of "an even more extensive upheaval" in the law, one that "sends a clear signal that scores of established liberties are now ripe for reconsideration." He rightly warned that the return of revenge could not or would not be contained, that it is part and parcel of an indignant, frustrated assault on those who have claimed the role of the victim in today's political discourse—"minorities, women, or the indigent." As a result, revenge returns with a vengeance. For Marshall, *Payne* was one major step toward the demise of a conception of law as "a source of impersonal and reasoned judgments."[73]

Conclusion

> *Retribution is vengeance in disguise.*
> —OLIVER WENDELL HOLMES, *The Common Law*

The demand to hear the voice of the victim in capital trials is but a symptom of the fragility and instability of the myths and stories that have been used to legitimate the killing state. That demand both expresses and precipitates a serious difficulty for the legal system because law seeks to replace one kind of violence—vengeful violence—with an economy of violence controlled and disciplined by legal norms. As Rene Girard reminds us in *Violence and the Sacred*, the emergence of both ritual sacrifice and ultimately of modern justice is rooted in the fear of an unending chain of "reciprocal acts of vengeance."[74] State violence on this account differs from and is superior to private violence because it is disciplined and subject to public accountability. Neither popular nor populist, it is different and superior because through public processes it ascertains guilt and fixes punishment and, in so doing, prevents an escalating cycle of injury-response-injury.

Payne is part of a larger movement that retells the myths and stories of American law and produces, whatever its intention, a new constellation of possibilities. It joins victims and offenders without acknowledging their complex interconnections. This landmark case brings passion to the house of reason and asks officials to reason as never before about grief and rage.[75] By personalizing an impersonal process, it exposes the personal to public judgment. While the return of revenge is a response to the complexities and contradictions of our era, it does not solve the problems that inspired it. Revenge brings its own complications.

In the narrative of the victims' rights movement, the state is a great source of danger; yet it is to the state that victims must turn for redress. The victims' rights movement is part of a historical moment in which the people heroically dismantle the apparatus of the Leviathan. And *Payne* seems, at first glance, to reflect Justice Holmes's view that "The first requirement of a sound body of law is that it should correspond with the actual feelings and demands of the community, whether right or wrong," and that "if people would gratify the passion of revenge outside of law, if law did not help them, the law has no choice but to satisfy the craving itself."[76]

The return of revenge in the United States comes at a time when some of our most fundamental beliefs seem particularly insecure, when we have conquered old enemies and are looking for new ones. Some believe that venting rage against the criminal class will put the pieces back together again.[77] As Minow notes, victim impact statements "persuade, when they do, because they invoke widely shared images of goodness, Christian piety . . . the 'little guy,' and American patriotism, all of which are talismans of the deserving person. Some degree of simplification is inevitable and no one should be surprised to find that victim impact statements do not reveal the uniqueness of the human being victimized by crime."[78]

We are, moreover, increasingly unable to agree upon a shared set of public values. The power of the victims' rights movement and the return of revenge are both indications of social conditions in which all institutions are judged by their responsiveness to private preferences. Ironically, the preferences to which institutions are supposed to respond are today recognizably shaped by those very institutions. In such a society we turn to "victims and their stories of suffering . . . to provide common grounds for certainty in the midst of profound alienation and doubt."[79] Nonetheless, those stories, when told as they are in and through the legal process, provide neither common grounds, nor, as the verdict in the criminal case against O. J. Simpson showed, can they replace doubt with certain knowledge.

The return of revenge is also a reminder that modern legal orders are built on the edge of fear and anger, and that they must walk a fine line in their efforts to allay that fear and calm that anger.[80] *Payne* is a misstep in that effort. Unlike Holmes, who could say with certainty that law's violence was superior to the "greater evil of private retribution,"[81] our era can speak with no such confidence. Throughout the West there is today a nagging doubt that public processes can be built on anything but rage and grief. That is what the call to hear the voice of the victim signals; that is what the return of revenge suggests.[82]

"Why is [the] sentiment of mankind indelible to the scandal of reason?" Beccaria once asked. His response increasingly marks the spirit of our age. "It is," he said, "that, in a secret corner of the mind, in which the original impressions of nature are still preserved, men discover a sentiment which tells them, that their lives are not lawfully in the power of any one, but of that necessity only which with its iron scepter rules the universe."[83] Perhaps this is what Justice Stevens understood when, at the end of his opinion in *Payne*, he observed, "Today is a sad day for a great institution."[84]

3

KILLING ME SOFTLY: CAPITAL PUNISHMENT AND THE TECHNOLOGIES FOR TAKING LIFE

There is no law that is not inscribed on bodies. Every law has a hold on the body. . . . Every power, including the power of law, is written first of all on the backs of its subjects.
—MICHEL DE CERTEAU, *The Practice of Everyday Life*

Make a good job of this.—WILLIAM KEMMLER, first person electrocuted in the United States, 1891

Do they feel anything? Do they hurt? Is there any pain? Very humane compared to what they've done to our children. The torture they've put our kids through. I think sometimes it's too easy. They ought to feel something. If it's fire burning all the way through their body or whatever. There ought to be some little sense of pain to it.
—Mother of a murder victim on being shown the planned death by lethal injection of her child's killer

People who wish to commit murder, they better not do it in the
state of Florida because we may have a problem with our electric
chair.—ROBERT BUTTERWORTH, Attorney General, State of
Florida, remarking on a malfunction that caused a fire during
 an electrocution

Though our brother is on the rack . . . our sense will never inform
us of what he suffers. . . . By the imagination we place ourselves
in his situation, we conceive ourselves enduring all the same
torments, we enter as it were into his body, and become in some
measure the same person with him.—ADAM SMITH, *The Theory*
of the Moral Sentiments

In March 1997 newspapers all over the United States announced
the "botched" electrocution of Pedro Medina, a thirty-nine-year-
old Cuban immigrant convicted and condemned for the stabbing
of a Florida high school teacher.[1] After the current was turned on,
as one newspaper put it, flames "leaped from the head" of the
condemned. "It was horrible," a witness was quoted as saying, "a
solid flame covered his whole head, from one side to the other. I
had the impression of somebody being burned alive."[2] Another
newspaper wrote, "The electrocution of Pedro Medina on Tuesday was the stuff of nightmares and horror fiction novels and
films. A foot-long blue and orange flame shot from the mask covering his head for about 10 seconds, filling the execution chamber
with smoke and sickening witnesses with the odor of charred
human flesh. One witness compared it to 'a burning alive.' "[3]
    Yet news reports also conveyed the "reassuring" reaction of Dr.
Belle Almojera, medical director at Florida State Prison, who said
that before the apparatus caught fire Medina already had "lurched
up in his seat and balled up his fists—the normal reaction to high

voltage. . . . I saw no evidence of pain or suffering by the inmate throughout the entire process. In my professional opinion, he died a very quick, humane death."[4] The Florida Supreme Court found that "Medina's brain was instantly and massively depolarized within milliseconds of the initial surge of electricity. He suffered no conscious pain."[5] And others defended even this botched electrocution by noting that it "was much more humane than what was done to the victim."[6]

Despite these attempts to contain adverse public reaction, the Medina execution made headlines because it suggested that the quest for a painless, and allegedly humane, technology of death was by no means complete. It did so, also, because it reminded us of the ferocity of the state's sovereign power over life itself. Yet these news stories also contained a hint of relief for supporters of capital punishment because most treated the Medina story as a mere technological glitch rather than as an occasion to rethink the practice of state killing. Florida, the Fort Lauderdale *Sun-Sentinel* opined, "is justified in imposing the death penalty. . . . But it has no justification for retaining a method . . . that is so gruesome and violent and sometimes flawed."[7] What might have been a challenge to the legitimacy of the killing state was quickly written off to the failure of one state to keep up with the technology of the times.

Almost immediately after the Medina execution some death penalty proponents denounced electrocution as an out-of-date, unreliable technology of death and called for its replacement in Florida by lethal injection, the current technology of choice when the state kills.[8] "Under lethal injection," one newspaper explained, "the condemned is first sedated, then injected with deadly chemicals that painlessly and quickly paralyze the lungs and stop the heart."[9] As one Florida judge commenting on the continuing use of electrocution in Florida observed, "other less cruel methods of execution are available; lethal injection is readily available . . . and is generally considered more humane."[10] In a similar vein the Florida Corrections Commission recommended a switch from electrocution to lethal injection, observing that "Florida has an obligation to ensure that modern technologies keep pace with the level of competence in this area, and, just as changes have occurred in Florida's past in carrying out the death penalty, changes should again occur."[11] Prompted by an impending U. S. Supreme Court hearing on the constitutionality of electrocution, in January 2000, the Florida legislature made lethal injection the default method of execution in that state.[12]

The botched execution of Pedro Medina clearly was an embarrassment to a legal order bent on killing people, but doing so quietly, invisibly, burcaucratically[13]—though at least one official, Florida's attorney general, was sufficiently *un*embarrassed to speculate that gruesome cruelty might be a better deterrent than a quick death. The Medina execution provided one of those periodic, though rare moments, in which the state's dealing in death makes headlines. The commentary on this execution is particularly revealing in what it says about how we understand the killing state. This commentary, first, is striking for what it did *not* say. Neither death itself, nor state killing, generated public horror; there was little investment in trying to understand either what it means for the state to deal in death, or for citizens of the United States to live in a state that kills.

That most executions in the United States are not newsworthy suggests that the killing state is taken for granted.[14] One of the few issues left in the public debate about capital punishment is *how* the state kills. As the news stories about the Medina execution suggest, concern about the state's dealing in death is displaced by a concern for technological efficiency in which we are invited, following Dr. Almojera, to imagine the body as a legible text that we read to understand the capacity of technology to move us from life to death swiftly, painlessly.[15] But one might ask, Why should the state be concerned about the suffering of those it puts to death? Painful death might be both more just and more effective as a deterrent than one that is quick, quiet, and tranquil.

As comments by the survivors and the families of the victims in the McVeigh case suggest, the search for a painless way of killing those who kill is somewhat unsettling and paradoxical. If McVeigh is eventually executed, he will be put to death by lethal injection. Yet the voice of vengeance demands that the pain inflicted in the crime equal the pain experienced in punishment. As Arlene Blanchard, a survivor of the bombing, explained after McVeigh's death sentence was handed down, "death by injection is 'too good' for McVeigh. She said he should be put in solitary confinement for life or simply hanged from a tree. 'I know it sounds uncivilized, but I want him to experience just a little of the pain and torture that he has put us through.' " Or, as William Baay, an emergency worker who helped remove bodies from the Murrah Building, explained, "I don't think conventional methods should be used. They should amputate his legs with no anesthesia . . . and then set him over a bunch of bamboo shoots and let them grow up into him until he's dead."[16]

When law commits itself to hearing the voices of victims and to satisfying their desires for vengeance, it will came under pressure to use it methods of killing that seem to many, including some of those who advocate them, "uncivilized." Thus even as it seeks to hear those voices, the state must be cautious about what they say. It must find ways of distinguishing state killing from the acts to which it is a supposedly just response and to kill in ways that do not allow the condemned to become an object of pity or to appropriate the status of the victim. In this chapter I examine the way law seeks to balance and respond to these contradictory demands. I am concerned, in particular, about what it means for law to imagine itself to be a master of the technologies of death, or whether the relationship that is imagined is really a relationship of mastery or of subservience.

Technology mediates between the state and death by masking physical pain and allowing citizens to imagine that state killing is painless. The language of law works hand in hand with this technology to veil the ugly realities of execution, separating cause and effect, and making it unclear who is actually ordering and doing the killing. In today's killing state, it has become too easy to believe that nobody in particular is responsible for capital punishment and that, in any event, execution is a "humane" procedure that need not unduly bother even the squeamish among us.

In this chapter I show how the search for ever more invisible, "humane" methods of state killing depends on certain assumptions about pain and our ability to understand what people feel as they are executed. I am concerned, in particular, to demonstrate that the legal construction of state killing, while it appears to reveal empathy or identification between the state and those it kills, works primarily to differentiate state killing from murder. In these efforts, we are invited to search for a way of taking life that signals our superiority and marks the distinction between state violence and violence outside the law, between a death we call capital punishment and a death we call murder. As one commentator on the Medina execution and its aftermath correctly observed, "Let's be honest: Seeking a 'humane' form of execution has nothing to do with it. It is not about sparing the condemned, but sparing ourselves. We like to keep the whole awful business at arms length, to tell ourselves capital punishment is civilized."[17]

Doing Death Silently, Invisibly

The recent history of state killing in the United States reads like someone's idea of the triumph of progress applied to the technologies of death.[18] From hanging to electrocution, from electrocution to lethal gas, from electricity and gas to lethal injection, the law has moved, gradually, from one technology to another.[19] At each stage the law has proclaimed its own previous methods barbaric or simply archaic. Thus, as one judge recently said about death by electrocution, "Execution by electrocution is a spectacle whose time has passed—like the guillotine or public stoning or burning at the stake. . . . Florida's electric chair, by its own track record, has proven to be a dinosaur more befitting the laboratory of Baron Frankenstein than the death chamber of Florida State Prison."[20] Responding to the advent of lethal injection, another judge characterized the continuing use of hanging as "an ugly vestige of earlier, less civilized times when science had not yet developed medically-appropriate methods of bringing human life to an end."[21] Nothing but the best will do in the business of state killing.

This search for a quiet technological fix contrasts starkly with the execution practices of previous eras. As Michel Foucault notes, in the past executions were "more than an act of justice"; they were a "manifestation of force."[22] They always revolved around display, in particular the display of the majestic, awesome power of sovereignty to decide who suffers and who goes free, who lives and who dies. Public executions functioned as public theater, but also as a school for citizenship.[23] Choosing the right method to kill was a matter of sovereign prerogative. Authorities chose methods for their ability to convey the ferocity of the sovereign's vengeance.

State killing produced a sadistic relation between the executioner, the victim, and the audience. Viewers obtained pleasure as well as schooling in their relation to sovereign power, by witnessing pain. The excesses of execution and the enthusiasm of the crowd blended the performance of torture with pleasure, creating an unembarrassed celebration of death that knew no law except the law of one person's will inscribed on the body of the condemned. The display of violence, of the sovereignty that was constituted in killing, was designed to create fearful, if not obedient, subjects.

The act of putting someone to death contained a dramatic, awe-inspiring pedagogy of power. "The public execution," Foucault explained,

> has a juridico-political function. It is a ceremonial by which a momentarily injured sovereignty is reconstituted. It restores sovereignty by manifesting it at its most spectacular. The public execution, however hasty and everyday, belongs to a whole series of great rituals in which power is eclipsed and restored (coronation, entry of the king into a conquered city, the submission of rebellious subjects). . . . There must be an emphatic affirmation of power and its intrinsic superiority. And this superiority is not simply that of right, but that of the physical strength of the sovereign beating down upon the body of his adversary and mastering it.[24]

Capital punishment was precisely about the right of the state to kill as it pleased. Sovereignty established itself by taking life. Executions were designed to make the state's ultimate power majestically visible to all. Live but live by the grace of the sovereign, live but remember that your life belongs to the state; these were the messages of the state killing of an earlier era.

Without a public audience state killing would have been meaningless. As Foucault put it, "Not only must the people know, they must see with their own eyes. Because they must be made afraid, but also because they must be witnesses, the guarantors of the punishment, and because they must to a certain extent take part in it."[25] In this understanding of punishment, the people were, at one and the same time, fearful subjects, authorizing witnesses, and lustful participants.

Today the death penalty, with some notable exceptions, has been transformed from dramatic spectacle to cool, bureaucratic operation, and the role of the public now is strictly limited and tightly controlled. The modern execution is carried out behind prison walls in what amounts to semiprivate, sacrificial ceremonies in which a few selected witnesses are gathered in a carefully monitored setting—to see and, in their seeing, to sanctify—the state's killing of one of its citizens.[26]

Capital punishment becomes, at best, a hidden reality. It is known, if it is known at all, by indirection. Hugo Bedau, a distinguished philosopher and ardent abolitionist, notes that "The relative privacy of executions nowadays (even photographs of the condemned man dying are almost invariably strictly prohibited) means that the average American literally does not know what is being done when the government, in his name and presumably on his behalf, executes a criminal."[27] What was public is now private. What was high drama has been reduced to a matter of mundane technique.

Whereas once the technologies of killing deployed by the state were valued precisely because of their gruesome effects on the body of the condemned, today we seek a technology that leaves no trace. Whereas in the past the technologies were valued as ways of making the sovereign power awe-inspiring and fearsome,

today the process of state killing is medicalized; it is less about
sovereignty than science. Executions

> were progressively stripped of their ritualistic and religious as-
> pects. . . . as Americans developed a keen dread of physical pain,
> medical professionals teamed up with . . . engineers to devise a pur-
> portedly "painless" method of administering the death penalty. . . .
> The condemned man . . . had now become simply the object of
> medico-bureaucratic technique—his body read closely for signs of
> pain. . . . The overriding aim of the state functionaries charged
> with conducting executions nowadays is to "get the man dead" as
> quickly, uneventfully, impersonally, and painlessly as Nature and
> Science permit.[28]

Since the earliest recorded execution in the Americas in 1608,
more than sixteen thousand people have been put to death at the
hands of the state.[29] "We've sawed people in half, beheaded them,
burned them, drowned them, crushed them with rocks, tied them
to anthills, buried them alive, and [executed them] in almost
every way except perhaps boiling them in oil."[30] Today, however,
five methods of execution are currently available: firing squad,
hanging, lethal gas, electrocution, and lethal injection. The first
two are authorized in just a few states, five states use lethal gas,
two more authorize electrocution as the sole method of state killing, and lethal injection is available in thirty-seven states.[31]

When, in 1888, New York became the first state to institute
death by electrocution, it did so because an expert commission
found it to be "the most humane and practical method known to
modern science of carrying into effect the sentence of death."[32]
States that eventually followed New York's lead "viewed . . .
[electrocution] as less painful than hanging and less horrific than
having the condemned swing from the gallows"; states that rejected hanging in favor of the gas chamber viewed it as "more
decent" than electrocution because it seemed less violent and did
not mutilate the body.[33] Thus the original legislation authorizing
the use of gas stipulated that the condemned was to be put to
death "without warning and while asleep in his cell."[34]

These same concerns have been echoed in the most recent fad among the technologies of state killing, lethal injection. Upholding the constitutionality of lethal injection, a federal district court recently noted that, "There is general agreement that lethal injection is at present the most humane type of execution available and is far preferable to the sometimes barbaric means employed in the past."[35] This is hardly the language of either the survivors and families of the victims of the Oklahoma City bombing or the awe-inspiring sovereignty about which Foucault wrote. Thus one might ask whether the killing state can respond adequately to the return of revenge epitomized by the push to make a place for victims in capital trials if it insists on using painless methods of execution. What is at stake in state killing when the state imagines itself killing decently, painlessly, humanely?

On the Invisible Body of the Condemned

Cases challenging the constitutionality of particular methods of execution are regularly, though not frequently, brought before courts in the United States.[36] In the first two such cases to reach the United States Supreme Court, that Court upheld first the use of firing squads[37] and then electrocution.[38] In the latter case, the Court proclaimed that no method of execution could be used that would "involve torture or a lingering death"; the state could kill so long as it used methods that did not impose "something more than the mere extinguishment of life."[39]

This statement is remarkable in the casual way in which it purports to limit sovereign prerogative, in the juxtaposition of the word "mere" with an awkward circumlocution for death, and in its seeming acquiescence in the view that "mere" death at the hands of the state gives no grounds for complaint. It condemns excess, "something more," as if state-imposed death itself were not already an excess.[40] The state can spare life, or extinguish it, but it cannot require its victims to "linger" between life and death. Law stands ready to police the excesses of sovereignty, but it still grants sovereignty its due. The domain of sovereignty extends to deciding who shall die who shall do the killing; law is left to police the technologies through which the state takes life.

Sometimes, however, even this jurisdiction has seemed more than the law could, or would, handle. Indeed, more often than not, the law has stayed its hand when the state has been accused of going too far. Perhaps the most famous instance of such inaction occurred in the case of *Francis v. Resweber*,[41] a case in which the United States Supreme Court allowed the state of Louisiana to execute a convicted murderer twice. As the Court wrote, "Francis was prepared for execution and on May 3, 1946 . . . was placed in the official electric chair of the State of Louisiana. . . . The executioner threw the switch but, presumably because of some mechanical difficulty, death did not result."[42] Sometime later Francis sought to prevent a "second" execution by contending that it would constitute cruel and unusual punishment.[43]

Justice Reed, writing for a majority of the Court, responded to these claims in what initially appears to be an unusual way. For him the cruelty of Louisiana's plan had little to do with Francis[44] or any pain he might have suffered during the attempted execution and in anticipation of being strapped into the chair again. The Constitution, as Reed understood it, clearly permits "the *necessary* suffering involved in any method employed to extinguish life humanely" (emphasis added).[45] Note how in Reed's formulation, suffering deemed "necessary" is fully compatible with humane killing. Something more than the mere extinction of life is permissible so long as that excess inheres in the "method" and so long as it is impossible for the state to kill without it.

What the Constitution permits, according to Reed, dutiful judges should not prohibit. If Francis had to undergo a second, more lethal, dose of electricity, it was because the rules, not the judges, allowed it. According to those rules, the fact of the first, botched execution would not "add an element of cruelty to a subsequent execution."[46] The constitutional question, as Reed saw it, turned instead on the behavior of those in charge of Francis's "first" execution, those authorized to unleash state violence.

Their acts and intentions were decisive in determining whether a second execution would be unconstitutionally cruel.

From the facts as he understood them, Reed found those officials to have carried out their duties in a "careful and humane manner" with "no suggestion of malevolence" and no "purpose to inflict unnecessary pain." He described diligent, indeed even compassionate, executioners frustrated by what he labeled an "unforeseeable accident . . . for which no man is to blame," and concluded that the state itself would be unfairly punished were it deprived of a second chance to execute Francis. Indeed, in the only place where Reed tries to come to terms with what the first execution did to Francis, he suggests, again relying on the image of the first execution as an accident, that Francis could only have suffered "the identical amount of mental anguish and physical pain (as in) any other occurrence, such as . . . a fire in the cell block." While Reed described Francis as an "accident victim," the issue for Francis was the future as much as the past.[47] For him what was constitutionally significant was the connection between the violence and horror inflicted on him during the first execution and the violence the state, with the Supreme Court's blessing, proposed to inflict on him in a second execution.

So remote was the Court's interest in Francis, in the death it was condoning, or in the pain that he had already experienced and would again experience, that only late in the dissenting opinion of Justice Burton was any reference made to the effect of the first execution attempt on Francis himself. There we are told that his "lips puffed out and he groaned and jumped so that the chair came off the floor." Nonetheless, even here the significance of Francis's impending death is deferred, as is his pain. References to that pain, taken from affidavits by witnesses to the first execution, were included solely to point out a "conflict in testimony" that made it impossible, in Burton's view, to determine whether any electricity had actually reached Francis during the abortive execution attempt. The conflict arose when those in charge of the electrical equipment testified that "no electrical current reached . . . [Francis] and that his flesh did not show electrical burns."[48]

Burton did worry about the number of failed executions the majority might tolerate before declaring subsequent attempts cruel and unusual. Yet while he labeled the state's desire to carry out a second execution "death by installments," he devoted most of his opinion to a careful scrutiny of Louisiana's death penalty statute. Death itself is not the object of attention. Instead Burton seeks to affirm the possibility of law's mastery over death as well as law's fidelity to its own rules for taking life. A proper execution is one whose occasions and procedures are prescribed by law, just as a proper judgment is one governed by the law and the law alone. Because the statute made no provision for "a second, third or multiple application of [electric] current," a second execution should not, in Burton's opinion, be permitted.[49] Though differing in their conclusions, Burton and Reed denied any connection between their acts of judgment and the fate of Willie Francis. They both treated the behavior of the state rather than the experience, and prospective death, of its intended victim as constitutionally significant.

The way Burton and Reed proceeded in *Francis* seems all too familiar and yet, from the perspective of the reactions to the Medina execution, somewhat strange. In *Francis*, the death that is the very business of the case is but a shadowy presence, barely acknowledged. Where it is glimpsed, almost inadvertently, Francis's return date with electrocution is presented as the deed of some abstract, impersonal set of rules; the judge's own hand is stayed. In the opinions of Burton and Reed, death is the absent subject, but so is pain and the search for a humane way of killing.

The Body in Pain

Today death still appears to be the absent subject when courts confront challenges to the state's technologies of death. However, unlike in the *Francis* case, where the question of pain was almost completely elided, courts faced with challenges to these technologies now focus, almost obsessively, on that question.[50] They sometimes treat the body as a text on which we can read the signs of excess—signs that the state's chosen method imposes something in addition to the mere extinction of life. At other times, however, they seek to read pain indirectly, hardly mentioning the body at all. Yet the law's increasing obsession with pain is really an obsession with pain as it appears to society—specifically those who serve as witnesses, real or imagined, of state killing. The experience of execution by its witnesses and a concern for their "suffering" fuel the search for painless death.

Let me focus on three recent examples to highlight this continuity and this difference. The first, *Campbell v. Wood*,[51] decided in 1994 by the Ninth Circuit Court of Appeals, dealt with the constitutionality of hanging as a method of execution; the second, *Fierro v. Gomez*,[52] decided later that same year, dealt with execution by lethal gas; the third, a 1999 decision of the Florida State Supreme Court, *Provenzano v. Moore*,[53] concerned the constitutionality of electrocution. The former upheld the use of hanging; the second prohibited the state of California from using gas to kill; the third found that death in the electric chair did not violate the Constitution.

Judge Beezer, writing for the majority in *Campbell*, framed the question presented in that case as "whether hanging comports with contemporary standards of decency." He noted that, while few states now use hanging, no court in the United States had ever found that it violated the Constitution. Nor, in his view, does the "mere" fact that hanging causes death render it unconstitutional. Instead Beezer argued that the question of whether hanging was acceptable depended on "the actual pain that may or may not attend the practice."[54] Determining the constitutionality of this method of execution required the court to read the body of the condemned for what it reveals of its suffering as it moves from the world of the living to the world of the dead. Beezer noted that the district court had heard extensive expert and eyewitness testimony about the way hanging causes death and about the pain that is associated with it.[55] He wrote confidently about the court's ability to know the pain of the condemned even as he noted that pain itself would not render hanging invalid. A method of execution, he claimed, relying on

Kemmler and *Francis*, is only unconstitutional if it "involves the unnecessary and wanton infliction of pain."[56]

With this as the standard, Beezer provided an extended discussion of the methods used in hanging, contrasting in particular the so-called long-drop with the short-drop method. He found that several factors make death by hanging "comparatively painless," namely the length of the drop, the selection and treatment of the rope, the positioning of the knot. Washington's use of the long-drop method of hanging, he said, is designed "to ensure that forces to the neck structures are optimized to cause rapid unconsciousness and death." The result of the methods deployed in Washington, Beezer argued, was that "unconsciousness and death . . . occur extremely rapidly, that unconsciousness was likely to be immediate or within a matter of seconds, and that death would follow rapidly thereafter." He ended his opinion by reiterating that "Campbell is not entitled to a painless execution, but only one free of purposeful cruelty."[57]

Here Beezer seems to return us, at least partially, to the world of *Francis* in which attention moves from the executed to the executioner, from the body in pain to the intentions of the executioner. But whereas the judgment in *Francis* almost completely avoids the subject of pain, in *Campbell* determining the pain associated with one or another technology of death is a necessary, though not sufficient, first step. If such a determination suggests that the condemned is subject to pain, the court must then, but only then, inquire into the purposes of the state in imposing death through that method. Evidence of pain suggests barbarism on the part of those who take life. Pain is thus the dangerous supplement of death, signaling excess or the sadistic pleasure associated with the willful taking of human life.

Judge Reinhardt dissented from Beezer's view in *Campbell* because it seemed to equate the "evolving standard of decency" of Eighth Amendment jurisprudence solely with an inquiry into pain and its purposes. In his view the development of "new and less brutal methods of execution, such as lethal injection" as well as the "risks of pain and mutilation inherent in hanging" make hanging constitutionally defective.[58] The fact that, by the time of

Campbell, all but a few state legislatures had abolished hanging provided, for Reinhardt, an additional but still crucial indicator of its incompatibility with contemporary standards of decency. Moreover, if the reduction of needless pain were to be taken as the exclusive measure of a technique's constitutionality, "barbaric and savage" forms of punishment such as the guillotine would not be constitutionally barred.

In the end, even if the Constitution were to mandate only an objective inquiry into pain and its purposes, judicial hanging would still, in Reinhardt's view, be unacceptable because it is "a crude, rough, and wanton procedure, the purpose of which is to tear apart the spine. It is needlessly violent and intrusive, deliberately degrading and dehumanizing. It causes grievous fear beyond that of death itself and the attendant consequences are often humiliating and disgusting." It carries with it a "high risk of pain far more than is necessary to kill a condemned inmate. If the drop is too short, the prisoner will strangle to death, a slow and painful process. . . . [If the drop] is too long the prisoner may be decapitated."[59]

A punishment can be cruel, Reinhardt contended, even if it is not painful. Cruelty can arise "from the relatively painless infliction of degradation, savagery, and brutality. . . . Indignities can be inflicted even after a person has died." The Constitution *obligates* the state, when it chooses to kill, to "eliminate the degrading, brutal, and violent aspects of an execution, and substitute a scientifically developed and approved method of terminating life through appropriate medical procedures in a neutral, medical environment."[60] Where science makes available technologies for ending life that serve the same goals, but with markedly lower risk of imposing pain, the Constitution *requires* that the state follow science. On Reinhardt's reading, the state is not master of technology but is subservient to it. Whereas Beezer imposed few limits on the sovereign's choice of the method of execution, Reinhardt would eliminate much, if not all, of the sovereign's discretion.

Although Beezer and Reinhardt differ on the sufficiency of pain as a standard in determining the constitutionality of a method of

execution, both assume that they can know the pain of another
and that they can represent it faithfully in their opinions. As
Reinhardt put it, "There is absolutely no question that every
hanging involves a risk that the prisoner will not die immediately, but will instead struggle or asphyxiate to death. This process, which may take several minutes, is extremely painful. Not
only does the prisoner experience the pain felt by any strangula-
tion victim, but he does so while dangling at the end of a rope."[61]
Though neither Beezer nor Reinhardt may know, or be able to
accurately represent, death, they write with confidence about
their ability to know the pain that precedes it.

This apparent displacement of death as well as this same confidence in the court's ability to read and represent pain is seen in
Fierro. Judge Patel notes, early in her *Fierro* opinion, that while
lethal gas had been the execution technology of choice in California since 1937, in the mid-1980s Warden Vasquez of San Quentin
revised the state's execution protocol. This statement takes on
significance later in her decision when she links it to the kind
of technological imperative hinted at in Reinhardt's opinion in
Campbell. As Patel put it, neither the warden nor his staff "con-
sulted scientific experts or medical personnel in formulating the
execution protocol nor did they examine records from previous
California executions"; she characterizes the result as an "unscientific, slapdash" execution protocol. When sovereignty exercises its power over life and death, it is not free to kill in a gruesome way to instill awe and fear in the citizenry. The availability
of lethal injection, which Patel characterized as "more humane
than lethal gas as a method of execution," renders the latter "anti-
quated" and incompatible with the Constitution.[62] Again, law requires that sovereignty be the servant of technology.

Taking *Campbell* as governing authority in the *Fierro* case,
Patel declared that the judgment makes it "clear" that the "key
question to be answered in a challenge to the method of execution
is how much pain the inmate suffers." *Campbell,* she argued,
"dictates that a court look first to objective evidence of pain."[63]
After an elaborate description of the gas chamber and the procedures used during execution by lethal gas, Patel reviewed contra-

dictory expert testimony concerning the effects of gas and the precise ways it kills.

As she summarized it, the basic disagreement between plaintiff and defense experts is "whether unconsciousness occurs within at most thirty seconds of inhalation, as defendants maintain, or whether, as plaintiffs contend, unconsciousness occurs much later, after the inmate has endured the painful effects of cyanide gas for several minutes." To resolve this conflict, she reviewed extant scientific literature but determined that, while "plaintiffs' theory of death through cellular suffocation has traditionally been the accepted viewpoint,"[64] the scientific community was neither uniform nor clear in its conclusions.

Next Patel discussed two types of eyewitness accounts of execution by lethal injection. The first, the observations and records of physicians who attended every execution by lethal gas, reads like an obsessive archive of death. The physician records when, during the course of an execution, each of the following events occurs: "'Sodium Cyanide Enters'; 'Gas Strikes Prisoner's Face'; 'Prisoner Apparently Unconscious'; and 'Prisoner Certainly Unconscious' and 'Last Bodily Movement.'"[65] The other eyewitness evidence involved observations by lay witnesses.

Patel prefaced her discussion of all of this evidence by noting that "neither consciousness nor pain is easy to gauge. Actions that appear volitional or appear to be a reaction to pain may in fact be unconscious and non-volitional."[66] Yet these cautions did not inhibit her interpretation of the testimony. She believed that pain, while difficult to measure, could be read on the surface of the body by untrained people as well as by medical personnel. Their observations provide the measure for constitutional judgment.

Beginning with the two California executions immediately preceding her decision, Patel noted that the physicians' records revealed that "certain unconsciousness" did not occur until three minutes after the gas hit the face of the condemned. Records of California's earlier executions contain similar results. The judge declared that the expert testimony, the scientific literature, the physicians' records, and eyewitness statements "unmistakably"

show that during a period of consciousness following the dispensing of lethal gas that "inmates suffer intense, visceral pain, primarily as a result of lack of oxygen to the cells." This pain Patel
asserted, moving from a calm balancing of evidence to vivid analogy is "akin to the experience of a major heart attack, or to being
held under water."[67] In this resort to analogy, Patel sought to conjure imagined horrors somewhat closer to home for the average
citizen than the particular horrors associated with death in the
gas chamber.

Like Judge Beezer and Judge Reinhardt in *Campbell*, Patel fore-
grounds the question of what the journey from life to death might
be like under one particular execution technique. She too focuses
on the presence of pain, carefully constructing a narrative from
different strands of evidence. She insists that the state kill as
softly, as gently, as painlessly as the minds of men and women
allow.[68]

Her opinion, like the opinions in *Campbell*, textualizes pain,
sometimes by focusing on the body of the condemned and sometimes by reading through it to understand consciousness and its
limits. A similar strategy was followed by the majority in
Provenzano,[69] which began by examining alleged errors in previous executions, in particular the execution of Allen Lee Davis.
"Allen Lee Davis," the Court claimed, "did not suffer any conscious pain while being electrocuted in Florida's electric chair.
Rather he suffered instantaneous and painless death once the current was applied to him." The *Provenzano* majority cautioned
against misreading the body, saying "The nose bleed incurred by
Allen Lee Davis began *before* the electric current was applied to
him, and was not caused whatsoever by the application of electrical current to Davis." It noted that "the record in this case reveals
abundant evidence that execution by electrocution renders an inmate instantaneously unconscious, thereby making it impossible
to feel pain."[70] Because it is painless, the court concluded, death
by electrocution is not cruel and because it is not cruel it is not
unconstitutional.

Justice Shaw, in his dissent, agreed about the centrality of pain,
though he reached strikingly different conclusions about its presence when electrocution is the method of state killing, reminding

us that legibility of the pain does not ensure that its presence will always be read accurately. But, like Reinhardt in *Campbell*, he insisted that the courts should not focus obsessively and exclusively on pain as the sole indicator of cruelty. They should also consider the crucial question of what he labeled "violence, mutilation, and disgrace."[71]

Choosing the guillotine as his example, he expressed a breezy confidence in his ability to read pain when he noted, "while beheading results in a quick, relatively painless death, it entails frank violence (i.e. gross laceration and blood-letting) and mutila tion (i.e. decapitation), and disgrace . . . and thus is facially cruel." Pain as well as violence, mutilation, and disgrace, Shaw claimed, also accompany electrocution. "Not only was every execution in Florida accompanied by the inevitable convulsing and burning that characterizes electrocution, but further, three executions were marred by extraordinary violence and mutilation. In two . . . smoke and flames spurted from the headpiece and burned the heads and faces of the inmates. In the third execution, the inmate bled from the nostrils and was at least partially asphyxiated by the restraining devices; and he too was burned."[72]

Shaw's opinion goes on for pages providing elaborate, detailed, and graphic descriptions of those three executions, paying particular attention to the third, the Davis execution. And, in a truly extraordinary gesture, he appended to his opinion "post-execution color photos of Davis before he was removed from the electric chair. These photos . . . provide a vivid picture of a violent scene . . . [and] show a ghastly post-execution scene." While he provided his own description of what those photographs show ("a stream of blood pours from his nostrils, flows over the wide-leather mouth-strap, runs down his neck and chest, and forms a bright red pool . . . on his white shirt"), he meant the photographic evidence to speak for itself[73] (see Figures 3, 4, and 5).

Appending such images to a judicial opinion transgresses convention in a way that ensures they will be the subject of considerable attention and commentary. They shock and draw upon a different register of understanding. They make pain and the violence associated with state killing into a matter of sight. Because they are "vivid," Shaw assumed that they would convey a reality more clearly transparent than any language could. Thus the presence of the photos is not only an almost unprecedented judicial effort to make state killing visible, it is also a stark reminder of the limits of language when it speaks about physical violence and physical pain.[74]

Pain, observes literary theorist Elaine Scarry, "has no voice. . . . When one hears about another's physical pain, the events happening within the interior of that person's body may seem to have the remote character of some deep subterranean fact, belonging to an invisible geography that, however portentous, has no reality because it has not yet manifested itself on the visible surface of the earth."[75] Pain is, according to Scarry,

> vaguely alarming yet unreal, laden with consequence yet evaporating before the mind because not available to sensory confirmation, unseeable classes of objects such as subterranean plates, Seyfert galaxies, and the pains occurring in other people's bodies flicker before the mind, then disappear. . . . [Pain] achieves . . . its aversiveness in part by bringing about, even within the radius of several feet, this absolute split between one's sense of one's own reality and the reality of other persons. . . . Whatever pain achieves, it achieves in part through its unsharability, and it ensures this unsharability through its resistance to language.[76]

"A great deal is at stake," Scarry herself suggests, "in the attempt to invent linguistic structures that will reach and accommodate this area of experience normally so inaccessible to language."[77] The cases on methods of execution surely confirm this view. Yet Scarry reminds us that the capacity of courts to understand and to convey the pain of the person being executed is limited, even as this capacity is foregrounded in these cases.

Scarry invites us to consider legal cases like *Francis, Campbell, Fierro,* and *Provenzano* for what they tell us about the use of languages of violence and pain, although she suggests that in law, as elsewhere, the languages that can be used face constraints. "As physical pain is monolithically consistent in its assault on language," Scarry writes, "so the verbal strategies for overcoming the assault are very small in number and reappear consistently as one looks at the words of the patient, physician, Amnesty worker, law-yer, artist." Those verbal strategies "revolve [first] around the ver-bal sign of the weapon." We know pain, in the first instance, through its instrumentalities—for example, hanging or lethal gas. Second, we know it through its effects. Here violence and pain are represented in the "wound," that is, "the bodily damage that is pictured as accompanying pain."[78] But, as Scarry suggests, these representations can provide no certain or reliable grounding for a jurisprudence that seeks to govern the technologies through which the state puts people to death. Yet it is precisely those repre-sentations that play a central role in death penalty jurisprudence.

If Scarry is right, then the courts in the United States have cre-ated for themselves epistemological and interpretive as well as legal and political problems. By deferring the question of death and foregrounding the question of pain, they are required to take seriously the empirical world of the body and its suffering even as they necessarily run up against the limits of their capacity to know that world and to render it in language.[79] Again we are driven back to the question of why pain and the search for pain-less execution would play so large a part in the law's confronta-tion with the killing state and whether this state can be both vengeful and humane.

Conclusion

At the beginning of the twenty-first century in the United States law seems reconciled to state-imposed death, but it is set on a quest to force the state to kill softly, gently, to impose no pain at all, or no more pain than is necessary. That the law requires the state to kill in this manner seems, in one way, counterintuitive; it may precipitate a crisis of legitimacy by distancing itself from the voices of victims and the demands of vengeance and, in so doing, by raising questions like those raised by the mother of a murder victim quoted in one of the epigraphs of this chapter: "Do they feel anything? Do they hurt? Is there any pain? Very humane compared to what they've done to our children. The torture

they've put our kids through. I think sometimes it's too easy.
They ought to feel something. If it's fire burning all the way
through their body or whatever. There ought to be some little
sense of pain to it."

Perhaps this strategy is less counterintuitive than it might otherwise seem. Legal scholar Alan Hyde argues that law's requirement that the state kill gently "follows a common pattern in
which the humanistic, sentimentalized body in pain emerges as
a site of empathy and identification" in the nineteenth and twentieth centuries. Sentimentalizing the body of the condemned establishes, Hyde notes, a bridge between the criminal and the public. The criminal, no matter how horrific his deeds, is like us in
his body's "amenability to feeling." The concern that punishment
not inflict physical pain and the empathy that it enables and expresses "lies behind the curious search in American legal history
for painless methods of execution." In an endlessly repeating ritual, Hyde says, "electrocution, gas chambers, lethal injections are
each introduced with tremendous fanfare as a painless form of
death, until each is revealed to promote its own kind of suffering
on the way to death." Yet, as Hyde himself recognizes, execution
marks the limits of empathy, reminding citizens of the ultimate
disconnection between themselves and the condemned, a disconnection that seeks to operate at the moral level.[80]

Thus the search for painless death might be better understood
as one way of keeping simplifying, sentimental narratives of
criminal and victim intact by not allowing those condemned to
die to assume the status of victims of outmoded technologies of
death, or as a response to one kind of crisis in legitimacy through
another legitimation strategy. Law imposes on sovereignty the
requirement that no matter how heinous the crime, or how reprehensible the criminal, that we not kill as those we punish have
killed. We give them a kinder, gentler death than they deserve to
mark a boundary between the "civilized" and the "savage" rather
than to establish a connection between citizens and murderers.
We kill gently not out of concern for the condemned but rather
to establish vividly a hierarchy between the law-abiding and the
lawless.[81]

The boundary-marking, hierarchy-establishing function of law's search for a painless execution was put vividly on display in Justice Scalia's response to Justice Blackmun's dissent from a Supreme Court denial of certiorari in a 1994 death penalty case. In that dissent, Blackmun announced that he no longer would "tinker with the machinery of death," and would, as a result, vote against the death penalty in all subsequent cases. Scalia responded by noting that while Blackmun had described "with poignancy the death of a convicted murderer by lethal injection," compared with what the condemned had done—"the murder of a man ripped by a bullet suddenly and unexpectedly . . . left to bleed to death on the floor of a tavern"—death by lethal injection was "pretty desirable." How enviable, Scalia continued, "a quiet death by lethal injection compared with that!"[82]

We may not be able to know death, or comprehend its possibilities or its horrors, but where law requires the killing state to kill softly, it restrains the state from fully and completely giving in to calls for vengeance and, in so doing, seeks legitimacy in an image of the hand of punishment humanely applied. It may be death we are doing, but it is a death whose savagery law insists it can, and will, control.

For the judges in *Campbell*, *Fierro*, and *Provenzano* close examination of the technologies of death takes the form of an effort to prevent the erosion of the boundaries between the state's violence and its extralegal counterpart. As Judge Shaw observed, "The color photos of Davis depict a man who—for all appearances—was brutally tortured to death by the citizens of Florida. . . . Each botched execution cast[s] the entire criminal justice system of this state—including the courts—in ignominy."[83] The killing state depends on law both to respond to and yet to restrain vengeance, to deploy and yet to mask power, to enable and yet to hide the violence on which that state ultimately depends. Yet the fact that the state takes life, and that it is everywhere a response to an imagined violence, generates an anxious questioning about the ways state violence differs from the violence to which it is, at least in theory, opposed. The effort to kill softly, gently, painlessly, humanely is one response to that questioning, one way of trying to show that the state, though it relies on violence, can transcend that violence.[84]

As a response to this anxious questioning, the courts insist on policing the technologies of death to ensure that sovereign power responds to scientific progress, that ferocity gives way to bureaucracy, that it proceeds judiciously, using no more force than is absolutely necessary. State killing, guided by the restraining hand of law, in this view should be rational, purposive, and proportional; the violence to which it responds is, in contrast, imagined to be irrational, anomic, excessive. In the face of scientific "progress" in the technologies of death, the forms of legal procedure cannot condone archaic displays of sovereignty like those demanded by the survivors and families of the victims of the Oklahoma City bombing or like the botched execution of Pedro Medina. The survival of state killing as an exercise of sovereign power depends on its ability to respond to the return of revenge, while being subject, even if against its will, to an unending search for technologies that in their capacity to kill with a pretense of humanity allow those who kill both to end life and, at the same time, to believe themselves to be the guardians of a moral order that, in part, bases its claims to superiority in its condemnation of killing.

FIGURE 1. Firefighter
Carrying Baby After
Oklahoma City Bombing

FIGURE 2. McVeigh under Arrest

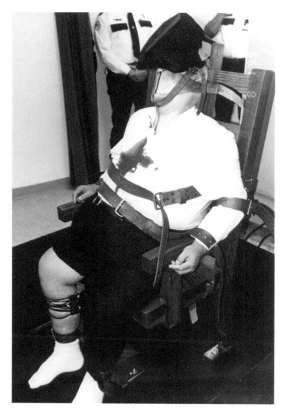

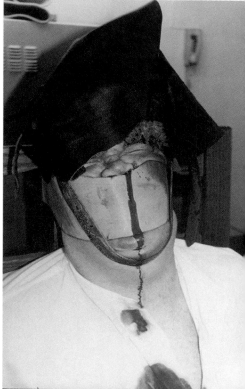

FIGURES 3, 4, and 5.
The Execution
of Allen Lee Davis

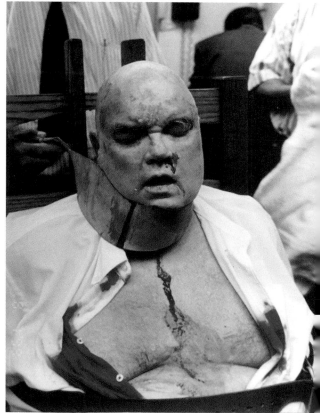

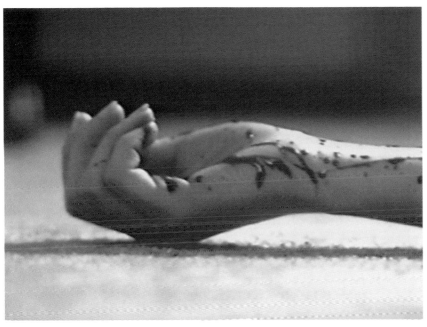

FIGURE 6. Hand of the Victim in *Last Dance*

FIGURE 7. Rick and Cindy in *Last Dance*

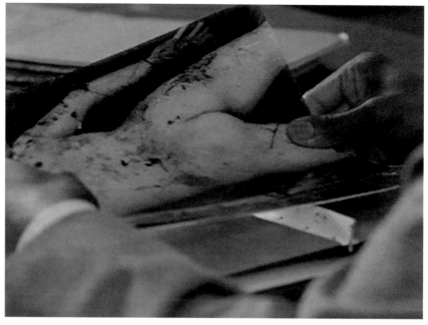

FIGURE 8. Photograph of Victim in *Dead Man Walking*

FIGURE 9. Sister Helen with Poncelet in *Dead Man Walking*

FIGURE 10. Poncelet Speaking His Last Words in *Dead Man Walking*

FIGURE 11. Wharton with His Victims in *The Green Mile*

FIGURE 12. Paul with John in *The Green Mile*

FIGURE 13. Witnesses in *Last Dance*

FIGURE 14. Poncelet with Faces of Hope and Walter in *Dead Man Walking*

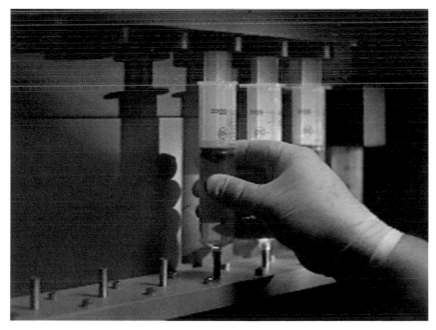

FIGURE 15. Vials Being Fitted into Lethal Injection Machinery in *Last Dance*

FIGURE 16. Botched Electrocution in *The Green Mile*

FIGURE 17. Protest in *Dead Man Walking*

part

STATE KILLING IN

two

THE LEGAL PROCESS

4

CAPITAL TRIALS AND THE ORDINARY

WORLD OF STATE KILLING

*The news lived in the air of the courtroom. It was
as if there had been one kind of existence in the
room, and now there was another: a man was
going to be executed. It was real but it was not
comprehensible. The man was standing there.*
—NORMAN MAILER, *The Executioner's Song*

*The way in which we choose those who will
die reveals the depth of moral commitment among
the living.*
—JUSTICE WILLIAM BRENNAN, *McCleskey v. Kemp*

At 8:30 A.M. on July 15, 1977, William Brooks accosted Carol Jeannine Galloway ("Jeannine" to her friends) at gunpoint and forced
her to drive to a wooded area behind a neighborhood school where
he raped her and shot her to death. Eventually Brooks was arrested and put on trial, charged with kidnaping, robbery, rape, and
murder.[1] If Timothy McVeigh is the poster boy for capital punishment, people like Brooks stand in his shadow, reminding us of
the dangers of the American condition.

Every day, all over the United States, capital trials like the Brooks trial are under way. There the business of the killing state is done beyond the glare of media attention. Unlike the McVeigh case, these trials generally are not the object of widespread publicity. Political leaders do not make public statements concerning appropriate punishments. Large teams of lawyers are not assembled to prosecute and defend an infamous accused.

It was precisely its everyday quality that made the Brooks case an ideal one to observe personally, drawing me from my New England home to Madison, Georgia, a classic southern town fifty miles from Atlanta. To sit in the courtroom would be to witness a case that exemplifies the mundane operations of the system of capital punishment in the United States. What I was going to see was, in fact, Brooks's second trial. His first had been notable because it was the first to be televised in Georgia. It ended with his conviction on all charges and the imposition of a death sentence. However, several years later an appellate court overturned his murder conviction and sentence, creating the occasion for the trial I was to witness. This time there would be no television coverage.

In the Brooks trial, and others like it, two different cultural narratives compete for prominence. One turns crime and punishment into a simplifying and reassuring story of individual responsibility, of evil people doing evil deeds and calling down upon themselves a just and inevitable punishment. The other, while not denying that individuals can and should be held responsible, tries to contextualize crime by focusing on the social conditions that bring it about. The former narrative authorizes punishment—severe punishment—as the right way to respond to crime; the latter insists on the complexity of the causes of crime and on the uncertainties about the right way to respond. Each characterizes its protagonist—the innocent person injured by crime or the criminal who himself has led a tragic life—as the real victim, evoking stock characterizations to create sympathetic identification.[2]

Trials of persons accused of capital crimes provide one vehicle through which to consider the complex relationship of law and

violence that state killing necessarily entails, as well as one opportunity to observe what Robert Cover called the "field of pain
and death" on which law acts.[3] Modern law traffics in and responds to aggression, force, and disruption, terrible acts, some
dramatic, like the bombing in Oklahoma City, some simply
tragic, like the rape and murder of Jeannine Galloway. Law de-
ploys violence every day, using its own force to deter and punish
acts that society brands as illegal.

The proximity of law to, and its dependence on, violence raises
a persistent doubt about whether state violence is different from
and preferable to the violence beyond its boundaries.[4] To address
that doubt is a continuing necessity, especially when the state
seeks to use death as a punishment. The opportunity to talk about
violence and to distinguish capital punishment from murder occurs in those rare moments—capital trials—when both are spoken about at once. As a result, such trials, whether celebrated or
not, are crucial and unusually revealing moments in the life of
the law.

Because capital punishment is irrevocable and unique, the
prospect of state killing challenges law to be fairer and more scru-
pulous than it would otherwise be. As we have seen, the challenge is potentially severe because it is in capital cases that the
call for vengeance is the loudest, the moral presence of the grieving family the weightiest. If legal institutions are to meet this
burden of fairness, they must resist those pressures while providing adequate representation for the accused and adhering to pre
scribed fact-finding procedures in the guilt and penalty phases of
capital trials.[5] They must also find a responsible way to talk about
the violence of both the crime and the prospective punishment.
Can they talk about killing without demonizing the killers? Can
they acknowledge the horror of murder without exiling murderers from the human community? Can they show restraint in the
face of evil?

Moreover, how does law respond to the difficulty of putting
physical violence and physical pain into words? Because violence
is visible and vivid, it speaks loudly, arouses indignation, and
threatens to overwhelm reason. Violence and its linguistic repre-

sentation are inseparable from pain and its representation. We know the full measure of violence only through the pain it inflicts; the indignation we experience at violence is a function of our imagining the hurt it imposes. In this sense, the problem of putting violence and pain into words is one problem rather than two.

It is the business of law in general and capital trials in particular to know violence and pain, and to find means to overcome their resistances to language. Scarry suggests that the courtroom and the criminal trial provide particularly important sites to observe how violence and pain "enter language."[6] In the criminal trial the problem of putting violence and pain into language is compounded by the fact that

> it is not immediately apparent in exactly what way the verbal act of expressing pain . . . helps to eliminate the physical fact of pain. Furthermore, built into the very structure of the case is a dispute about the correspondence between language and material reality: the accuracy of the descriptions of suffering given by the plaintiff's lawyer may be contested by the defendant's lawyer. . . . For the moment it is enough to notice that, whatever else is true, . . . [a trial] provides a situation that once again requires that the impediments to expressing pain be overcome. Under the pressure of this requirement, the lawyer, too, becomes an inventor of language, one who speaks on behalf of another person . . . and attempts to communicate the reality of that person's physical pain to people who are not themselves in pain [the jurors].[7]

As I noted in the preceding chapter, Scarry sees capital trials as occasions for lawyers to try out languages of violence and pain. But she warns that as violence and pain are put into language, we may be tempted to forget that their metaphorical representation as weapons and wounds cannot truly capture the meaning of violence and pain themselves. And in the process of putting those things into language, physical violence and pain that are palpable to us (those engendered by particular weapons and those that leave visible marks on the body) take priority over systemic cruelties and hardships that can cause much suffering (racism, poverty, and despair) but may leave no visible traces.

My analysis of the Brooks case focuses on how law copes with the challenges posed by the killing state and in particular on how it responds to the difficulties of talking responsibly about violence in capital trials. How does law overcome the resistance of violence and pain to language? How is the direct, physical violence done by William Brooks to Jeannine Galloway—the violence of kidnapping, rape, and murder, the violence that extinguished a life—spoken about? How is the more diffuse violence that pervaded Brooks's life from childhood onward known and understood? However, capital trials involve more than the presentation of violence beyond law's boundaries. In such trials the specter of state killing is real and immediate, and, as a result, we must be reassured that state killing is different from and preferable to the violence that is used to punish and deter.[8]

In this chapter I turn to the ordinary world of capital punishment to describe the ways boundaries are constructed between state killing and the other forms of violence—for example, murder and abuse—with which the law deals. Just as it does in its choice of technologies of death, law seeks in capital trials to distinguish the killings it opposes and avenges from force used in the name of justice.[9] In such trials violence of the kind done to Jeannine Galloway is juxtaposed with the "legitimate force" of state punishment. In the eyes of the law, violence is "the illegitimate or unauthorized use of force to effect decisions against the will or desire of others. Thus murder is an act of violence, but capital punishment by a legitimate state is not."[10]

Moreover, prosecutors seek to instantiate and vividly portray the violence beyond law's boundary—the killing of such innocents as Jeannine Galloway—while muting racial injustice, poverty, and abuse that often shape the life of killers as well as the violence of state killing. This is done in the hope of affirming the social value of law, reassuring citizens that the state's use of violence is somehow different from and better than illegal violence, alleviating anxiety about state killing by identifying a more terrifying Other and, in so doing, facilitating the willful use of violence and infliction of pain as an instrument of the state itself.

Those gestures coexist, but their coexistence is an uneasy one because, in capital trials, they are so often replete with racial symbols.[11] The narratives of violence and victimization that appear there frequently are racially charged; they suggest the boundary between law and nonlaw runs along a racial divide of us versus them, order versus disorder, reason against the mob. In the Brooks case, because Galloway was a hardworking, young white woman from a respectable family, and Brooks was an unemployed, drug-using, black male from a broken home, the trial (re)enacted a familiar American story in which young black men are demonized and state killing is authorized as a response to imagined racial savagery.[12]

The juxtaposition of the images of Galloway and Brooks told a simple story of lost innocence and racial danger. Thus, even as we are reassured about the legitimacy of state killing and its difference from violence outside the law, the racialization of that difference arouses other fears that encourage an acceptance, if not a warm embrace, of state violence as a necessary tool in a struggle between "us" and "them."[13] Do we feel safer as a result? Do we feel more secure in the embrace of the killing state? The Brooks trial may suggest some answers to these questions.

The Life and Death of Jeannine Galloway

The courthouse in Madison, Georgia, is an impressive building that sits on the edge of the town's gracious central square. To get to its main courtroom I walked up the wide, creaky stairway that empties out onto the second floor just down the corridor from the room where Brooks was on trial. That room was much too large for this sparsely attended event. Its size and relative emptiness inspired no majesty; instead they mostly invited glances when any new face appeared.

I entered hoping to be mistakenly identified as a journalist doing the unpleasant job of covering this trial rather than as an academic studying the real world of capital trials. Throughout the trial I felt uncomfortable, out of place in a setting most people would prefer to avoid. I felt that way partly because what I was seeing was but a tiny glimpse of lives forever changed by a terrible crime. The Brooks trial, like most capital trials, revealed few details about the life of the victim, Jeannine Galloway. She, after all, was not on trial. The first (guilt) phase of the trial centered, instead, on a story about the lawless violence that Brooks perpetrated and that Galloway endured.

As the trial unfolded, Jeannine's white, female body and the attack on it became a symbol for what the prosecutor—Douglas Pullen, then district attorney of Muscogee County where Jeannine's killing occurred—called "the body of mankind." The violence unleashed against her body was, at the same time, unleashed against a body that was not her own, the disembodied body of "everyone." Her death became a Hobbesian tale of anomic violence against a supposedly universal body. As in the McVeigh case, the death of an ordinary person became a trope for the American condition, one in which each of us could suffer the tragic fate of Jeannine Galloway.

Yet the displacement of Jeannine and her life story could not be and was not complete. That story was of a life of innocence, purity, and virtue. Throughout the trial the innocence of Jeannine's body provided the context for the discussion of the violence and pain she suffered. Her innocence became the true measure of her worth and of the horror of her body's violation.

It was the white, good Jeannine who was slain by the black, evil Brooks; good was assaulted and sullied by evil. Although Pullen denied the significance of race ("This isn't black versus white"), the imagery on which he consistently relied was racial, as in his repeated claim that Brooks had led his life in "dark places," or as in the contrast between those, like Jeannine, who embrace the "American way, play by the rules, and work hard" and those, like Brooks, who are "mean and lazy."

Good people versus bad people, virtue juxtaposed with vice— this simple morality tale, a reassuring sentimental narrative, fuels the engine of state killing. The Brooks case was for Pullen and, he hoped, for the jury an opportunity to vindicate, if not restore, Jeannine's fallen innocence and to assert the value of white life against the devaluing acts of black men.[14] Brooks's lead defense lawyer, Stephen Bright—a tall, redheaded man with a southern accent, which grew deeper and more pronounced the minute he entered the courtroom—told me, in an interview after the trial, that "This was a classic sort of race case with the young white woman, a virgin according to the newspapers, who was taken from her home by a black man. Your classic southern death penalty case is the rape of a white woman by a young, black man."

The prosecution constructed the image of Jeannine's innocence and of the value of her white life by calling attention to particular facets of that life and emphasizing certain of her attributes: her place as the "child" in a loving family and her virginity. Both play on prominent themes in contemporary culture wars, putting Jeannine on the "right side" in contests about family values and sexual promiscuity. At the time of her death, she was a twenty-three-year-old piano teacher at a local music store and engaged to be married to Harold "Bob" Murray, though she still lived at home with her parents, Earl and Heddie.

On the day of Jeannine's death Heddie, a frail, soft-spoken woman in her sixties who worked for an optometrist, was home on vacation. Jeannine went out the door at 8:30 A.M. to meet her friend Ann Overton for breakfast. As Heddie put it in her testimony,

> A: Jeannine went out to the carport. I was beginning to relax after breakfast, and I put the chain on the door because I was alone in the house. I looked out the window and saw Jeannine's car with the door to the driver's side open. . . .
>
> Q: At that time did you see anyone?
>
> A: No. I didn't see anyone. I opened the kitchen door and went outside. I called to her, but no one answered. So I went back into the house to see if she was there. And then I walked back out to the carport. That's when I heard her say "I'm in here." Her voice came from the utility room.

Q: Where is this?

A: The utility room is just off to the left of the kitchen door. I
heard a voice say "I'm in here." And I said, "What are you
doing in there?" She said, "I'm just looking for something."
She said, "Go back in the house. When I find what I'm looking
for I'll let you know." So I went in the house and called my
neighbor. I knew something was wrong, but nobody answered.
Then I went outside again. The door to the utility room was
closed. I started to go back in the house again and the phone
rang. I picked it up and it was Ann Overton wanting to know
where Jeannine was and whether she was coming to breakfast.
I told her that someone had her in the utility room and I said
she should come over here fast. As soon as we hung up I tried
my neighbor again. Then I heard the car start up and I ran to
the door.

Q: What did you see?

A: I saw her in her car with a black man on the passenger side. I'd
never seen him before. I looked inside the car and I got very
close to it. She began to back down the driveway. I walked
along as she backed out, and I kept my eyes on him. I called
out to her to "Please wait." "No," she said, "I'll be back.
Don't worry."

There is something nightmarish and terrifying in this testimony of the mother's witnessing of Jeannine's kidnapping and
her excruciating inability to stop it. Both prefigure and foretell
the murder to come. It is as if the violence done to Jeannine was
already present, symbolically displaced, and expressed in Heddie's disbelief of Jeannine's reassurances. Heddie's recollection is
like a terrible dream in which she is forced to look at the living
corpse of her daughter.

In Heddie's testimony race makes an overt appearance when she volunteered the race of the man in the car next to Jeannine. The danger that first appears as a disruption of domestic routine is thus a racial danger. At an early stage in the trial, in the voice of the victim's mother, a portrait of the violence on the other side of law's boundary and of its association with race begins to emerge.

Lawless violence invades the unworried, safe space of home and family. Yet that space is less unworried than it first appears. Even where there has been, as yet, no invasion, the specter of violence is already looming. Mrs. Galloway's testimony contained a stark reminder of our collective anxieties about criminal violence. She was sufficiently aware of the possibility of violence that she chained the door to protect herself. Hers was a diffuse anxiety about the particular vulnerability of a woman alone. Her response was to lock the world out so she could "relax."

In addition, anxiety about violence was sufficiently part of Jeannine's life that, according to the testimony of her fiancé she "went to seminars about what to do if you are raped." For Jeannine lawless violence could not be locked out; hers was a life in which neither law nor locks could provide security or certainty. Yet in her world of innocence, preparation to meet such lawless violence seemed nearly incomprehensible to some. As Bob Murray explained to the court, "I couldn't understand why she went [to the seminars on rape]. I treated it lightly."

Here, as in the Oklahoma City bombing, violence is so bold and powerful that no preparation is adequate. It takes the innocent daughter right out from under her mother's eyes. Thus Heddie watched helplessly as Jeannine drove away with an unidentifiable "black man" beside her, and as a nightmare of racial victimization was played out. Implicit in the testimony about this nightmare is a contrast between domestic routine and the known, but unspoken, fate of Jeannine Galloway.[15]

Not only was Jeannine's the innocence of a dutiful daughter, it was, in addition, a virginal innocence. Jeannine's virginity was admitted into evidence over the defense's strenuous objection. Bright contended that it was irrelevant and inadmissible, that it went to no material issue in the case. Pullen responded by claim-

ing that the fact of her virginity went to the issue of noncon-
sent; it showed that there "was no consent to the crime of
intercourse."

Once admitted, Jeannine's virginity would quickly become important. It became an essential part of the story of the "wounds"
that the prosecutor would use to bring Brooks's violence and Jeannine's pain into the trial. Once admitted, virginity helped fur-
therto racialize the story of Jeannine's rape. It became the unsub-
tle symbol of her innocence and worth, and Brooks's crime became an incorporation of the stereotypical racial attack on white
womanhood.[16]

In a statement given to the police at the time of his arrest
Brooks said that after he had intercourse with Jeannine he asked
her "Was it your first time?" and that she responded that it was.
According to Brooks's own account, "I didn't believe her."
Against his disbelief the trial provided the occasion for affirming
the truth of what she had uttered, as if her virginity were itself
on trial.[17]

If the story of Jeannine's life was a linear narrative of racial
innocence and gendered purity, the story of her violation was
complex. From the beginning of the trial the prosecution painted
a picture of the violence committed against Jeannine Galloway
as gruesome, wanton, cruel, and unnecessary. In Pullen's words,
"Jeannine died a horrible death. . . . She did nothing to deserve to
die." Using these words, he presented an implicit contrast between violence outside the law, which is visited upon the deserving and the undeserving alike and which respects neither innocence nor virtue, and state killing, which is reserved for those
who by their acts deserve death. Unlike the indiscriminate use of violence against the innocent Jeannine, law provides
elaborate procedures (in Brooks's case, a trial, an extended process of review and appeal, and then a retrial) and uses them to
ensure that state violence is visited only on the guilty. What is
unspoken here is that unlike Jeannine, Brooks has done something to warrant death, and that the death to which Brooks might
be subject at the hands of the state will be neither wanton, nor
cruel, nor unnecessary.

Throughout the trial, Pullen referred to the irrationality of the crime committed against Jeannine Galloway and tried to describe the full measure of the pain she had endured. He returned again and again to the issue of her blamelessness. "What did she do?" he asked repeatedly. "She just went outside her home. She was not running around in skimpy clothes, and she was taken from her home." In his effort to describe the senseless horror of Brooks's crime, Pullen used the dress of other rape victims—suggesting that clothing can invite the crime—as a foil to highlight Jeannine's innocence. Thus Jeannine's virtue became a standard against which the flaws of other women, less pure and innocent than she, could be measured.

In his opening statement the prosecutor told the jury that Jeannine was

> accosted by the defendant at gunpoint. She was forced to drive with him to the woods behind Dawson school. There she was forced at gunpoint to disrobe. She was raped. And then she was shot in the neck at a downward angle. Some time later she died from the gunshot and the fact that she received no medical attention. . . . Behind the school at gunpoint the defendant had Jeannine strip and then he raped her. She was begging "Let me go." But he taunted her about her virginity. And then he shot her in the neck because she was screaming and she wouldn't shut up.

With these words Pullen sought to make violence and pain speak, though he acknowledged to the jury that "it is not easy for us to appreciate the horror" of Jeannine's suffering. "Shot in the neck at a downward angle" and "begging 'Let me go'" suggest that Jeannine was on her knees when she was shot. The violence unleashed by the shot was designed to silence its victim who was by then so desperate that she could only beg for a mercy that was not forthcoming.

The violence that Brooks inflicted on Jeannine Galloway was, in Pullen's narrative, "done in the course of rape, in the course of armed robbery, in the course of kidnaping with injury. Kidnaping is horrible but this involved an injury to the breast and vaginal area. This was a crime of torture. The defendant wasn't content with just the physical act. He taunted her with his cruel question about her lack of sexual experience." Pullen told the jury that Jeannine had been shot at close range and that the medical examiner had "found that she had been raped and had been torn up in her private parts. Her panties were very bloody, and on her breast were bite marks. She bled to death over an extended period of time." Brooks's lawless violence is attached to particular parts of her body. It is inscribed as a hole in the neck, bite marks on the breast, blood from "her private parts."

But it is not vision or the visibility of her wounds that dominate in the re-creation of the lawless violence done to Jeannine Galloway. It is speech that carries the burden of capturing violence. Three speech acts were central to the narrative of Jeannine's suffering. First is the statement Brooks made to the police at the time of his arrest. Second is Jeannine's speech as well as her silence. Third is the testimony of the medical examiner, Dr. Weber.

Although Brooks did not testify in his own defense, his statement set the scene and the action of the crime.

> We drove down the dirt road by the Dawson School into the woods. When we got there I told her to stop the car and get out. She asked me to let her go, but I told her to take her clothes off. Then I had sex with her. When we got done I told her to get dressed. I asked her if it was her first time, and she said yes. I told her that I didn't believe her, and she started to scream. I pointed the gun at her and told her to be quiet. I cocked the gun and it went off. She fell. She was still screaming but I couldn't hear her.

In this account, Jeannine's movement from silence to speech caused her death. She was unable or unwilling to silently endure, to acquiesce to Brooks's demand for silence in the face of his disbelief in her lost innocence. She spoke in the only way she could, first in an audible and then in a quickly silenced scream.

Her silence was treated, throughout the trial, as a kind of heroism, even as its end marked the end of her life. As Pullen put it,

> the defendant came up to her, but she didn't scream. She was scared to death but she didn't scream. She had taken a course, but

she didn't scream. The defendant hid Jeannine when her mother came outside looking for her. She wanted to say "Momma save me," but she didn't because she knew what would happen. She didn't scream when she was forced to strip naked as a baby or when she was forced to lay down in the woods or when she was penetrated and her body was torn. Still she didn't scream. Then he taunted her about her virginity. It was only then, only when she saw her death in his eyes that she screamed. And then he killed her.

A third speech act played an important, if unusual, role in representing the lawless violence of William Brooks and in giving words to Jeannine's pain. This was the testimony of Dr. Weber, the medical examiner who, as it happened, died shortly before the trial. In a strange reenactment, a member of the prosecution team took the stand equipped with the transcript of testimony that Weber gave previously. As if from beyond the grave, the doctor became an embodied speaker. Another prosecutor asked the same questions as had been asked in Brooks's first trial, and Weber's answers were read verbatim. Those answers suggested Galloway had been killed by a bullet fired from short range that entered the base of her neck, "tore away the trachea, hit a rib and the spinal column, lacerated a lung and exited between the third and fourth rib."

Weber stated that Galloway had not died quickly; in his opinion she lived for between one-half hour and two hours after being shot. During this time, he suggested, she had suffered greatly. In addition, Weber indicated that he found "teeth marks on the left nipple, injuries to the vagina including a lacerated hymen . . . and hemorrhaging around the pelvis." He noted that Jeannine was a virgin prior to the assault and that her injuries were "associated with violent sexual activity." In his account, virginity becomes the context for understanding the overt marks of violence and pain. Here again violence and pain speak, as Scarry argues they must, through their visible effects—lacerations and hemorrhaging.

The context of a capital trial ensures that the difficulty of talking about violence and pain is compounded because at every turn "the accuracy of the descriptions of suffering" given by one lawyer will be "contested" by the other.[18] This was clear in the way the defense reacted to the testimony of Dr. Weber and his representations of Jeannine's pain: by calling another medical examiner as an expert witness to contest those representations.

That witness put the words of Dr. Weber on trial; he called particular attention to the language of Weber's autopsy report and his testimony. "Dr. Weber," the defense expert contended, "used words in his report that I would never use and that I've never seen before. He didn't use the standard scientific terms to describe what he was seeing. He talked about rips and tears. As a result, I don't know what he actually saw. . . . And while he described the hymen as virginal, you can't ever tell that."

On cross-examination, this witness persisted in his analysis of Weber's language.

> Q: Have you ever found rape in a murder victim?
>
> A: I prefer to call it sexual battery, not rape. The presence of sperm in and of itself doesn't equal rape.
>
> Q: What is the difference between sexual battery and rape?
>
> A: Well, a stick or a finger would do injury, and sexual battery takes all this into account
>
> Q: The defendant said he raped her. Are you arguing with that?
>
> A: No. But Weber's testimony said more than he said in his report. Sometimes medical examiners say more than they should in order to help prosecutors. Anyway his testimony and his report are inconsistent.

While there would be no argument about Brooks's self-incriminating words, Weber's words could be doubted and argued.

Quickly, however, Pullen turned his attention to the language of the expert himself.

Q: Are you saying Jeannine wasn't raped?

A: No. But you can be raped without being injured. There is still plenty of evidence to indicate that she was raped.

Q: Does the blood on her panties indicate the trauma associated with this rape?

A: Yes.

Q: Does it suggest the presence of brute force?

A: No. What we know is that someone had intercourse with her, caused a laceration, and it bled. Many people are, in fact, raped gently.

Q: Was Jeannine raped gently?

A: The bruise on her nipple may or may not have come from a bite. Other than the gunshot wound and the small tear in her vagina there is no evidence she was beaten or choked. There is evidence she was raped but not beaten up.

Q: She was kidnaped and forced to strip at gunpoint, then raped. . .

A: The defendant said he had sex with her.

Q: The girl said she was a virgin?

A: Yes.

Q: Was this a pleasant situation to lose her virginity?

A: No.

Q: Is this the way virgins choose to lose their virginity?

A: Some might. She did not.

Q: Would this have been painful?

A: Yes.

In this sequence of questions and answers the focus quickly shifts from Weber's speech to the expert's use of the phrase "gentle rape." His introduction of this absurd idea rendered oxymoronic the very idea of rape itself, and it gave Pullen a chance to remind the jury again of Jeannine's violated innocence, the wounds she had suffered, and the pain spoken through those wounds.

As in the defense expert's testimony, the question of the adequacy of language in describing violence was critical throughout the trial. Brooks's defense insisted that his statement should be taken literally, that it should be treated as an honest, full, and precise account of the events surrounding Jeannine Galloway's death, and that the agent of her pain was the gun that "went off" on its own.[19] The prosecutor, in contrast, suggested that the words of that statement, especially the words "it went off," should not be taken literally. As Pullen explained to the jury, "That's just how he happened to say it. That's just what his lawyer picked up on." Against the literalism of the defense was juxtaposed a theory of linguistic accident, of happenings rather than intentions, of words given meaning only by interpreters with purposes quite foreign to those of the original speaker.[20]

To Pullen, what was not said in Brooks's statement was as revealing as what was. "I want you to think about committing crimes and if you were telling the truth when you got to the part about the shooting you'd speak pages. 'I didn't mean to. I was going to let her go.' But none of that was ever said."

The defense responded that the statement was accurate and complete, and it appealed to a rather conventional idea of what makes a persuasive narrative.[21]

> The first thing to look at is the statement itself. . . . It is long and detailed. It tells about everything that happened. It said that she was made to get into a car with a gun. The defendant didn't make

things up. The statement tells about the crimes he committed in great detail. Those details are, in addition, corroborated by other evidence. Those details are the kind of things that no other person could have known. And every detail paints as bad a picture of the defendant as could be. Everything says it is true. And the prosecution wants you to believe everything but one sentence. Well they can't have it both ways. The whole statement is truthful.

Taking the statement literally would mean that the gun would become the personified agent of death. "The gun went off."

The literal reading of the defendant's statement with its personification of the gun was bolstered by the testimony of a firearms expert.

Q: Is it possible for a gun to go off by itself?

A: Yes.

Q: Is it possible for a 357 Charter Arms to discharge inadvertently?

A: Yes.

Q: How can a revolver discharge accidently?

A: It depends on the condition of the revolver and whether the safeties are operative. If the weapon is in poor condition the trigger pull might be much too tight so that when a person doesn't intend it, it might fire. You might pull back the trigger accidently after having the hammer back.

Q: Could the shooting in this case have been accidental?

A: Yes. There was one shot from close range. And the statement of the defendant that the hammer had been pulled back and that it went off. These things are all consistent with the conclusion that the gun in this case could have gone off accidently.

While the defense treated the gun, not Brooks, as the agent of death, the prosecution presented another story.

> Guns are dangerous, but they have their place. We all know that they don't just sit there looking to go off. The gun that snuffed out her life didn't really do it. That defendant did it. He pulled the trigger. . . . The mouth that marked her breast is that mouth there. The sex organ that penetrated her is on that man right there. The hand that fired the fatal bullet is on that man.

"Mouth," "sex organ," "hand"—each is a weapon used against Jeannine Galloway, each is an agent of the violence done to her, each is a sign of the pain unjustifiably imposed on her. "Mouth," "sex organ," "hand"—these signify a power brutally abused, a power able to silence Jeannine. But they also signify the dismemberment of Brooks's own body, a symbolic dismemberment in which each part of his body is linked with a discrete injury to his victim.

Where the defense portrayed the violence of Jeannine's death as tragic and accidental violence that knew no logic and for which no one could be held responsible, the prosecution portrayed it as the painful deliberate, humiliating violence of torture and slow death. But most of all it was an unnecessary violence. "If he wanted her to shut up he could have hit her with a big hand. When she woke up he would have been gone." This violence was, moreover, the willful, immoral, predatory gesture of an evil will transgressing against innocence itself. "One thing keeps coming back. It was all so unnecessary. If one person hadn't decided to use another for his lust she would still be alive. This is not the age of disposable people."

The phrases "It was all so unnecessary" and "to use another for his lust" bring together two different narrative strands in the prosecution's argument. The first is the story of violence outside the law with its implicit comparison to state violence, and the second is the story of race. In the first story, the violence outside law is senseless, random, almost inexplicable. Why did Brooks pick Galloway as his victim? Why that woman at that time? "We don't know whether he had staked out the Galloway house," Pul-

len noted, "or whether he was just looking for anybody to rob."
Thus the horrifying quality of Jeannine Galloway's murder was
that it was a

> chance encounter between strangers, in which what . . . [was] casu-
> ally exchanged happens to be death. . . . The radical disjunction, or
> discontinuity, between the immeasurably great value of what is
> being destroyed . . . and the minuscule, trivial, "perceived gain" that
> prompted the murder . . . leaves . . . a palpable, profound and almost
> physical need to reestablish sense and meaning in the universe.[22]

Galloway's murder, as described by the prosecution, was an instance of what law professor Robin West has called "post-modern
murders." Such murders, West claims, "strip the natural world
of its hierarchy of values—life, love, nurture, work, care, play,
sorrow, grief—and they do so for no reason, not even to satisfy
the misguided pseudo-Nietzschean desire of a Loeb or Leopold to
effectuate precisely that deconstruction. They are meaningless
murders."[23]

If there is meaning in Galloway's death, it is found only in a
racial narrative in which the "animal" passions of the young
black male lead him to use another person to satisfy his "lust."
"How," Pullen asked, "did the defendant treat Jeannine—like
some mother's baby, some daddy's little girl, or like something
disposable?" The question invites us to recover meaning by reas-
serting the significance of individual responsibility and by as-
serting the difference between lawless violence and official violence necessary to control or deter it, between the inability of
black men to control their "lust" and respect the sanctity of
human life and the human need for self-respect and self-control.[24]

The invitation is to reject meaninglessness in favor of a racially
coded meaning, and to see Brooks and his act as "inexplicably
alien, horrendous and inhuman."[25] The jurors in the Brooks
case—seven men and five women, nine blacks and three whites—
accepted that invitation and rejected what the prosecutor had dis-
paragingly called the "I didn't mean to" version of Jeannine Galloway's death. They convicted Brooks of malice murder, and the
trial moved into the second or sentencing phase.

The Life and "Death" of William Brooks

Jeannine Galloway's murder exemplifies one way in which the killing state depends on simplistic cultural oppositions embedded in a sentimental tale—good versus evil, virtue versus vice, offender versus victim—as well as a broadly shared narrative of racial danger. Complexity dissolves in the story of Brooks's crime. The dangers of this world can be readily explained. In such a conception we accord the status of victim "to someone who loses something—property, physical safety—because of the predation of someone else. Victimization, then, results from concrete, individual acts by identifiable transgressors."[26]

In the penalty phase of Brooks's trial the focus shifted to the life of the defendant. Brooks, a quiet, unassuming presence in the courtroom, did not graduate from high school. Indeed he spent most of his life between the ages of seventeen and twenty-one in jail for various crimes. In his life we see another story about violence that emphasizes the complexity underlying criminal acts and focuses on social structure as well as individual responsibility in explaining those acts. This story, too, depends on the cultural power of the idea of victimization even as it tries to refigure and complicate that idea.

Here we catch a different glimpse of the American condition, one that depends on another act of racialized tropes. In contrast to the equivalent stage of the McVeigh case, the sentencing phase of the Brooks trial revolved around a narrative about violence that the defendant himself had endured. Here again a racial narrative emerged, only this time constructed by the defense, a narrative of pain and victimization in which the rage of the young black male is portrayed as an understandable, if not justifiable, response to the constitutive violence of an America beyond his making.

In contrast to the direct, personal, decontextualized violence that Jeannine suffered at Brooks's hands, the defendant's life story was marked by a more diffuse, systemic violence, spread over a longer period of time. In contrast to the violence that took Jeannine's life, the suffering that Brooks had endured made his life what it is. In this alternative conception of violence and victimization both become matters "of the sweep of history, not the actions of individual transgressors. . . . In this vision of victimhood, the criminal behavior of so many black males is itself a mark of victimhood, a victimhood virtually determined from birth."[27]

In the penalty phase of most capital trials "the overall goal of the defense is to present a human narrative, an explanation of the defendant's apparently malignant violence as in some way rooted in understandable aspects of the human condition."[28] Defense strategies are premised on the belief that one cannot reliably judge a person's character simply by what they do. Identities are more complex than actions. In the common refrain of defense lawyers in the penalty phase, "Everyone is more than their worst act."

Here, too, an appeal to sentiment plays a key role. In this appeal the defense itself is a kind of "solemn memorial to ruin."[29] Thus defense lawyer Bright began his opening argument in the penalty phase by saying,

> It is hard to get up in front of you. You reached a verdict on Saturday that is not what we had hoped, but I accept it. To this point, however, all you've heard about is one terrible incident. Now you must consider the larger picture of William Brooks' life as you decide about the most extraordinary and extreme punishments—life in prison and being electrocuted by the state. The fact of his conviction for murder is not enough. The state must prove particular aggravating circumstances in this case. And even if those circumstances are established you still have to consider whether this person is so beyond redemption that he should be eliminated from the human community. To do that you must look at his whole life— good and bad. . . . We are going to tell the story of a life. In court we usually talk about just one incident. . . . Now we are going to talk about a life.

The plea in this argument is to consider the person behind the crime, to put the crime in context. In addition, through his rhetorical insistence that it is a "life" that must be talked about, Brooks's lawyer reminds the jury of the reality of state killing; he reminds them that there is now another life at stake, a life that can be extinguished through a legal gesture with as much crushing finality as Brooks's own life-destroying gesture. By naming that gesture "electrocution," Bright makes the violence of state killing at least momentarily visible by making it specific and concrete. He urges each juror to take full responsibility for a life-or-death decision that is now unavoidable. "Each of you," he says, "is the Supreme Court today. It is your decision whether he lives or dies."

This is an anxiety-laden and anxiety-producing exhortation. In describing the violence in Brooks's life and the context in which his crime should be judged, the defense must struggle to explain that its narrative does not undo or diminish the seriousness of the murder. If the defense fails, or suggests that context explains everything and character nothing, it invites the jury to reaffirm its judgment of guilt by imposing the death penalty. What the defense must provide, then, is a narrative of violence and pain and a context for understanding that explains but does not excuse, "that could respond to the need to assign responsibility . . . to the defendant, society, or history,"[30] and that helps the jury understand and empathize with the sources of Brooks's crime without suggesting that they forgive it. Bright's argument asks Americans to think in a nuanced way about the dangers of, and problems in, the society of which they are a part.

> The defendant has hurt people and sinned against man and God. What you need to consider is what forces pushed him in that direction. But will any of this excuse what happened? Nothing excuses or justifies his crime. . . . Let me remind you what is not before you. This isn't about whether the defendant will be excused. There is no excuse for what William Brooks did. When you consider mitigating evidence it isn't to excuse or justify. He is responsible for what he did. That's why we are here, why we are at this point. That's been decided. . . . Mitigating evidence is offered to help you understand what he did and why, not to excuse or justify it.

Instead of excusing the crime, the narrative of Brooks's life was presented as a reason for showing mercy.[31] Bright appealed to the jury to be better than the killer, who showed no mercy to Jeannine Galloway, by following "feelings of mercy and sympathy that flow from the evidence." "As Christians," he argued,

> we learn about the place of mercy and compassion. Here the law makes room for mercy and compassion. We are proud of our law because it allows us to show mercy. If you find mitigation that can be a reason to give life—anything about William Brooks' life and background, or about his life in prison that makes him worthy of not being killed. If anything you think merits mercy whether I've told you or not, you can vote for life.

This appeal to mercy suggests that state killing can and should be different from Brooks's violence and that law can and should show compassion even for the undeserving. It suggests that the jury itself must ultimately decide whether state killing, in the end, will be different. To establish its difference and to legitimate state violence, the jury must show the very restraint that Brooks himself did not show; it must heed the call of mercy as Brooks himself did not when Jeannine Galloway begged for her life. It must resist the voice of vengeance. In making this argument Bright gave the state "its moral victory by acknowledging this crime" while trying to "persuade the jury that it can accommodate the crime into the assumptions of a social order it wants to reaffirm."[32] At the center of those assumptions is the idea that law must be different and better than those over whom it exercises the power of life and death.

The story that Bright told about Brooks to elicit mercy was one of abuse, cruelty, and victimization. This story itself is a reminder of the American condition. It calls attention not to law's victories but to its defeats, not to its capacity to protect, but to its frustrating limits. Throughout his life Brooks was the object of a lawless violence that showed no mercy. In contrast to the untroubled innocence of Jeannine Galloway's life, "the defendant's life," Bright contended, "was one nightmare after another." His family was torn apart by violence and abuse, violence first directed at his mother by an alcoholic father who was himself murdered on the streets of Columbus, Georgia, and then against Brooks by his stepfather.

In this narrative of violence and victimization, the defense faced the same daunting task of talking about pain that had confronted the prosecution in its efforts to speak about Jeannine Galloway. Here again the appeal was to wounds and to weapons. As Bright put it, "The defendant carries scars on his back from the beatings he received from his stepfather who would take him in a room, lock the door and whip him on his back with a belt buckle. Gwen [Brooks's sister] used to come home and hear William screaming. When the beating was done William would come out of the room, his back bloody from the beatings. Such beatings were a daily event."

The violence done to Brooks emerged from a domestic life starkly different from that of Jeannine Galloway, though all too familiar in contemporary America. Whereas her home was a fortress against lawless violence, Brooks's home was the continuous scene of such violence. Whereas Jeannine's mother was called to the stand to speak about lost innocence, the disruption of domestic tranquility, and the one horrific time she was unable to rescue her child from harm, Brooks's mother was called to testify to her continuous inability to prevent pain.

> Q: What happened after you moved to Columbus?
>
> A: My husband began to drink heavily. And then he would try to hit me and we would have fights. He'd hit me and we would tussle. William saw all of this. He saw everything and he'd get very upset. Once [my husband] broke my nose and I had to go to the hospital. Another time he hit me and I began to beat him with the heel of my shoe. All the kids were there.
>
> Q: Did you ever inflict injuries on your husband?
>
> A: Well, once I scalded him with hot coffee once when we had a fight. And the children they saw it. They were all at the table.

Q: How frequent were the fights?

A: Every weekend. Pretty soon I had to leave every weekend and take the kids to my parents' house. . . . Later my father bought me a shot gun and told me to use it if he tried to beat me again. . . . Once my oldest daughter took the gun and shot him in the hand.

Three of William Brooks's sisters also testified about the violence he and they had experienced as they grew up. Brooks's sister Gwen provided the most vivid portrait of William's victimization.

Q: What was life like with your stepfather?

A: It was a kind of holy terror. He was abusive and when he wasn't being abusive he made us feel unwanted. He'd curse us and make us feel out of place in our own home. He'd always have a house full of young men drinking, smoking and being fresh. He could get away with all that being abusive because my mother was at work.

Q: How did he treat William?

A: He really hated him. He beat him all the time with his belt buckle or with an extension cord. He was always hitting him and pushing him against the wall. More than once I'd heard my brother screaming when I came home. Once I pushed against the door in the room where the screams were coming from. My brother was lying on the mattress and there was blood all over the walls. William begged me to make him stop, but he threw me out of the room and started beating William again.

There is no lost innocence, no fall from grace, in this story because there was never an innocence to be lost. The brutality Brooks faced at the end of the "belt buckle," the "extension cord and other instruments" was continuous and inescapable. Like many other young black men, Brooks lived beyond law's protection and suffered pitifully for doing so. Looming over this story is the specter of violence generating violence, aided and abetted by law's inability to provide protection or defense.

But the language of law could neither fully contain nor explain the lawless violence that brutalized Brooks or the impact of that violence in causing or explaining what he did to Jeannine Galloway. For such an explanation the defense turned to a social worker experienced in issues of child development and in child abuse and neglect. As she put it,

> William Brooks was subject to persistent and brutal abuse throughout his childhood. He saw explosive tempers all around him, and they became for him a model of how to behave. . . . To say the least, he grew up in the absence of a nurturing environment. . . . The abuse and neglect which he suffered caused fear, anxiety and anger. He was left alone to deal with these things. He needed but did not get professional help. Through no fault of his own the very volatile feelings inside him were left to fester. . . . He did not develop internal controls or mechanisms for dealing with his anger. He never found a place to put it.

The introduction of this testimony turned the penalty phase of the Brooks trial into a contest of high culture and scientific discourse versus low culture and common sense, elitist indulgence versus populist understanding. At issue was the extent to which violence had made Brooks the kind of person he was, the extent to which it had shaped him and contributed to his own violent acts. The high-culture, scientific-discourse explanation implied that Brooks's behavior was complex and hard to disentangle from the violence he had experienced. The low-culture, commonsense rendering searched for a more parsimonious explanation. Thus in the midst of his cross-examination of the social worker, Pullen asked

> Q: Do you believe in the Christian principle of free moral agency? Do you believe that God gave us the capacity to choose right from wrong?

> A: Yes, that can happen if one has a nurturing environment that would support that capacity and allow it to be used.

> Q: Do you believe that Almighty God gave us the capacity to know right from wrong?

> A: Almighty God gave us the potential. . . .

> Q: How do you explain why some people who come from bad homes do well in life?

> A: We all have different innate endowments and ability to tolerate frustration. One can't just look at people and know who will turn out good and who will turn out bad. You have to look carefully at the environment and especially at family dynamics.

> Q: Are you saying that people are not responsible for what they do?

> A: What William Brooks did was the product of interaction between himself and his environment.

> Q: Can a child be spoiled?

> A: Yes.

> Q: Can someone be just plain mean?

> A: No, not without reason. Children aren't born mean. Children are responsive to their environment.

In this denunciation of Brooks and counterexplanation of his actions, the prosecutor sought to identify with what sociologist Harold Garfinkel calls the "dignity of the supra-personal values of the tribe," a community of persons committed to the theological principle of free choice.[33] "Just plain mean" is presented as the community's commonsense response to a "scientific" discourse that seemed to make the explanation for violence disappear or to locate it outside the acting subject. What was at stake for the prosecution was pinning the responsibility for violence to a freely acting person—the very idea of responsibility itself. As the cross-examination continued this theme reappeared.

Q: Was the defendant a time bomb? Was violence inevitable?

A: He had no way of expressing what was happening to him. His feelings were just festering inside him. He could have learned to channel those feelings and the violence if he'd gotten help.

Q: Suppose he confronted a young woman in her yard, twenty-three years old, a small woman, and he heard her mother coming. Would he be able to transport his victim to a place of seclusion so as to be able to continue his criminal enterprise?

A: One could not have predicted how he would act out. His anger was there. How it would be expressed could not be predicted. . . .

. . . .

Q: Whose fault was it that Brooks kidnaped Jeannine?

A: He would have to take responsibility for that.

Q: And for all his other voluntary acts?

A: He would be responsible. . . .

. . . .

Q: Isn't it true that heaven helps those who help themselves?

A: That capacity, like any other human capacity, needs to be acti-
vated by outside sources.

Q: Not even God could help him? It would take counseling?

A: The counselor would be an instrument of God. . . .

. . . .

Q: Aren't you saying that he wasn't responsible?

A: I'm not saying that. I'm not saying that he wasn't responsible
for what he did. I am saying that things in his childhood
caused problems and that he needed professional help that he
never received.

The language of responsibility again provided the building
blocks for Pullen to construct a narrative about violence, about
the life and crimes of William Brooks. Those acts have to be assigned to a particular individual for law's response to have any
pretense of efficacy. Pullen treated the narrative of violence be-
getting violence, of an abused person reenacting his abuse, sarcas-
tically, calling it a "Devil made me do it" defense. Such a defense
"had" to be rejected. Ironically, the prosecutor used the language
of compulsion to authorize or require the idea of responsible
choice that he sought to defend. "We *have to* believe that God
gave everybody the ability to know right from wrong, good from
evil. . . . It is the American way to play by the rules, work hard.
That's what he rejected. . . . The defendant, by his own volition,
selected to live his life in dark places" (emphasis added).

Pullen denied that there was anything special about Brooks's
life. The violence of his origins did not determine his actions; his
own willed choices did that. Brooks had to be judged and punished in the same way as anyone else who made such choices.
For the defense, however, Brooks's life was a story of difference,
not similarity. It was a life entirely contained by violence, not

one of free decisions made in the bright light of God's will or the American way.

> People aren't all the same [Brooks's defense lawyer argued]. Free will, yes, but we are not all the same. . . . Some people grow up in good ground, but William Brooks' seed was sown among the thorns. Yes, some sown among the thorns will grow up well. Some will survive, but even they aren't like those that are planted in the field. This little seed tried to struggle through the thorns. And the fact that some make it, well, that's life. You've got to look at where his seed was sown. "Just plain mean"—some people are just plain mean. When we see new babies do we see anyone who is just plain mean? When kids are two or five are they just plain mean? Do they exercise free will in deciding whether they are going to turn out to kill people?. . . People who are abused and neglected, it isn't surprising that they get in trouble. We know there's a road to that even though it doesn't make it okay. . . . It doesn't make it okay. . . . We are not saying if you are abused you can kill.

Violence and pain shaped Brooks's life. The appeal to understand his suffering was an appeal to see how a young man who had only known the world as a source of pain would act in such a world. Bright sought to convince the jury that Brooks, too, deserved the status of victim.[34] It was an appeal not to privilege and power but to recognize how powerlessness and racial deprivation act out their powerful rage. The appeal is to a shared, though not equally shared, responsibility for Jeannine Galloway's death. Brooks was not, as Bright said to the jury, "Ted Bundy. He didn't go to law school. He isn't somebody who had all that smarts. You've got to ask yourself, is this some poor kid who had never been taught values? You punish those people differently." The recognition that a life had been violated required the imposition of less violent punishment.

Ultimately the contest between the two narratives of lawless violence—Pullen's narrative of Brooks's violence against Jeannine Galloway and Bright's story of Brooks's own suffering—had to give way to another contest: one between different ways of understanding the lawful violence of the state. Each side completed its narrative by representing in carefully chosen words the possibility of state violence as the end of the story.

Naming State Violence

Seeing the penalty phase of a capital trial is a truly remarkable experience. Here (as I discuss in the next chapter) our system uses a legal proceeding solely for the purpose of asking twelve ordinary people to consider ordering the death of a fellow citizen. As if drawn by this disquieting prospect, the courtroom where Brooks's fate would be decided filled with many new faces, providing me the comforting anonymity I had sought throughout the trial.

In the penalty phase of a capital trial, participants talk about the violence of the killing state openly, and the disposition and use of the state's ultimate power over life and death becomes the subject of contention. In this moment when the legitimation of that power is most pressing, law enlists citizens to exercise its power over life and death. It seeks to make its violence our violence.

Yet even then it is striking that so little was actually said in the Brooks trial about the nature of that violence. In contrast to their detailed descriptions of the violence outside the law, neither Pullen nor Bright presented a detailed account of the violence to which the jury might commit William Brooks. This is, of course, not surprising as a tactic of the prosecutor; one would expect him to foreground the violence done to the victim and the pain she endured and to tread lightly on the terrain of the state's own violence. It is, however, not what one would have expected from the defense, until one considers that in all death cases the defense confronts a "death qualified" jury—that is, a group of persons who as a condition of their service in a capital case must have attested to their ability and willingness to impose the death penalty.[35] Given such an audience, with its known dispositions, to attack the death penalty frontally and repeatedly, to highlight its gruesome violence, even if the rules of evidence allowed it, would be to take on the burden of conversion.

Nonetheless, although neither prosecution nor defense details the nature of state killing, the question before the jury in the penalty phase of a capital trial is, What kind of violence is the jury being asked to authorize? And how does that violence differ from the violence it opposes? The prosecution in the Brooks case consistently called the state's violence "the death penalty," as if death here did not involve killing. The prosecution passed over in silence the weapon the state would use in its killing and gave no expression to the pain the state's violence would inflict.

The defense, not surprisingly, named both the weapon and the act. What Pullen called the "death penalty," Bright called the "most extreme and extraordinary punishment." The latter insisted that what was at stake was the "elimination of life by 2200 volts of electricity"—not a penalty abstractly called "death" but the question of whether the state should "kill" William Brooks. The insistence that state violence is a killing violence seeks to blur the distinction between the act of the criminal and the act of law itself. And it suggests that the legitimation of state violence cannot rest securely in any sanitized renaming of the death-doing, life-destroying instrumentalities of the state itself.

Pullen addressed the question of the legitimacy of state killing by making explicit what had been left unspoken earlier in the trial. Here the violence of the law is overtly labeled purposive, measured, and necessary. "We have a right," he claimed, "to be vindicated and protected." "We" is a naming that is both inclusive and violent, fraught with racial meaning. Who is included in the "we"? While this "we" reaches from this world to the next as a remembrance of and identification with Jeannine, at the same time it makes the black Brooks an outsider in a community that needs protection from people like him. Yet the meaning attributed to Brooks's race surely has a complicated resonance in an appeal to a multiracial jury. The racialization of his crime invited black jurors to choose sides, to identify themselves as members of the community of the law-abiding, or to express solidarity with Brooks.

By speaking the language of "we," Pullen sought to invest himself with the authority to speak for, as well as to, the jury and the community it represented. He reminded the jurors that the trial that had brought them to the point of considering a capital sentence "has been conducted according to the rule of law." He identified himself with the jury and the community while distancing himself and them from the defendant, whom he denounced.[36] The prosecutor claimed that the state's violence could properly be used to vindicate Jeannine's lost innocence and to protect those who lead innocent lives from those who, like Brooks, live in "dark places" and have "forfeited their place in the human community."

Pullen argued that this vindication and protection would be—again seeking to legitimate state killing by differentiating it from violence of the kind that Brooks visited on Jeannine Galloway—a proportionate response to a horrible and horrifying violence.

> It fits the crime. Jeannine was taunted and tortured. It wasn't like TV. When it was all over she didn't get up and walk away. . . . When the defense says "mercy," think of what the defendant did to Jeannine. . . . Go back behind Dawson School when Jeannine was screaming, begging for her life, and the defendant shot her and she was screaming and no scream came out. I want you to hear that silent scream when you hear him [the defense lawyer] say "mercy and mitigation."

But in the end the most powerful authorization and the most unquestionable legitimation of state killing rests with those who would die at its hands. Unlike Jeannine, who did nothing to earn the violence that was done to her, Brooks had, by his own choice and acts, put himself in harm's way. "Some," the prosecutor argued, "by their own acts forfeit the right to breathe the air we breathe. If he had left Jeannine alone none of this would have happened. Mr. Brooks showed in what he did to her that he believes in the death penalty."

The defense countered this argument with the contention that the death penalty would be neither necessary nor rational *in this case*. To apply it would reveal state violence to be excessive; to apply it would be to reduce that violence to the level of the violence the jury had condemned by its earlier verdict. Killing Brooks would be a vindictive desecration of someone who was already leading a life on the other side of a line that separates the incarcerated from the free, those in laws custody from those beyond its confinement. In some sense Brooks was already dead. Here Bright addresses jurors as "the possessors of successful, family-defined identities . . . and superior domestic comforts" and encourages them to look down on Brooks in pity.

> What's at stake in this case isn't life as we know it. We are not talking about someone who can go home and play with his kids. We are talking about life lived inside a prison. I know the defendant is here because I hear the chains rattling. A life in chains and in prison, that is already an extreme and harsh punishment. . . . This is not about not being punished. You are choosing between two punishments. And you should remember that society has ways of punishing without killing people.

This questioning of the necessity of another killing lay at the heart of the defense's argument. For state killing to be different and better than lawless killing it has to meet the test of necessity and, in so doing, live with its own restraint. According to Bright this threshold had not been, and could not be, met in the Brooks case.

> We don't need to kill this defendant. The law doesn't require us to do so. There may be times when we need to but this isn't one. . . . No case requires the death penalty. There is no automatic capital punishment. There was no death penalty for the people who murdered those young, black children in Atlanta, or for the man who killed Dr. King or Medgar Evers. . . . No case has to bring the death penalty. . . . Society can be protected without killing William Brooks. . . . You don't have to kill. . . . Brooks' crimes were terrible, evil, and vile. But Jeannine Galloway's life can't be brought back. If we could bring Jeannine back I would electrocute William Brooks myself. . . . For everything there is a season. This is a time to punish, but not to kill.

In contrast to his repeated refrain, "You don't have to kill William Brooks," Bright's statement that "If I could bring Jeannine back I would electrocute William Brooks myself" was extraordinary in marking the nature of state killing. It served to identify Bright with the jurors; like them, he suggested he had no conscientious objection to the death penalty. Rather than seeking to turn them against the death penalty, this lawyer insisted that state killing must be used in measured ways to achieve purposes that can be achieved by no other means, and that each use of state violence must be justified on its own terms. In this case, he challenged the jury to maintain the legitimacy of that violence by exercising restraint and by ensuring that it is not used where unnecessary.

This was a persuasive appeal. The jury decided on a life sentence for William Brooks.[37]

Conclusion

For me the conclusion of Brooks's trial was not a stirring vindication of law. It was simply too sad to bring anything but relief that it was over. This trial, like all capital trials, from the best known to the least noticed, reminded me that the state's violent nature does not end with the establishment of the legal order. The law, constituted, in part, in response to metaphorical violence, traffics with literal violence. In the Brooks trial, I saw how different kinds of violence are incorporated into legal discourse and then differentiated from each other within a set of familiar narrative styles and racialized conventions.

First is the violence of the murder. In constructing a narrative of violence and pain prosecutors, like Pullen, project a sociologically simple world of good and evil, and a morally clear world of responsibility and desert. The prosecution seeks to create a binary opposition between the "angelic" character of the murder victim, who did not deserve to die, and the "evil" character of the perpetrator, who does not deserve to live. This is the dominant cultural motif for representing violence and victimization. Instead of confronting complex social problems, we are invited to see them in stark and simple terms.

The second kind of violence whose "reality" runs through capital trials is that done, in their childhood and throughout their life, to defendants like Brooks, the violence of an abusive home and family. Examining this violence forces up to confront a more complex, though equally tragic, aspect of the American condition. Inventing a language to accommodate and express this kind of violence and pain involves challenging the dominant cultural conception of violence and victimization. Defending a murderer like Brooks requires the construction of a more complex narrative of causation and accident, of mixed lives and mixed motives.[38]

The third kind of violence is the violence of the killing state. Whereas lawyers present the other kinds as weapons and wounds and describe them in vivid, concrete, gory detail, they hardly present this violence at all. It is named, when it is named, in the most general, abstract, and impersonal ways. In this process, state killing is barely perceivable as violence.

Capital trials express and embody a deeply felt anxiety about the proper relationship of law and these three forms of violence. This anxiety is reflected in the enormous efforts put into the rationalization and justification of the apparatus of punishment, efforts that efface the violence of the state by renaming it. Thus Stanford law professor Robert Weisberg recently observed,

> Anglo-American law has traditionally suffered a serious identity crisis over its awkward relation to violence. . . . Our system assumes that law is to hold a monopoly on violence, but this is a monopoly viewed as both necessary and discomforting. It is necessary because it is viewed as the alternative to something worse—unrestrained private vengeance—and it is discomforting because those who make and enforce the law would like us to believe that, though they may be required to use force, force is somehow categorically distinguishable from violence. . . . The efforts of modern jurisprudence to finesse or deny the role of violence have not ceased.[39]

In all capital trials the juxtaposition of narratives about violence is disquieting, if not destabilizing. This is especially true of the juxtaposition of violence outside law with the state's own violence. Putting lawful violence alongside lawless violence threatens to expose state killing as essentially similar to the antisocial violence it is supposed to deter and punish. As Walter Benjamin notes, "In the exercise of violence over life and death more than in any other legal act, law reaffirms itself. But in this very violence something rotten in law is revealed, above all to a finer sensibility, because the latter knows itself to be infinitely remote from conditions in which fate might imperiously have shown itself in such a sentence."[40]

The killing state threatens to expose the facade of law's dispassionate reason, of its necessity and restraint, as just that—a facade—and to destabilize law by forcing choices between its aspirations and the need to maintain social order through force. Violence threatens to swallow up law and leave nothing but a social world of forces arrayed in aggressive opposition.[41] Where violence is present can there be anything other than violence? This question puts enormous pressure on legal rituals such as the capital trial to demonstrate and affirm the difference between state killing and the violence that law condemns.

Here, then, we find the most intense efforts to gloss over and deny the role of violence in law, to mark the differences between the world beyond law's control and what law itself authorizes, and to transform the latter into legitimate force. Capital trials are occasions for overcoming doubt and regaining stability. The cultural resources for doing so are both internal and external to law itself. Whereas the prosecution describes violence outside the law as unnecessary, irrational, indiscriminate, gruesome, and useless, it portrays the violence of the death penalty as rational, purposive, and controlled through values, norms, and procedures external to violence itself. In capital trials, the force of law presents itself as the community's bulwark against the anomic savagery lurking just beyond law's boundaries. Elaborate rituals and procedures allegedly give evidence of the care and concern with which law traffics in violence. The case of the condemned proceeds with a seriousness equal to, if not greater than, any other in law. Thus the procedures and purposes of law come to the fore while its instrumentalities and wounding effects are kept in the background.

Externally, however, law draws all too often on cultural symbols of race and danger. The violence of the killing state is, thus, "our" violence against "them." As former Supreme Court Justice Powell implied in *McCleskey v. Kemp*, the racialization of capital punishment and its disproportionate use against black men and especially those who kill white victims is not sufficiently disturbing in this culture to be "constitutionally significant."[42] State killing is viewed as the civilizing violence of white order against savage disorder. Thus in the Brooks trial and in others like it, the price our society pays for such efforts to alleviate anxiety is extraordinary. In addition to the actual violence often unleashed and the linguistic violence done in the process of rendering state killing abstract, capital trials regularly reaffirm racialized social conventions as well as flat narratives of purity and danger, responsibility and excuse, and innocence and guilt.

Yet the anxiety surrounding state killing does not end. Capital trials place several narratives of violence side by side: a narrative of violence that has already taken life, a narrative of abuse and poverty that has shaped another life, and the abstract narrative of a prospective killing. Whereas the first seeks to justify and strengthen the last, the last stands as an internal reminder of the artifice and artificiality of the distinctions on which law's anxiety-alleviating legitimacy depends. Each narrative of lawless violence—whether of Brooks's crime or of the abuse he suffered— reminds us of the failure of state violence to guarantee security. Each narrative of violence turns us into anxious citizens caught between a fearful aversion to one kind of violence and a fearful embrace of another.

5

THE ROLE OF THE JURY IN

THE KILLING STATE

Let's do it.
—GARY GILMORE

Let's get on with it.
—WILLIAM REHNQUIST

At no time in American history has the role of the jury been as controversial as it is today.[1] In celebrated case after celebrated case—from the first Rodney King verdict to the mistrials of the Menendez brothers and the acquittal of O. J. Simpson in his criminal trial—the media has called our attention to the unexpected and, according to some, incomprehensible decisions that juries have rendered. Confused by complicated testimony, led astray by the "abuse excuse" and the continuing contest to identify real victims, placing racial solidarity ahead of the clear weight of evidence, these and other juries seem to have failed, in some profound way, to do their duty.

As controversial as the role of the jury can be, it stands at the center of the complex efforts to rationalize state killing in and through capital trials. As we have seen in both the McVeigh and the Brooks cases, in most states and in the federal system juries not only decide on questions of guilt or innocence, but act as the conscience of the community, deciding whether those accused of capital crimes live or die. Writing about the continuing importance of the death penalty in the apparatus of criminal justice in the United States, Supreme Court Justice John Paul Stevens has remarked on the essential role of the jury in both administering and legitimizing that punishment. "If the State wishes to execute a citizen," Stevens wrote,

> it must persuade a jury of his peers that death is an appropriate punishment for his offense. . . . If the prosecutor cannot convince a jury that the defendant deserves to die, there is an unjustifiable risk that the imposition of that punishment will not reflect the community's sense of the defendant's "moral guilt." . . . *Furman* and its progeny provide no warrant for—indeed do not tolerate— the exclusion from the capital sentencing process of the jury and the critical contribution only it can make toward linking the administration of capital punishment to community values.[2]

By highlighting the jury's place in the administration of capital punishment, Stevens called attention to something that is widely taken for granted but is nonetheless remarkable—the fact that ordinary citizens are regularly enlisted as authorizing agents for the state's own lethal brand of violence. This kind of democratically administered death penalty is a reminder of a venerable yet enduring problem in social life, namely the question of how people come to participate in projects of violence, of how cultural inhibitions against the infliction of pain can be overcome in the acts of otherwise decent persons. What factors come into play in capital trials such that ordinary citizens can authorize and lend themselves to the project of using lethal violence as an aspect of state policy?

Despite the support of persons as seemingly different as Gary Gilmore and William Rehnquist, and the substantial public approval that the death penalty continues to garner, it is nonetheless unsettling, as I note in chapter 1, that the United States clings tenaciously to such a punishment long after almost all other democratic nations have abandoned it. It is unsettling because the conscious, deliberate killing of citizens as an instrument of state policy is always an evil but never more so than in a democracy. Today the formality, complexity, and ritual of capital trials displace, at least symbolically, execution itself as the site of the state's violent majesty. In capital trials we focus on the case rather than the body of the "condemned."

As a result, the Supreme Court, until relatively recently, invested enormous effort to regulate the conduct of capital trials, insisting more than two decades ago that because "death is different"[3] capital trials must be conducted according to special procedures designed to ensure their reliability.[4] Capital trials are thus both the "field" of pain and death on which law plays and the field of its discursive representation. As Robert Weisberg argues, such trials provide "a representational medium that . . . serves as a grammar of social symbols. . . . The criminal trial is a 'miracle play' of government in which we carry out our inarticulate beliefs about crime and criminals within the reassuring formal structure of disinterested due process."[5]

In this structure the jury provides the means through which the death penalty becomes an instrument of popular sovereignty; it provides the mechanism through which citizens are enlisted to authorize the life-ending violence of the state. A jury's decision to impose a death sentence expresses public condemnation for the violence that exists just beyond law's boundary while muting state violence, shading and toning it down, and rendering it acceptable, thus making the act of the executioner violence that can be approved and rationally dispensed. The jury's role is crucial because in and through jury decisions the law seeks to define the boundary between life and death, guilty killing and innocent execution. Moreover, law embodies a precarious hope that words can contain and control violence, that unspeakable pain can be made to speak, and that jury decisions tame aggression and put it to useful public purposes. If law is to succeed it must always conquer force and calm turmoil, or at least appear to do so. Here again, as Justice Stevens suggested, what the jury does and how it acts is crucial.

The Centrality of the Jury in the Jurisprudence of Death

In the killing state the jury represents the fullest actualization of popular sovereignty, of the right of the people to exercise power over life and death. Thus Judge Patrick Higginbotham correctly notes that "the history of the death penalty and the history of juries are entangled."[6]

> This should not be a surprise. The choice between a sentence of life or death is uniquely laden with expressions of anger and retribution. . . . By its nature it is a decision that we instinctively believe is best made by a group of citizens, because a group of citizens better represents community values and because responsibility for such a decision is best shared. Equally the ultimate call is visceral. The decision must occur past the point to which legalistic reasoning can carry; it necessarily reflects a gut level hunch as to what is just.[7]

The jury, in Higginbotham's view, both stands in for and represents the vengeful anger of the democratic community and is the truest expression of its values. The jury's justice is itself a kind of violent transgression of both reason and law. Owing to the gravity and uniqueness of a decision to sentence someone to death, the juror voting whether to authorize a killing by the state must go beyond law.[8] "In the final analysis," Justice Stevens states, "capital punishment rests not on a legal but on an ethical judgment. . . . And . . . the decision that capital punishment is the appropriate sanction in the extreme cases is justified because it expresses the community's moral sensibility—its demand that a given affront to humanity requires retribution."[9]

Because the juror allegedly gives voice to the community's sentiments, she helps to diffuse responsibility for the punishment of death. Here then is an important reformulation of the problematic of popular sovereignty and the death penalty. On the one hand, the juror speaks in the powerful, retributive tones of a sovereign assaulted; on the other hand, the juror speaks in the muted, restrained tones appropriate to popular sovereignty.

Since 1970, the Supreme Court has struggled to come to terms with this contradictory image of the jury in capital cases. The Court has, alternatively expressed expansive faith in the jury as a reliable, trustworthy repository of the sovereign right over the lives of citizens, and profound doubt about the jury's capacity to exercise that power responsibly.[10] Throughout, the Court has struggled to define the jury's role as the crucial decision maker in the capital punishment process.

McGautha v. California set the debate of the past three decades in motion and defined its terms.[11] In that case, the defendant alleged that a California statute that left the "decision whether the defendant should live or die . . . to the absolute discretion of the jury" violated due process of law.[12] This claim evoked two very different responses: one, from Justice Harlan, embraced the California scheme and with it expansive power for the jury in capital cases, while the other, from Justice Brennan, rejected that scheme in the hope of encouraging legislatures to provide standards or guidelines to limit jury power.[13] Both Harlan and Brennan, however, used the language of sovereignty and consent to speak about the jury's role in capital cases, and both recognized the jury, not the legislature, as the locus of law's power to kill.

For Harlan the comparison between legislature and jury clearly favored the latter. If the final decision in capital eases were to be acceptable, it had to be based on a highly individualized assessment of a myriad of factors peculiar to each crime and criminal. The detailed and subtle judgments of juries were, in Harlan's view, precisely the kind that legislative assemblies were incapable of making. Unbridled jury discretion to decide who shall die from among all those who commit capital offenses was both just and necessary given what Harlan saw as legislative disability.

> Those who have come to terms with the hard task of actually attempting to draft means of channeling capital sentencing discretion have confirmed . . . [that] [t]o identify before the fact those characteristics of criminal homicides and their perpetrators which call for the death penalty, and to express these characteristics in language which can be fairly understood and applied by the sen-

tencing authority appear to be tasks which are beyond present human ability.[14]

Harlan worried that words would be unable adequately to contain and convey the requisites for authorizing capital punishment. Language fails in the face of death. As a result, legal authority must respond to linguistic inadequacy. If legislatures are unable to speak about the pain and death the state dispenses, the only choice is to legitimate the de facto discretion of the jury.

But the impossibility of specifying, in advance, standards to determine which particular criminals should be executed was not enough to justify a sovereign role for the jury. We must also have an image of how the jury would use its sovereign power. Here the best Harlan could do was to engage in a Tocquevillian imagining of the jury ennobled by the responsibility given to it.[15] In this imagining

> jurors confronted with the truly awesome responsibility of decreeing death for a fellow human will act with due regard for the consequences of their decision and will consider a variety of factors. . . . For a court to attempt to catalog the appropriate factors in this elusive area could inhibit rather than expand the scope of consideration. . . . The infinite variety of cases and facets to each case would make general standards either meaningless "boiler-plate" or a statement of the obvious that no jury would need.[16]

In Brennan's view, by contrast, there was neither persuasive evidence of legislative inability to provide structuring guidelines nor reason to assume that unbridled discretion would not, like all exercises of unfettered power, produce arbitrariness and discrimination rather than reason and responsibility. Brennan countered Harlan's theory of linguistic failure by surveying a variety of means and mechanisms that legislatures might employ to communicate with the jury and to guide it in its interpretive task.

> A legislature that has determined that the State should kill some but not all of the persons whom it has convicted of certain crimes must inevitably determine how the State is to distinguish those

who are to be killed from those who are not. Depending ultimately
on the legislature's notion of wise penological policy, that distinction may be hard or easy to make. But capital sentencing is not the
only difficult question which legislatures have ever faced.[17]

In addition, Brennan rejected Harlan's Tocquevillian optimism
about jury sovereignty and substituted a hardheaded kind of due
process realism. The power and responsibility that Harlan saw as
ennobling, Brennan believed to be fraught with the danger of
abuse. As he put it, "the Due Process Clause of the Fourteenth
Amendment is fundamentally inconsistent with capital sentencing procedures that are purposely constructed to allow the maximum possible variation from one case to the next, and provide
no mechanism to prevent that consciously maximized variation
from reflecting merely random or arbitrary choice." Brennan suggested that Harlan would ask us to choose between "the rule of
law and the power of the states to kill. . . ." and to resolve the
conflict "in favor of the states' power to kill."[18]

Two years after *McGautha* this choice was repudiated and undone by *Furman v. Georgia*. Consistent with Brennan, *Furman*
held that the unbridled discretion that Harlan had embraced in
McGautha was constitutionally unacceptable. Yet the justices
in *Furman* continued to wrestle with the problem of defining the
jury's proper role in capital trials. Like Brennan, Justice Douglas
feared that leaving juries with the untrammeled discretion to
decide who should live and who should die ensured "selective
and irregular use" of the death penalty and allowed the punishment of death to be reserved for "minorities whose numbers are
few, who are outcasts of society, and who are unpopular, but
whom society is willing to see suffer." Instead of Tocquevillian
responsibility, Douglas suggested that jury sovereignty meant
that "People live or die, dependent on the whim of one man or of
12."[19]

Against Douglas's doubt, Chief Justice Burger took up Harlan's
defense of jury sovereignty in capital cases. Burger suggested that
"trust in lay jurors . . . [is] the cornerstone of our system of criminal justice" and that juries as the "conscience of the community"

are properly "entrusted to determine in individual cases that the ultimate punishment is warranted." Jurors in capital cases, facing the awesome decision about whether one of their fellow citizens should live or die are, on Burger's account, "meticulous" in their decisions, and "cautious and discriminating [in their] reservation of . . . [the death] penalty for the most extreme cases."[20]

The Harlan-Burger advocacy of complete jury sovereignty was finally put to rest by the Court when, in *Gregg v. Georgia*, it upheld a Georgia statute whose purpose was to provide guidance to jurors in selecting those who should actually receive the death penalty from among the class of convicted capital murderers. Justice Stewart, writing for the majority, held that jury discretion "on a matter so grave as the determination of whether a human life should be taken or spared . . . must be suitably directed and limited so as to minimize the risk of arbitrary and capricious action." Absent such direction he claimed that "juries imposed the death sentence in a way that could only be called freakish."[21]

Stewart, finally completing the work begun by Brennan in *McGautha*, rejected Harlan's arguments about the linguistic impossibility of formulating standards to provide such direction by saying that "while some have suggested that standards to guide a capital jury's sentencing deliberation are impossible to formulate, the fact is that such standards have been developed." He argued that it was particularly important to provide such standards for a jury because "members of a jury will have had little, if any, previous experience in sentencing." Standards that direct the jury's attention to the specific circumstances of the crime and of the person who committed the crime would, in Stewart's view, be sufficient to "produce non-discriminatory application" of the death penalty.[22]

In a line of later cases, however, the Court imposed on the states little more than formal requirements for statutory sentencing guidelines.[23] Thus, despite Stewart's apparent confidence in the efficacy of legislative standards in ensuring the rationality of life and death decisions made by ordinary citizens, how those decisions are made, especially how jurors understand their own responsibility and the violence they are asked to authorize, re-

mains a mystery in the jurisprudence of death. "Individual jurors," Justice Powell has written, "bring to their deliberations
'qualities of human nature and varieties of human experience, the
range of which is unknown and perhaps unknowable.' The capital
sentencing decision requires the individual jurors to focus their
collective judgment on the unique characteristics of a particular
criminal defendant. It is not surprising that such collective judgments often are difficult to explain."[24]

Authorizing Death

From the perspective of someone interested in understanding the
killing state as well as the relationship of democracy and the
death penalty, how ordinary citizens, in their roles as jurors,
could allow themselves to use their sovereign power to authorize
death is indeed almost inexplicable. This is because "to any person endowed with the normal inhibitions against the imposition
of pain and death, the deed of capital punishment entails a special
measure of reluctance and abhorrence."[25]

The work of the late Yale law professor Robert Cover, however,
provided some insight into both the nature of that reluctance
and how it is overcome. Cover noted that while for most people
"evolutionary, psychological, cultural and moral considerations
inhibit the infliction of pain on other people . . . in almost all
people social cues may overcome or suppress the revulsion to violence under certain circumstances." Because the provision of
such cues is the peculiar work of law, Cover called attention to
distinctive features of the "organization of the legal system [itself
that] operate . . . to facilitate overcoming inhibitions against . . .
violence."[26]

Two features of that organization have special relevance for understanding how ordinary citizens become the authorizing agents
of state violence in capital trials. First, those who authorize violence, in this case the death penalty, do not themselves carry out
the deed that their verdict allows. The juror is asked only to say

the words that will activate a process that at some considerable remove may lead to death. These words do things. Like many other kinds of language the juror's language is performative. Yet jurors are encouraged to think that it is not. Were they required to witness the full consequences of their verdict or were they required to pull the switch on those they condemn to death, the law would find it radically more difficult to get their authorization to kill. As Cover puts it, "The most elementary understanding of our social practice of violence ensures that a judge knows that she herself cannot actually pull the switch. This is not a trivial convention. For it means that someone else will have the duty and opportunity to pass upon what the judge has done."[27] What Cover says about the judge is surely no less true of jurors. Second, jury decisions are subject to review on appeal.[28] The judge or juror who initially authorizes execution is able to transfer responsibility for his authorizing act and, in so doing, to deny the very authority of that act.[29] The consequences of this ability to transfer responsibility have been well understood in the jurisprudence of death. They are, in fact, detailed by the Supreme Court's opinion in *Caldwell v. Mississippi*.[30]

In *Caldwell* the question before the Court was whether comments by a prosecutor to the effect that a jury should not view itself as finally determining whether the defendant should die because a death sentence would automatically be reviewed by the state supreme court violated the Eighth Amendment. Reviewing those comments in light of its prior holdings, the Court found that it is constitutionally impermissible to rest a death sentence on a determination made by a sentencer who has been led to believe that the responsibility for determining the appropriateness of the defendant's death rests elsewhere.[31]

Justice Marshall, writing for the majority in *Caldwell*, explained that,

> This Court's Eighth Amendment jurisprudence has taken it as a given that capital sentencers would view their task as the serious one of determining whether a specific human being should die at the hands of the State. . . . Belief in the truth of the assumption

that sentencers treat their power to determine the appropriateness
of death as an "awesome responsibility," has allowed this Court
to view sentencer discretion as consistent with—and indeed indispensable to—the Eighth Amendment's "need for reliability in the
determination that death is the appropriate punishment in a specific case."[32]

The question of how juries sentence is, in Marshall's view, central to the question of whether they may constitutionally exercise
the sovereign power to make life and death decisions.

Marshall then went on to paint a picture of the capital sentencing jury as

> made up of individuals placed in a very unfamiliar situation and
> called on to make a very difficult and uncomfortable choice. They
> are confronted with evidence and argument on the issue of
> whether another should die, and they are asked to decide that issue
> on behalf of the community. Moreover, they are given only partial
> guidance as to how their judgment should be exercised, leaving
> them with substantial discretion. . . . Given such a situation, the
> uncorrected suggestion that the responsibility for any ultimate de-
> termination of death will rest with others presents an intolerable
> danger that the jury will in fact choose to minimize the importance
> of its role.[33]

Marshall, echoing the insights of Cover, suggested that anything
that encouraged the sentencing jury to believe that it was not
responsible for authorizing death would make it more likely that
juries would provide such authorization. The jury thus unbur-
dened might use a death sentence, even when it is "unconvinced
that death is the appropriate punishment" to "'send a message'
of extreme disapproval for the defendant's acts."[34]

Yet the mystery of how jurors are enlisted as agents of the killing state remains. This mystery is, as I have already suggested, in
one sense a problem of popular sovereignty and in another sense
a problem of understanding how humans relate to the imposition
of pain and violence on other humans. It can be explored only by
carefully attending to what jurors actually do in, and say about,
capital trials.

The Case of John Henry Connors

Convenience stores are, despite their reassuring, welcoming name, some of the most dangerous places in America. Late at night such stores provide, as much as anything else, convenient settings for robbery and murder. This is as true in small towns like Bowling, Georgia,[35] as it is in big cities throughout the United States. The case of John Henry Connors is an apt illustration.

At 10:30 P.M. on a hot July night two friends picked up John Henry Connors from his modest home on the outskirts of Bowling. Connors, twenty-six years old, worked in a local auto body shop. He had been married for seven years but was now having serious marital problems. As a result, he frequently sought the company of his friends to escape his troubled relationship. On the night of July 23, they spent several hours driving around, smoking marijuana, and drinking. Each had a gun.

There was, however, nothing unusual in any of this. It had become a regular leisure activity for these men to drive along back country roads, get high, and fire shots into the night until they got bored, or sick, or sleepy. Three hours after they first went out, Connors and his friends stopped at the local Jiffy Store to buy "Do-It-Yourself Microwave Meals" and some beer. The two friends went to the back of the store while Connors waited for them near the counter where Andy Donaldson was working at his job as a cashier. After Donaldson finished ringing up the friends' purchases and opened the cash register to make change, Connors suddenly pulled out the .357 Magnum pistol that he had brought with him and shot Donaldson in the chest.

Connors's friends, who would later be offered the chance to plead to reduced charges in return for their testimony against him, were, by their own account, taken totally by surprise. At the sound of the shot they ducked and then ran for the door. Meanwhile, Donaldson fell to the floor in a bloody heap, moaning and writhing in pain while Connors took ten one-dollar bills and some food stamps from the register. Connors then leaned over

the counter and fired a second shot, which hit Donaldson above
the left eye. After firing the second shot he joined his friends in
their car and escaped into the night.

Eight days later Connors was arrested when his two friends
turned themselves in to the police. At the time of his arrest, the
gun that killed Andy Donaldson was found in Connors's home
along with the food stamps and nine of the bills he had taken
from the Jiffy Store.[36] Connors was charged with, and subsequently convicted of, robbery and malice murder in the death of
Andy Donaldson. He was sentenced to death.

In what follows I recount what the jurors in the Connors case
said about that case and explore how they made the decision that
John Henry Connors should be sentenced to die.[37]

Imagining Violence

As noted in chapter 4, one of the crucial tasks of the prosecution
in a capital case is to answer two questions: what was done by
whom to whom and why does the killer deserve to die. To answer
these questions the prosecutor has to portray, in a vivid and compelling way, the circumstances and nature of the killing. He has
to make what is for most people quite unreal—namely, a scene
of violent death—real.

As the jurors in the Connors case talked about that case, vivid
images of the scene of death and the violence that surrounded it
were most prominent in their recollections. Words and photographs were used in the Connors case, as in most other capital
trials, to bring to life the violence outside law. No comparable
effort, however, was made to enable jurors to imagine the scene
of the violence and death that they were being asked to authorize.
No one showed jurors images of the scene of the prospective execution, of the violence of electrocution, like those contained in
Justice Shaw's opinion in *Provenzano*.[38] No such images were ad-
missible or available for the juror eager to understand what he
was being asked to authorize.

Images of the weapons and wounds made the violence that Connors had visited on Donaldson real and pressing. As Joseph Rane, one of the Connors jurors, put it,

> Connors shot the man—I don't remember the man's name, I can see his face, I don't remember his name—he shot him. If I'm not mistaken it went into his chest and came out by his shoulder blade with a .357 Magnum, if I remember correctly. He leaned over, got some money out of the cash register. The clerk of the store was laying on the ground, moaning and moving around from . . . you figure a maximum of three feet with a high-powered weapon like that. It had knocked him against the back . . . he was on the floor bleeding. And he reached over the counter as he was retrieving the money and shot him again. It went in, if I'm not mistaken, over his eye and out behind his ear on the opposite side.

Like other jurors, Rane was able to speak in a detailed way about the murder weapon as well as about the entry and exit wounds that it caused, and about its ballistics and bullet trajectories. When asked if there was anything specific about the case that stuck out in his mind, Rane, a twenty-eight-year-old salesman, said, "What I remember is seeing the pictures of the man laying behind the counter, laying in a puddle of blood probably bigger than this table. And the pictures—the other jurors and I had to . . . It was difficult for some of them to look at the pictures. They'd take them up so close and they'd show the clear shots and all. Then we handled the weapon and a lot of them really didn't want to do that." When asked if he still thought about those pictures and the gun, Rane replied, "Surely."

Another juror in the Connors case, a seventy-three-year-old retired grandmother, Belle Givens, recalled the violence that Connors had done in terms of "a big gun. Right that's it. He used a big gun." Confronting the instrument of death was a horrifying experience. She described herself as an unwilling victim of a process that would not respect her squeamishness in the face of violence. "Reason I say big gun is because they passed it around and made me look at it and touch it, and I didn't want to. They made me look at it and touch it." The image of the violence done by the big gun "followed us into the jury room and it bothered me very much."

For her, like Joseph Rane, the image of violence also was fixed in the photographic evidence of the crime scene. "These photographs," cultural critic Luc Sante argues, "lack the functions that are usually attached to images of death. They do not memorialize, or ennoble, or declare triumph. . . . As evidence they are mere affectless records, concerned with details, as they themselves become details in the wider scope of police philosophy, which is far less concerned with the value of life than with the value of order. They are bookkeeping entries, with no transfixing mission, and so serve death up raw and unmediated."[39]

Once seen, the image was deeply imprinted on Belle Givens.

> But what did this idiot do. As the guy fell down behind the counter he hit the shelves right in back of him, and John Henry took the gun and leaned over the counter—bam—and another shot killed him. And they showed a picture of the man to the jury. I didn't want to look. They insisted I had to look. If I don't look, what they decide, well. I didn't want not to look and then have to have another trial. So I had to look, and that's still following me into that deliberating room.

In the system of state killing, while the execution is hidden and the violence jurors are asked to authorize has no image, and while no one can claim an entitlement to see the deadly deed,[40] it is compulsory to view representations or instruments of the violence to which they are asked to respond. Jurors must view such graphic representations and grasp the death-producing instrumentalities, which are given special evidentiary value in the state's case against the accused. To refuse to consider all the evidence is tantamount to defying one's oath as a juror. Because the gaze cannot be legitimately averted, the juror becomes a "victim" of viewing.[41]

Images and instrumentalities, in their evidentiary guise, engender a vivid and immediate confrontation with illegal violence and its consequences by emphasizing a particularized focus. As another juror, Charlotte Howles, explained, "The only thing we saw were pictures they had taken of the scene and they were just from the head up. You know, of where the gunshot wounds were at. That's all we saw of him." The victim is presented only in the violent images of the wounds that ended his life.

Being forced to confront those images has dramatic consequences in enlisting jurors to authorize execution. The victim will often be remembered as nothing other than the wounds that ended his life. As Sante says, "If photographs are supposed to freeze time, these crystallize what is already frozen, the aftermath of violence, like a voice-print of a scream. If photographs extend life, in memory and imagination, these extend death, not as a permanent condition the way tombstones do, but as a stage, an active moment of inactivity. Their subjects are constantly in the process of moving toward oblivion."[42]

Indeed, so powerful are those images that Charlotte Howles, when asked if she could remember what Donaldson looked like, said, "No, because to be honest I didn't look directly at the picture of his face because we were looking at where the bullets went in and came out. I didn't really look in his face." Or as Ms. Givens put it, "Normally I consider myself a liberal easterner transplanted here to Georgia and against capital punishment—always was—but after I saw that picture of that man, something popped. I saw the pictures of him slumped down behind the counter and he was shot at somewhere around here and behind the ear, that was terrible. . . . I think about it even now and it bothers me very much."

Assigning Responsibility and Explaining Motivation

But the juxtaposition of images of murder made vivid and the virtual invisibility of the state's own violence does not, in itself, explain how jurors allow themselves to be enlisted as authorizing agents of capital punishment. The testimony of the Connors's jurors suggests that two other factors are crucially in play. The first of those factors is what I call the "compulsion" to assign responsibility and explain motivation.

The origin and force of this "compulsion" in the case of John Henry Connors can perhaps be appreciated if we first understand that the story of his killing of Andy Donaldson is a seemingly random, meaningless death.[43] Events like the shooting of a clerk in the context of a ten-dollar robbery produce an intense effort to restore meaning, to answer the kind of question put by juror Howles when she asked, "Why? Why did he do it? Why, for such a small amount of money? I would love to have confronted him, face-to-face, and asked him why he committed such a senseless [act. It is] stupid to me to take another human life." Howles's questions express "a simple primal fear that our collective attempt to reassert meaning and value in a world deconstructed by random violence . . . will be . . . fleeting and unsuccessful. . . . [The juror] is swamped by a physical as well as psychic need not to succumb, not to be drawn, not to be sucked under, not to be seduced by the meaninglessness of such murders, into the falsely sophisticated, David Lynch-ian belief in the meaninglessness of the particular lives ended." The response is a virtually overwhelming desire to "assign personal responsibility for the murder and its consequences—including the arrest, trial and its outcome-imposition of the death penalty—squarely and irrevocably on the defendant."[44]

The Connors jurors voiced a strong desire to fix personal responsibility on the defendant, to make him a moral agent capable of being held to account for what otherwise seemed unaccountable. For each of those jurors the capital trial was, in fact, a drama dominated by the question of Connors's responsibility. As Ranes said, "There really wasn't much of a question about Connors' guilt. He was there. He never denied that. His gun fired the shot; he never denied that. There was just a lot of talk as if, you know, the fact he was drinking, as if the bottle left Connors behind, got out of the car, went into the Jiffy, and fired the shots." As Howles explained,

> They [the defense] said that alcohol had taken hold of his mind at
> the moment and that, if he had not been under the influence of

alcohol, he wouldn't have been where he was at. They were blam-
ing it on the alcohol because that's when they were questioning us
as jurors . . . that was the one question they asked us, did we think
that alcohol could make you do things that you normally wouldn't
do. It was one of the questions that the defense asked when they
were selecting the jurors.

Another juror, Sylvia Mann, a forty-nine-year-old high school
social studies teacher, rejected the argument that alcohol could
provide a sufficient explanation of why Connors killed Donaldson or that it should somehow diminish his responsibility.

It did come up that he was under the influence of alcohol and drugs
even though they told us from the beginning that that was not a
defense. I felt that the defense really pushed it a lot. They kept
talking about it a lot even though they said it was not a defense.
When we deliberated it was brought up fairly often that the person
was under the influence. But so what? I mean a lot of people get
drunk, but they don't take guns and go shoot up the Jiffy Store. I
don't think anybody really ever felt it was much of a defense. . . .
He shot someone because he wanted money. Like lots of people
want money but they don't kill other people to get it. And he knew
what he was doing. Because he'd already shot the man and the
man was on the floor and unconscious and there was no need to
shoot him a second time. Apparently he intended for the man
to die.

For this juror, Connors was a moral agent despite his alcohol
problems, fully capable of knowing what he was about, one
whose actions suggest an inexcusable intention to kill. "Bottles,"
she continued, "don't kill people. Only people, people like Connors, kill people." By insisting that Connors was both legally
guilty and morally responsible for the murder of Donaldson this
juror and her colleagues refused to accept the picture of a social
world of events governed by causes beyond human control; instead, they constructed a moral world of free agents making
choices for which they could be held to account.

As Joseph Rane saw it,

> There is a simple explanation for why he [Connors] did it. He made
> a really bad choice. He valued human life for ten dollars. And
> whether he was under the influence of alcohol or drugs or what-
> ever, he's still responsible for what he does and that's something
> that was brought out. . . . He wanted money though if you are fa-
> miliar with convenience stores you know that after eleven o'clock
> they don't even carry twenties in the drawer. And being under the
> influence of drugs and alcohol, there's no telling what it'll make
> you do. But you still do it. I think he just saw an opportunity to get
> some money to go get whatever and he just took that opportu-
> nity. . . . There was no reason in the world why somebody under
> the influence of alcohol or drugs should take anybody else's life.
> Why should he be any different from the rest of us?

In these narratives we see jurors confronting what Ranes himself called "just one of them whimsical things." We see their need
to "reassert responsibility and human agency for a momentous
act and momentous deprivation; so that we can again feel in
control of destiny."[45] To his jurors Connors seemed enough like
them that he could be justly subject to their judgment. Yet, at
the same time, he was different enough that his "cold-blooded,"
"vicious" act seemed to deserve the most severe, and thus unusual, punishment.

But as the jurors in the Connors case contemplated whether to
authorize such a punishment, another question of responsibility
having to do with their own responsibility as jurors arose. As
Robin West argues,

> The juror's responsibility for his fellow citizen, and responsibility
> to reach the morally right decision, is precisely what defines the
> juror as citizen. . . . That capacity gives the juror a stake in the
> affairs of others and makes him care about the consequences of his
> decision. The juror's capacity for doing so, his duty to engage this
> capacity, and his responsibility for the outcome are all necessary
> contributions . . . to the vitality of a liberal, participatory, and non-
> apathetic society.[46]

If Marshall's speculations in *Caldwell* are correct, responsible jurors, those who see themselves directly and personally responsible for the executions their decisions authorize, would be less likely to support state killing, whereas those who convince themselves that the responsibility lies elsewhere would be more likely to do so. Three jurors in the Connors case conformed to Marshall's expectation; even as they insisted on Connors's responsibility for murder, they refused to see themselves as agents of death.

Jurors Mann, Givens, and Rane each talked about their decision to condemn Connors to death as if that decision was somehow made elsewhere, as if they were not really making choices or authorizing anything. Each of them echoed an argument made by the legal philosopher Herbert Morris, namely, that the person who is truly responsible for the punishment is the defendant himself.[47] In this view the murderer, by his own acts, determines the death sentence. Thus the juror who votes for such a punishment is merely the agent of the defendant.

However, the efforts of Mann, Givens, and Rane to avoid responsibility for authorizing violence did not end there. Each was acutely aware of a point made by Cover, namely, that "the social organization of legal violence . . . [ensures that] responsibility for the violence must be shared." Cover noted, "Law . . . manifests itself in the secondary rules and principles which generally ensure that no single mind and no single will can generate the violent outcomes that follow from interpretive commitments. No single individual can render any interpretation operative as law—as authority for the violent act."[48] This is, of course, readily apparent from the group character of jury decision making, but it is also apparent to jurors from law's hierarchical social organization.

The jurors in the Connors case knew, or at least believed, that their decision was not the last word. Each knew or believed that it would be reviewed by the judge who presided over the trial and/ or by an appellate court. All thought that the appeals courts were as likely to reject the death penalty imposed on Connors as to accept it, and Mann, Givens, and Rane said that the fact that their death sentence would be reviewed by other actors in the legal process meant that, should Connors actually be executed, they would not have his death on their consciences. For them, the very structure of "super due process," and of extended review and appeal, which had been put in place to ensure heightened reliability in capital cases, made it easier to impose the death penalty.

Only Charlotte Howles saw herself as directly and personally responsible for the death sentence for which she voted. As she put it,

> I was really surprised when I could go in and vote for death because really and truly, before I was on this jury I had never given it a lot of thought. And I didn't have any strong convictions one way or the other. It is a big responsibility, and hard to accept, but I think that's why they have juries so people like me have to make those hard decisions. I felt from the beginning that it would be my call, and I thought that if the facts are there . . . I would have no problem going in and finding somebody guilty and giving them the death penalty. I think that if it's a heinous thing and if it warrants it, then I would certainly vote again for the death penalty. . . . My opinion was that, hey, I'm not going to let this guy [Connors] out. I would feel the same way if he was guilty, electrocuted later on, and they found him innocent. I'd feel bad, but not as bad as if I didn't give him the death penalty and he somehow got out and killed again. For me, my job was to make sure that that didn't happen again.

The moral responsibility that Howles felt most acutely was to use the death penalty to address a social crisis engendered by the kind of random, valueless violence perpetrated by Connors. In contrast to the act for which Howles was prepared to hold Connors responsible, Howles saw state killing, and her participation in the authorization of death itself, as meaningful and purposive, as being necessary to protect innocent others from him.

When "Life Doesn't Mean Life" and "Death Doesn't Mean Death"

As we saw in the Brooks case, not all jurors vote for death and not all juries impose it. Nonetheless, when people like Charlotte

Howles accept responsibility for imposing the death penalty, one might still ask, What is the meaning of the penalty they are voting to impose? When jurors lend their voice and vote for capital punishment, how do they understand the act they are authorizing?

My conversations with the jurors in the Connors case suggest that glaring inadequacies in the arsenal of criminal punishment as well as in the processes of review and appeal that automatically accompany a death sentence combined to push them to authorize such a sentence, although most were neither enthusiastic about their decision nor convinced that Connors would ever be executed. These conversations point to the instability and unpredictability of the responses of readers-listeners-jurors to the stories presented at trial. The jurors in the Connors case "rewrote" or supplemented the stories of both prosecution and defense, insisting that another story had to be told, this one a story of the unreliability of the state and the inadequacies of its penal policies.

That unreliability and those inadequacies make the death penalty seem to some jurors necessary and, at the same time, a highly improbable event. Focusing on the unreliability of the state and the inadequacy of its policies allowed jurors in the Connors case to decide one thing, that Connors should be sentenced to death, as a way of achieving another—namely, that he should spend the rest of his life in jail. While Connors's violent act could not be undone, the jurors responded by ordering a violent act that they thought would not be done at all.

The jurors in the Connors case were overwhelmingly concerned with incapacitation as a goal of criminal punishment. None of them believed that executions served as a deterrent to others, and none embraced a purely retributivist rationale for capital punishment. Each of them was, however, deeply concerned with the possibility that Connors might someday be back on the streets of Bowling. Each seemed sure that Connors's vicious, bloody acts qualified him to die under the laws of Georgia, yet each believed that what was necessary to achieve justice was something less than his death at the hands of the state.

Because, at the time of the trial in the Connors case, Georgia law did not provide for a sentence of life without parole, each was persuaded that unless they voted for death John Henry Connors would soon be out of prison posing a threat to innocent others. For these jurors, then, sentencing someone to die was the only way of insuring that he would live the rest of his life in prison. As juror Howles explained, "If he had not been found guilty of capital murder he would have gotten life. But that doesn't mean that he would have served a life term. It means he would have gotten out in however many years it is you have to serve before you get out on parole. Isn't it something like seven years. I think I'm just going by what I hear on TV, you know." Like the other jurors, Howles voted for death as a form of insurance: "If we didn't give him the death penalty, if he did get back out into society, he would hurt someone else. And I really didn't want that."

Rane and Mann stated that they would have preferred an alternative to the stark choice of death or a life sentence that did not really mean life in prison. Both said that they would have preferred it if they could have voted for life in prison without the possibility of parole. Both suggested that they chose death because this alternative was not available.

In fact, Rane reported that a substantial part of the jury's initial deliberations about Connors's fate focused on the meaning of life in prison.

> We were concerned that if he got life in prison he would serve only a few years and then be turned loose. There was one woman who was particularly adamant that she didn't want that, only problem was she said that she couldn't vote for death. So that's when the question of life in prison without the possibility of parole came up and that's when we sent a note to the judge asking if we could give that. And he called us back out and had us in the jury box again and he read the question and then told us that we couldn't, that that was not one of the options given. It would either be the death penalty or life in prison which meant he would have a possibility of parole.

This turned out to be a decisive moment in the Connors case. As Sylvia Mann said,

I was truly amazed because many of the people that were on the jury did not really seem to understand that life does not mean life. And I was astonished that a good number did not realize that when they started it. Those of us who did understand that, it took us to explain it to them because they really did not understand that. A lot of them would have liked to have given John Henry Connors life if it had really meant life, you know, that he was going to go to jail and stay there forever. When the judge told us it was either life that didn't mean life or death that changed things for most of us. But there were still a couple who didn't want Connors to die. . . . That meant that we had to talk about the fact that this, just for the reason that we voted for death, did not necessarily mean that Connors would die. . . . And I think we talked a good bit about the fact that this would go to the Georgia Supreme Court and it would be reviewed and that if anything was out of the ordinary then it would be thrown out, and that even after then the man would have many opportunities to appeal. And I think that probably that discussion helped more than anything to persuade the two that was reluctant. Just because we voted death didn't mean he would die.

Life that doesn't mean life and death that doesn't mean death—given these alternatives jurors in the Connors case struggled to find a way to express their view that the appropriate response to Donaldson's killing would be to put Connors away and to throw away the proverbial key. Indeed, no one—not Howles, Mann, Givens, or Rane—believed that execution was a likely result of a death sentence. As Howles put it, "We all pretty much knew that when you vote for death you don't necessarily or even usually get death. Ninety-nine percent of the time they don't put you to death. You sit on death row and get old."

This belief is typical of the views and attitudes of Americans.[49] Interviews with jurors across the country who have served in capital cases suggest that they often come to court believing that the law grants excessive and undue protections to defendants, which result in endless appeals in capital cases. As one juror who sat on a case that resulted in a life sentence said about persons given the death penalty, "They go back and appeal, appeal, appeal, so they die of old age." Or, as a juror who voted for death in another case explained, "Just because someone is sentenced to the death penalty doesn't mean he'll ever die. They don't put people to death. For example, [name of defendant] has now been on death row for many years. He's still there. Every time you turn around he's appealing again. . . . I'm very unhappy. I think the man should be put to death."

Still another juror talked about the influence that the allegedly prolonged appeals process had in the deliberations of the jury on which he sat. "There was," he said, "a lot of discussion about the appeals and the money it would cost to keep him trying and in the end he might still get life after years of appeal. . . . So, this came up that there could be appeal after appeal after appeal and in the end you still get life." Finally, another person suggested that for the jury on which he sat the issue of endless appeals was very important. "If this guy gets death," the jury hypothesized, "they are going to appeal the hell out of it on all kinds of grounds because [name of defense lawyer] is that good. . . . If we say he gets the death penalty there is no guarantee that he'll get it. He'll appeal all the way up through the Supreme Court for the next ten years. And who is to say that through some technicality he won't get off scot free." Thus if a life sentence doesn't necessarily mean life, it is also not clear that a death sentence will mean death.

In this context it is important to note that, since the mid-1960s, uneasiness about social disorder generally, and about criminal behavior in particular, has given rise to what political scientist Stuart Scheingold calls the "myth of crime and punishment." This myth stresses punitiveness as the appropriate response to crime, in contrast to seemingly out-of-vogue alternative scenarios he labels the "myth of redemption" and the "myth of rehabilitation."[50] The so-called myth of crime and punishment provides the rationale for scapegoating and stereotyping entire categories or classes of people as the "criminal element."[51] It calls for harsh and lasting punishment as the appropriate solution—indeed, the only adequate solution to the frightening scourge of allegedly random, predatory criminal violence.[52]

Mistrust of the criminal justice process is inherent in public support for harsh punishment. It is reflected in a cultural common sense that holds that courts do not punish severely or effectively enough, that prisons release incarcerated offenders "far too soon."[53] Underlying these sentiments is the view that the criminal justice system has been and continues to be "faulty," especially those agencies responsible for the imposition and administration of criminal punishment.

The impression of leniency owing to the breakdown of the criminal justice system is conveyed best, perhaps, by news accounts of the recidivism of ex-convicts or persons on probation, parole, or furlough from prison—in the worst case, by the nightmare of the murderer released to murder again. In Georgia, where the Connors jury sat, as in the rest of the nation, the mass media play a key role in reinforcing and reproducing the perception that early release is endemic to the criminal justice system. Throughout the 1980s and 1990s the media in Georgia have repeatedly reported that murderers not given the death penalty will be eligible for parole in seven years. They have done so despite the Georgia State Parole Board's explicit statement in 1985 that class I murderers, persons sentenced to life for capital crimes, are considered for parole only after fifteen years,[54] despite official reports of the parole board indicating that class II murderers who do become eligible for parole in seven years are extremely unlikely to actually be paroled in seven years,[55] and despite legislation in 1994 that altogether abolished parole for capital offenders not sentenced to death.[56] The extremely infrequent use of parole after seven years for noncapital murderers and the explicit rejection of parole consideration before fifteen years for capital murderers not given the death penalty have received virtually no publicity and have thus been ignored in political rhetoric and news accounts of murders. As a result, the realities of the justice system have had little chance of penetrating the consciousness of even the most attentive Georgian.

The most visceral confirmation or "proof" of a defective criminal justice system and of the need for more severe punishment is the early release of criminals who return to violent crime. Such cases easily become the focal points for public debate about the "crime problem" and how it should be dealt with. In this debate, what the public knows or thinks about the release of criminals in general and murderers in particular may well be reinforced and reproduced by politicians and others in the "law and order marketplace" with a stake in having the public see the issue in one way or another. The public's apprehension about crime and punishment invites politicians to assume a "get tough" posture in their political campaigns, and to tell stories of early release and what they will do about it as a way of garnering support from a public ever wary of crime.[57] Especially when the crime is murder and early release is blamed, politicians will be tempted to use emotionally laden media accounts accompanied by allegations of the contributing role of early release to present the crime problem to the public.

Perhaps the most striking example of such accounts were the two "Willie" Horton ads in the presidential campaign of 1988.[58] Those ads proved to be ideal fodder for an election year media rampage that turned the tide for then vice president Bush. They created a narrative nightmare of escape from punishment that resonated with public fears of criminal violence. They have provided the bedrock for both political rhetoric and the consciousness of crime and punishment ever since. The Horton narrative did so by making a black man who senselessly brutalized a white couple the symbolic representation of Michael Dukakis (the Democratic candidate for president) and the alleged failure of his criminal justice policy,[59] a racial theme also echoed in media crime coverage.[60]

In this context it should not be surprising that jurors like those in the Connors case were extremely vocal in articulating concern about early release. Their statements provide strong evidence of a cultural common sense focused on "undue solicitude" for defendant's rights and "insufficient severity" in dealing with the most dangerous criminals. Time and again, jurors in the Connors case, and in others returned to those issues. As one man put it, "The prosecution and the judges. . . . It's the pardons and parole people and the judges that keep interfering with the system that turn them loose." This language is interesting in its separation of particular actors in the criminal justice system from that "system" itself, suggesting that the source of problems is personal rather than institutional. In contrast, another juror's analysis moved from the personal to the systemic as he explained his thinking about crime and punishment; "I feel like our justice system has gotten—now I can get on the soapbox—that our justice system has gone way too much for the criminal instead of the victim. I think they definitely have gotten more."

So pervasive is the belief about early release that some jurors regard any contrary belief as frivolous.[61] One juror explained how he had responded when he encountered such a belief during his jury's deliberation.

> One of the women, she was under the impression that if you gave someone life in prison they would be in prison for the rest of their life and myself and a couple of other jurors had to explain to her that if he did get life in prison, he would stand a chance of parole in years to come and that they would be back out on the streets again. There was only one way to actually stop him from doing what he did again. It was to give him the death penalty.

When asked if he explained that to the other juror, he replied "Myself and someone else, because she wasn't aware that a life sentence means you can be released in 7–9 years." The female juror's view is attributed to ignorance, to a lack of awareness of what the respondent takes as an established fact.

Still another juror talked about how he had confounded the judge and the lawyers during voir dire.

> They asked something about life in prison and I said "Well, there's really no such thing," and of course they all went "uhhhh." And they said "What do you base your opinion on?" I said "I read a lot while I was growing up. I got the impression that when you were sentenced to life in prison and you died in prison, you weren't killed, but you died in prison." But I said "This is not true. You get out in seven years, you know, even for the most heinous crimes."

So deep is this belief that it is not clear that some jurors are prepared to hear or accept a view that contradicts it. "If we could definitely determine," one juror suggested, reflecting on the deliberations of the jury on which he sat, "that he would not get out of prison rather than being electrocuted that might have been allowed, but the fact that a life sentence would mean but a few years in jail meant that we had to go the other way. . . . The judge was saying that life in prison means life in prison period. *But we knew better.*"

Thus where state killing is concerned, saying yes does not necessarily mean yes. To the jurors in the Connors case, and in others in the everyday world of the killing state, saying yes to the death penalty meant both more and less than it seemed. For the Connors jurors it was a way of expressing moral horror and revulsion at the violent and "whimsical" killing of Andy Donaldson and of ensuring, as best they were able, that Connors would himself never be an agent of such violence again.

Conclusion

The capital sentencing decision is, at least in theory, distinctive. It is a state-authorized collective choice made by citizens under legally prescribed procedures with explicit rules to govern, or at least guide, the decision-making process. The decision is supposed to be a "reasoned moral choice" between life and death informed by aggravating and mitigating considerations in accord with retributive standards.[62]

As the Connors case illustrates, the realities for those called upon to make this decision are different. Jurors in capital trials are asked to participate in a set of complex rituals through which the state seeks to gain the right to exercise the ultimate power of sovereignty, namely the power over life itself. They are asked to cast the weight of citizenship on the side of state killing. It is, as I have said, a remarkable and troubling aspect of democratic politics that jurors regularly do so. The Connors case helps us understand how and why this happens.

In the Connors case, and other capital trials, the representation of violence is as difficult and as uncertain as it is anywhere else. Yet capital trials make some kinds of violence vivid and visible while effectively hiding others and rendering them invisible. The violence made visible is the murderous violence of people like John Henry Connors whose acts are graphically displayed and the consequences of which are eagerly described to jurors. While the prosecution makes great efforts to persuade jurors that such violence is unnecessary, irrational, indiscriminate, gruesome, and useless, the violence of the death penalty is described, when it is spoken about at all, as rational, purposive, and controlled through values, norms, and procedures external to violence itself. The jury's verdict, the spoken truth of the community, is the ultimate affirmation of the meaningfulness of that difference. Thus death sentences, some might assume, speak for themselves. They intermingle a politics of vengeance with a fearful concern about dangerous persons and convey the authority and the desire that someone should be put to death by the state. They represent the ultimate public embrace of the killing state.

In the Connors case, while the death sentence did authorize the state to extinguish the life of John Henry Connors, it is by no means clear that the jurors truly desired this result. The death sentence was not simply a linguistic command whose integrity depended on Connors's execution. It was at one and the same time a powerful condemnation of Connors for his vicious crime and a way of ensuring that he would be imprisoned for life. Where death sentences are not imposed, it may be because jurors feel that execution is disproportionate and perhaps, as in the Brooks case, because they believe, contrary to the weight of public opinion, that a life sentence means what it says.

The Connors jury verdict was also an expression of distrust in the criminal justice system. It has now become conventional wisdom that state policy is too lenient and ineffective—in particular, that murderers not condemned to death will be back in society far too soon. The Connors case shows the way such beliefs may help shape legal action in the killing state.

Though represented in state law as a strictly regulated and formally guided exercise of reasoned moral judgement, in practice the capital sentencing decision is often a negotiated social transaction fraught with tactics of persuasion, advocacy, rhetorical claims, and intimidation. In this context, jurors' claims about the timing of release become potent tools in negotiations over the right punishment. These claims empower citizens, giving them a conception of how state law does, and should, operate, whose source is independent of those whose legal authority derives from formal training or official position. Instructing jurors in capital cases not to think about what the sentence alternatives would be when they are deciding guilt and refusing to explain to them what the death penalty alternative would be when they are deciding punishment may make sense within the highly structured ideology of due process, but doing so defies cultural common sense and, as such, is regularly resisted.[63]

Lawrence Friedman, of Stanford Law School, observes that "The jury's power to bend and sway, to chip away at the official rules, is built into the system. Juries are not supposed to be lawless, but the system is set up in such a way that lawlessness . . . cannot be prevented—cannot even be detected."[64] But how can law tolerate death as a punishment when prevailing public attitudes compromise the constitutional protections required by state law? It can do so only by ignoring this fact. By "deregulating death" the Supreme Court is able to ignore the sacrifice of legal protections, while insisting that lower courts exercise heightened care and reliability in the handling of capital cases.

Yet the Supreme Court has recognized the difficult position capital jurors are put in when they are not informed about sentencing alternatives prescribed by state law.[65] As a result, the Court held that it is the defendant's right to have jurors know what the alternative to the death penalty would be, though under limited conditions.[66] But would telling jurors about the alternative override their anxieties about early release and their mistrust of the criminal justice system?

While some may argue that beliefs about early release with their adverse impact on defendant's rights can be dispelled by jury instructions, the evidence presented here raises serious doubts. Jurors' ideas are embedded in more general folk beliefs about early release. They are the product of a perception that murderers get out of prison far too soon, which, in turn, is rooted in a deep-seated mistrust of the criminal justice system and its punitiveness and in the belief that due process unfairly tips the scale in favor of defendants.

Evidence inconsistent with taken-for-granted assumptions about the right way of dealing with criminals and the dangers of deviating from those methods does not penetrate.[67] Given the repeated and insistent political and media emphasis on the prospect of early release in murder cases, and jurors' beliefs in the unreliability of evidence about parole practice in such cases, they are not apt to trust court pronouncements that run contrary to their deeply ingrained folk knowledge. Thus a public enlisted by the state to impose death may do so, but not in the way required by the Constitution as a condition for using that punishment. The killing state, in spite of the formal protections of the law, may end up being a lawless state.

6

NARRATIVE STRATEGY AND DEATH PENALTY ADVOCACY: ATTEMPTING TO SAVE THE CONDEMNED

I'd make my Supreme Court down in Texas,
and there wouldn't be no killers getting free.
If they were found guilty,
then they would hang quickly,
Instead of writin' books and smiling on TV.
—HANK WILLIAMS JR., "If the South Would Have Won . . ."

Holmes was . . . wrong: The life of the law is neither logic nor experience, but narrative.
—DAVID LUBAN, "Difference Made Legal: The Court and Dr. King"

You can never forget that whatever decision you make could well determine if your client lives or dies. How you cast the issue, whether you are going to interview a witness or not. . . . It doesn't matter if you live from now until eternity, there would always be more to do. . . . It is just an overpowering sense of pressure to have to deal with making decisions that determine whether someone lives or dies. . . . If we don't present their cases in an effective story then we can't save them. It's just something that you are not prepared to deal with. Some people believe that we've done our job if we represent our clients vigorously and if we tell their story. But saving their stories is little consolation if you can't save their lives. A surgeon knows every day that he or she is going to be doing something that saves somebody's life or could not save somebody's life. That's just not what lawyers are trained to deal with.—A death penalty lawyer who worked in a death penalty resource center

I am a human rights lawyer like my colleagues in Guatemala who are butting their heads against a government that won't allow free speech. . . . A lawyer in Guatemala or Iran, no one has any trouble labeling what they do as human rights work. But is it clear that death penalty work in the United States is also human rights work. . . . There is an international trend toward abolition, but not here. So it is one of the very few jobs in the United States where you are truly a human rights lawyer because it is an area of law where we are butting our heads against a domestic law that is going against a larger human rights norm. We now have to find ways of telling our clients stories that will appeal to an international audience. To win in the long run we will have to broaden the audience for the stories we tell and hope that that audience will bring pressure to bear in the United States.—A death penalty lawyer working in a public interest setting

The battle to stop state killing often does not end after the jury renders its verdict in a capital case, whether that case is as politicized as McVeigh's or as seemingly routine as the Brooks and Connors cases. The battle carries on in other venues where the byzantine rules governing the American appellate process make it possible to raise legal challenges. This process, jurors believe, is the major hurdle that stands between their verdict and the ultimate responsibility for state violence. For those anxious to see death sentences turned into executions, the process can sometimes be infuriating.

At the center of this stage of the death penalty system in the United States stands a small group of lawyers who dedicate their professional lives to saving condemned persons from being killed by the state.[1] Over the course of several years I met and talked with forty of them in their offices, their homes, and in courtrooms across the country.[2] I wanted to see for myself the people who some see as villains and others as saints. In fact, the people I met were mostly neither villains nor saints. Some seemed unusually dedicated and selfless; others had more common motives for doing the work they did.

Whatever their differences, these lawyers all specialize in appellate and postconviction procedures and, as such, are the last line of defense in the effort to prevent executions. These men and women carry the burden of representing some of the most hated persons in American society. Unlike trial lawyers, who defend a legally innocent person against the most serious criminal charges, these lawyers seek to save the lives of those already found guilty and sentenced to death. The success of their work is crucial in determining when the state kills and how much state killing there will be in the United States.

Crucial is their ability to craft persuasive narratives, which they present before reviewing courts in order to demonstrate the legal inadequacy or the injustice of the conviction or sentencing of their clients. Much of this work occurs in habeas corpus proceedings. In those proceedings, often framed as challenges to the competency or adequacy of the trial lawyers who originally represented their clients or as allegations of prosecutorial misconduct arising from the illegal withholding of evidence, these lawyers are afforded an opportunity to retell the client's story. Like all lawyers, they specialize in organizing facts into a clear and believable chronology, with a compelling narrative line.[3] The stories they craft are crucial because narrative can be a source of consolation in a world that knows violence and pain.

The history of narrative is, in part, a record of the way humans respond to the violence and pain that can threaten to tear down our carefully constructed but fragile webs of signification and structures of meaning. Only the rare person—the martyr, Robert Cover claims—is able, through an individual assertion of will and commitment, to hold on to meaning in the face of suffering.[4] For most of us, doing so requires a shared effort. Thus the impulse to narrate flourishes. Narrative can heal. It provides the comforting assurance that meaning can survive. Our ability to narrate wards off despair.

Narrative provides a link between what Cover called law's "jurispathic" and its "jurisgenerative" qualities,[5] between the daily reality of violence in which the killing state traffics and the normative ideals—justice—to which law aspires. It is in the stories that we tell, and that law tells to us, that state violence is called to account. Narrative provides one device for critique; it also provides a vehicle for law's renewal and regeneration because the aspiration to justice is maintained and revitalized in narrative.[6]

Death penalty lawyers challenge our nation to live up to its commitment to fairness and to protect individual rights for the most despised among us. They insist that America attend responsibly to social problems that lead to violence. For them, the fight against state killing is but one part of an ongoing political struggle to ensure fairness to the poor, the downtrodden, the dispossessed. Fighting against a punishment disproportionately imposed on persons of color is at the turn of the century what the struggle for racial equality was to earlier generations. Lawyers for the condemned say that they are fighting for the soul and the future of America. What we do to those who deserve our just condemnation will, they believe, go far in determining whether we can deal responsibly with our society's most serious problems. While they neither forgive nor excuse those whose lives they defend, they insist that we should not answer violence with violence. They reply to calls for vengeance with calls for healing, to the clamor for killing with calls for social reconstruction.

Death penalty lawyers use the legal process as an archive, a place to record and preserve their deeply held views of justice so that, someday, they may be retrieved and so that the killing state someday may be dismantled.[7] They turn to the law to carry on a political struggle because at least in that arena their voices, even when they are not needed, will not be drowned out completely by the escalating intensity of demands for executions.

As public support for capital punishment, the large number of people on death row, and the growing number of executions show, death penalty lawyers often fight a lonely and losing battle. They are widely blamed for unfairly complicating the process of moving from death sentences to state killings. They are said, by conservative leaders in the culture wars, to exemplify elitist indifference to the lives and pains of ordinary people. Death penalty proponents and grieving relatives of murder victims regularly ask, What kind of people are these who would give aid and comfort to murderers?

Today, in a hostile political climate, death penalty lawyers seek to protect legal rights that, not a generation ago, were thought essential to guaranteeing fairness in capital cases. Their work pits them against the increasing fear and frustration that mark the American condition and that fuel our national appetite for state killing. They call on all of us to see beyond evil deeds to the desperate lives that produce those deeds and not to give in to our fears and frustrations. They do so in the name of a justice beyond or outside the purview of the killing state. In this chapter I focus on the political and legal context in which death penalty lawyers now work and describe the different narratives that they construct to humanize those who have been condemned to death. Although death penalty lawyers, in the current political and legal climate, often cannot save their clients' lives, perhaps saving the client's story may be valuable for the political effort to end capital punishment.

Political and Legal Context

If the impulse to narrate flourishes, as I have argued, in the face of violence and pain, then one would expect to see a flourishing of narrative in what I call the death penalty bar. As I noted in chapter 1, these are complicated and difficult times for opponents of the death penalty. Advocacy against capital punishment thus takes on particular salience, both as a type of political lawyering aimed at the abolition of state killing and as a type of traditional lawyering, the goal of which is to save the lives of individual clients.[8] Opposition to the death penalty in the United States bridges these categories even as it reveals the tension between them. Representing individual clients against whom death sentences have been imposed provides one vehicle through which lawyers can make abolitionist arguments; yet in the current legal climate making such arguments may not be the best way to persuade a court that any particular client should not be executed.

A generation ago, death penalty lawyers might have been called the "abolitionist" bar,[9] but today is a different time.[10] Toward the end of the heyday of the Warren Court and the era of sustained civil rights activism, a favorable judicial response to the abolitionist movement seemed quite possible. In 1972 in *Furman v. Georgia*, the Supreme Court provided such a response, holding that the death penalty as then *applied* was unconstitutional.[11] While the Court did not find that the death penalty was per se unconstitutional, there was a reasonable expectation that it might very well soon do so. As Philip Kurland wrote at the time, "One role of the Constitution is to help the nation to become 'more civilized.' A society with the aspirations that ours so often asserts can't, consistently with its goals, coldly and deliberately take the life of any human being no matter how reprehensible his past behavior. . . . In the *Furman v. Georgia* decision the inevitable came to pass."[12] Jack Greenberg of the NAACP Legal Defense Fund expressed a similar understanding of the significance of *Fur-*

man when he said, "There will no longer be any more capital punishment in the United States."[13]

Then something unexpected happened. Whereas in other Western nations the formal abolition of the death penalty was followed by a downturn in public interest and support for it, in the wake of *Furman* a dramatic backlash occurred. State legislatures quickly reenacted death penalty laws designed to cure the problems identified by the Supreme Court. Public reaction followed a similar pattern, "with a hostile response all over the country."[14] Thus, four years after *Furman's* limited abolition of capital punishment the Supreme Court, in *Gregg v. Georgia*, found that "it is now evident that a large proportion of American society continues to regard . . . [capital punishment] as an appropriate and necessary criminal sanction." As a result, it held that "the punishment of death does not invariably violate the Constitution."[15]

Since the mid-1970s chances for abolition of the death penalty have dramatically declined. Today the United States uses state killing more and more frequently and for a wider variety of reasons.[16] We do so in the face of a clear international movement toward abolition, a movement that not long ago saw the abolition of capital punishment in South Africa.[17] The United Nations Commission on Human Rights recently cited America's continued use of capital punishment as a source of concern.[18] American courts are now in the embarrassing position of hearing arguments in which our practices are described as violating basic principles of human rights and in which the United States is compared unfavorably with the South African regime, which, for years, was the epitome of everything that the American legal system claimed to oppose and claimed not to be.[19]

Despite its surprising prominence in the early part of the 2000 presidential campaign, there are few signs of a complete rethinking of our attachment to capital punishment. In both the legal and political processes continued attachment to state killing seems well entrenched. In fact, as I noted earlier, the Supreme Court has moved step by step to cut off all systemic, "wholesale" challenges to the constitutionality of capital punishment.[20]

Moreover, it has imposed technical obstacles designed, in part, to *prevent* death row inmates from raising constitutional claims in repeated habeas petitions to the federal courts. The Court has grown impatient with the complex legal process that it had constructed itself in earlier years to ensure fairness in the administration of law's ultimate penalty.

Several years ago, in the most significant sign of that impatience, the Court declared that defendants generally must base their habeas petitions on asserted violations of the federal law as it existed at the time of the original state proceedings.[21] In a follow-up case, it held that if the federal law was unclear at that time, any reasonable, "good faith" interpretation of the federal law by the state courts immunizes the conviction and sentence from later habeas attack.[22] Even more recently, the Court extended the same principle to the method of application of the federal law to the facts of a particular case; if the state courts' method of application of the federal law was proper in view of the precedents that existed at that time, then federal habeas relief is unavailable (even if those precedents are later overruled or changed).[23] These decisions have made it much more difficult for a defendant who receives a death sentence to obtain federal habeas review of the merits of whatever decisions or rulings might have been made by the judge during his capital trial.[24] For the current Supreme Court "finality is more important than hearing every meritorious legal claim; there simply comes a point when legal proceedings must end and punishment must be imposed."[25]

Outright abolition now has little support, and the abolition movement has become virtually invisible.[26] Congress has passed legislation that further limits the ability of federal courts to review constitutional defects in death penalty cases,[27] and postconviction defender programs and capital resource centers have been defunded in eighteen states. As a result, it will be increasingly difficult for inmates on death row to secure legal representation to challenge their death sentences. By limiting habeas and cutting funds for death penalty lawyers, the political battle over state killing has now been carried to the heart of the Constitution's guarantees of due process and equal protection. Capital punishment has now changed from a largely symbolic sanction to an almost regular occurrence.

In these circumstances death penalty lawyers can carry on only guerrilla campaigns, fighting with increasingly limited legal tools on terrain defined and fortified by those who want to use state killing as part of a war against crime or as a resource in their effort to win the culture wars. As one death penalty lawyer put it,

> When I started there was still so much hope, we were actually still winning cases. But now the cases that are in the system, the train is coming and everybody's jumping off the track, but we are there waiting. The law has gotten so horrible. The Supreme Court has continued to put up a barrier every time you go down a road. It's a legitimate road, but then they say "Oh yeah, we said you could go down that road, but we were just kidding. We don't mean that anymore." So you stop and you go down the next road that they told you that you could go down. Then they say, "Haven't you figured it out. We were just kidding, you can't go down that road." So things have changed. The hope has changed. The political feeling, the atmosphere, the environment that we are litigating in today is one where people think that capital defendants have too many avenues of appeal and are going to stop it. Cases that fifteen years ago would have been reversed are no longer reversed. The result is that we are now prepared to kill our minorities, brain damaged indigents, and people who don't have competent lawyers. It's an injustice, an absolute injustice.

Or as another, well-known veteran of the campaign to abolish the death penalty said,

> We were beating them as long as they took the Constitution seriously. Then they could never get by us. They couldn't do it. So they changed the rules. They began burying habeas. They took away substantive issues and made it a series of technical bars so they could kill people. They had to take away basic due process. The point still remains that if they had held the line on due process, care, reliability, we would win. But no more.

In this climate death penalty lawyers have not themselves escaped condemnation.[28] Rather than being respected as the guardians of important legal values rooted in the Fourteenth Amendment guarantee of due process of law, or the Eighth Amendment's prohibition of cruel and unusual punishment,[29] they are vilified as rogues who violate the canons of their profession by conducting an ideologically motivated campaign against capital punishment. As the Supreme Court put it when it refused to grant a stay of execution to Robert Alton Harris,[30]

> Harris seeks an equitable remedy. Equity must take into consideration the state's strong interest in proceeding with its judgment and Harris's obvious attempt at manipulation. This claim could have been brought more than a decade ago. There is no good reason for this abusive delay, which has been compounded by last-minute attempts to manipulate the judicial process.[31]

To oppose the death penalty through the legal process in the United States at the turn of the century is not unlike fighting against apartheid in the courts of South Africa in the 1970s, or litigating in behalf of Palestinian rights in the occupied territories in the 1980s.[32] In the face of a state intent on imposing violence, death penalty lawyers turn to narrative. Their work is increasingly the work of recording the stories of their clients' lives, of the poverty and abuse that breeds violence, and of the indifference of a state intent on doing its own kind of violence. As the prospect of saving lives diminishes, the importance of saving the stories of those whose lives are lost grows.

The Construction of Narrative

Death penalty lawyers use particular types of narrative both to criticize state killing and also to tell an alternative story, a story of violence renounced, of human rights vindicated, of the death penalty defeated. Like Scheherazade in *The Arabian Nights*, they use narrative to forestall death.[33] They remind us that narrative

has always been a way of holding on to life, of distracting or satisfying those with the power to end life.[34]

Death penalty lawyers use narrative to buy time for their clients, but even when they fail, they seek to preserve their clients'
stories. Through narrative these lawyers fix their gaze, not only
on the possibilities (or impossibilities) of the present, but on the
future with its uncertain and as yet unkept promises. In their
use of narrative they address two different audiences; first is the
present, usually a court to which they appeal to save the life of
their client; second is the future, an indeterminate audience of
citizens to whom they petition for an end to capital punishment.
For each audience they deploy a different set of narrative strategies; to each they tell a different story.

In their address to the present, death penalty lawyers serve as
witnesses to injustice; in their address to the future, they serve
as historians memorializing the injustices they witness. Through
both of these activities, death penalty lawyers refuse to recognize
the violence of the present as the defining totality of law, and
they become the carriers of a vision of a future in which justice
prevails over that violence. Their refusal takes place through the
construction of "realist" tales.[35] This appeal to realism is not surprising because it is the appeal most congenial to the legal process
and because "the natural form of mimetic narrative is eye-witness and first-person. Circumstantiality, verisimilitude, and
many more of the qualities that we recognize as identifying characteristics of realism in narrative are all natural functions of the
eye-witness point of view."[36]

Death penalty lawyers use eyewitness accounts, "realist" stories, to try to persuade their audience of the "truth" and salience
of facts not previously known and circumstances either ignored
or underappreciated. As is true of trial lawyers in capital cases,
these lawyers try to bend realism to the service of a sentimental
tale and seek to play on the terrain of a cultural contest about
victims and victimization. In so doing, they speak in a prophetic
voice even as they supply the argumentative and interpretive resources to bridge the gap between present and future.[37] They in-

sist, in the face of their current inability to end state killing, that the future will remember as well as judge the present.

Death penalty lawyers use legal processes to record a history that preserves the present's pained voice. Because they can, indeed, take advantage of one of the legitimating promises of law, namely its commitment to due process, they can use the litigated case to create a record, and to turn the court into the archive in which that record serves as the materialization of memory.[38] The legal hearing provides an opportunity both to witness and to record history by creating narratives of present injustices. Death penalty lawyers put state killing in a narrative context that juxtaposes it to the Good, and they use narrative to preserve memory in the face of an obliterating violence.

In their roles as both witnesses and historians of the present, death penalty lawyers self-consciously and strategically deploy and depend upon narrative. As one death penalty lawyer who practices in a southern state told me:

> I think of what I do as constructing and using narrative. I think that that phrase—narrative—actually describes a lot of what I do both inside and outside the courthouse. In court, my pleadings and briefs have to be constructed to tell a story. . . . My strategy for telling the story is, in fact, pretty much the same inside court and in the court of public opinion. If my client did the crime, the narrative must put it in context. I have to tell a story that explains why he did the crime, what brought him to that, and why he's still a good person in spite of it. And if he didn't do the crime then I have to put together a pretty dramatic story of why all the people in the system are screwing him and why all this compelling evidence that says he didn't do it never made it into his trial. And again it's storytelling. It's like going back to *To Kill a Mockingbird* or something like that. . . . I see what I do as playing into certain standard accepted stories that flow through our society. What I do is take my client's story and fit it into one of those narrative paths that make people go, "Okay. Yeah." You see my job is to come up with a narrative that is going to work.

This lawyer calls attention to the artificial, constructed, audience-driven quality of narrative by reminding us that there is never only a single narrative that can be told. Rather narrative strategy depends, in the first instance, on choosing among the available repertoire of stories. As a lawyer from another southern state put it,

> My theory of this work is that you have a terminal patient. . . . If you are going to cure any of them you have to, not to mix a metaphor, think up a good story. You breath new life into the case first by finding new facts, but the facts by themselves won't do the job. You've got to change the way the case appears. You've got to find a good story that will get the attention of the court. They saw it once and they didn't like it so we need to come up with a new narrative. Your job is to breath new life into a dead case. . . . It's as simple as that, and I am convinced beyond any doubt that you don't do that by doing law or technicalities. If you do it at all, the story is the thing.

Both of these lawyers understand their work as crafting persuasive stories. They present sentimentalizing accounts of lives of misfortune, like the life of William Brooks, that lead to and explain, though do not excuse, a single murderous incident. Both also think about narrative in a strategic sense. Facts do not speak for themselves, and stories do not tell themselves. The good lawyer fits the story that he has to tell into the available stock of culturally recognized narratives that connect his client to familiar and recognizable themes.[39] Because the plot is known and predictable, however, the audience may not be fully engaged. To get attention death penalty lawyers must fashion narrative elements that evoke curiosity yet are, at the same time, both commonplace and comfortable.

These narrative strategies have changed dramatically over the past thirty years in response to the increasing difficulty of persuading conservative judges and a tough-on-crime public. Today, if they are to have any hope of success in keeping their clients alive, they have to adopt "discrete" rather than "universalistic"

narrative styles: discrete narratives are "keyed to an isolated incident as experienced by a single litigant, and universalistic stories
are keyed to broader issues and shared experiences."[40] The former
emphasize the idiosyncratic issues found in a single case; the latter focus on the patterns unifying classes of cases. As one experienced death penalty lawyer explained,

> Systemic challenges are not likely to succeed. The nineties are not
> like the seventies. No one—not the Supreme Court, not state legis-
> latures—is going to take the whole thing down all at once. No
> court is going to grant relief on an issue if they know that two,
> three, or five hundred people are going to be relieved of their death
> sentences. . . . The country is simply not willing to accept that. So
> I think that that means that our focus as lawyers is to find a hook
> in each of our cases that can get relief for your client in a way that
> isn't going to be broad based. You have to put things together into
> a story that works. And each client's story has to be presented as
> a unique thing. We save lives, when we are able to save lives, if we
> can tell about broken lives, systematic abuse, you know, the stuff
> of pathos. It isn't dramatic. It is tragedy that we work with.

The narratives that death penalty lawyers construct in addressing the audience of the present are what literary theorists
Robert Scholes and Robert Kellogg refer to as "empirical."[41] Such
narratives replace "allegiance to the *mythos* with allegiance to
reality."[42] The reality that dominates in such stories is biographical. "We are like our clients' biographers," a young death penalty
lawyer said,

> in the sense that we have to construct a story that broadens the
> focus from the single act of violence to a whole life. We have to
> tell a life story in such a way that puts the killing in context. We
> attempt to go to the past, you know, to show who this person was
> in the context of his family, in his life. I keep waiting for some
> justice on the Supreme Court to have their child commit a murder.
> Then our stories will really hit home. Because we feel so differently
> when we know the people. So we have to make the judges feel as
> if they know our clients. We have to tell their lives.

Or as another, more experienced lawyer put it,

> My strong feeling is, if you can't convince a judge in the first five
> pages of a one hundred fifty page petition that this is a life worth
> saving, you've already lost. You've already lost because you have
> to be able to bring home to the fact finder or to that tribunal what
> has gone terribly wrong in this person's life. I am convinced that
> you cannot just talk about the legal chain of events and say "Isn't
> this outrageous. This person deserves relief." No, you have to start
> and really about ninety-five percent of what you say is in those first
> five pages. They should be doing biography. Well-done biography is
> what wins hearts and minds.

Making judges "feel as if they know" the person who has been
condemned to death or winning "hearts and minds" places the
emphasis not on the facts of the case but on the skill with which
those facts can be narrated.[43] In this sense the lawyer's skill is
rhetorical; narrative must evoke feelings sufficient to persuade.
Their narratives test the power of the victims' rights movement,
making space to claim that their clients too are victims.

Not everyone agrees, however, that the best narrative strategy
is to emphasize only the discrete and separate facts of their client's life. Some believe that it is important, in every case, to use
narrative to generalize from this particular client into an overtly
political argument against capital punishment. As one such critic
told me,

> I always am looking for ways to move from the particulars of my
> client to say something, you know, about the death penalty. I think
> that too many lawyers are afraid today, because of the really horri-
> ble political conditions, to make the wholesale argument. But I
> haven't given up on that. But you have to be subtle. Each story has
> to suggest not that this is the only story, but that it is an example
> that could be repeated hundreds of times. A good story is a story
> that highlights the vulnerability of my client and the fact that he
> was led to the actions in his situation. But it also has to universal-
> ize the experience in a way that makes the political argument
> against the death penalty. This means I have to tell a story that

convinces people that no one is outside the human community so much that they need to be executed.

That a death penalty lawyer can say, with no hint of irony, that they must look carefully for opportunities to talk about capital punishment itself is just another indication of America's attachment to state killing.

Despite the emphasis on "discrete" stories, the one overriding strategic goal in all narratives is to humanize the client,[44] under the assumption that jurors and judges will only condemn those whom they see as fundamentally Other, as inhuman, as outside the reach of the community of compassionate beings. "The key to your job," one Midwestern death penalty lawyer noted,

> is to give your client a human face. Judges, just like the rest of us, don't want to think that humans kill other humans. It is as if the client who kills is really of a different species. Our job is to make the judges see something of themselves or, if not themselves, at least to recognize the human condition in the lives of our clients. It is your job to make them feel legitimate sympathy, based on real facts. . . . If you tell the whole story so they know what led up to the murder, . . . people will understand how that whole scenario would lead any one of us down a path of increasing anger and frustration to a killing somewhere down the line.

"Death cases," another well-known member of the death penalty bar argued,

> are all and always about the humanity of somebody who is about to be put to death. They are not about that in a technical legal sense, but they are if we are doing what we should. We have to tell their stories so that judges see them as people, people who have done a terrible thing. . . . I suppose what we are trying to do is make it harder to kill by reminding everyone that our clients are not just drug-crazed, twenty-five-year-olds who prey on little old ladies. We have to turn them into brain-damaged, mentally retarded, sexually abused, discriminated against people who end up over their heads in situations where they don't know what to do.

Humanizing the client requires that death penalty lawyers engage in fact-intensive investigations designed to show that the mitigation stages of death penalty trials were constitutionally deficient.[45] But the facts, once collected, do not speak for themselves. They must be put into a story line, with its own characters and plot. As one lawyer put it,

> If we allow the argument to be carried on at the abstract level, you know, "Is capital punishment moral or immoral?" we will always lose. So we have to counter the abstract arguments with the stories of our clients and their lives. They've usually led tragic, terrible lives. Most people think of death row as filled with Charles Mansons. But that's not the case. Once you say, "Let me tell you about the life my client led before he committed the crime" the whole thing changes. You need to fill the conversation with details, with who did what to brutalize him so that he would later do what he did. Once you move the discussion about the death penalty in the abstract to killing an individual, you really can change the way people look at the punishment. You can ask people, "Do you support the death penalty?" and eighty percent say yes. But if you force them to see that the question is whether you want to kill this brain-damaged, mentally retarded African American, then we have a chance. You just have to keep telling stories.[46]

If there is to be a successful address to the audience of the present, the client must be given a unique human face, and an inhuman act must be put into a distinctive narrative of human tragedy.[47] If that address is to be successful, death penalty lawyers must shift genres, turning the narrative attached to their client from a horror story to a sentimental tale, from a story that evokes fear and disgust to one that evokes pity or identification.[48]

When these narratives succeed, they give new life to those condemned to die. But even when they don't save the life of the client, narratives still may have a redemptive quality. They give meaning to the work of death penalty lawyers at a time when telling stories is the one thing that they can assuredly do for their clients. And they save their audience of judges from failing to see humanity in all its complexity and with all its failings, even if that audience remains unpersuaded that the particular person whose humanity is portrayed is worthy of continued life. That narrative has these redemptive qualities makes it especially valuable to death penalty lawyers at a time when saving the lives of their clients seems an increasingly remote prospect.

Speaking to the Future

The movement from being a witness to the humanity of the condemned to writing history is a movement from one audience to another and from one kind of narrative strategy to another—from the audience of the present to that of the future.[49] It involves a shift from the audience of the present to the audience of posterity, and from using sentiment to draw attention to the client as an individual to using it to emphasize the broad social and political conditions that shaped the client's life. In addition to testifying to the human qualities of those they represent and the abuses they suffer in the legal process, death penalty lawyers link their client's case to political and social conditions that explain both the crime and the persistence of death as a criminal punishment.

The history written by these lawyers is mediated through the abstract, impersonal categories of law, but it is itself neither abstract nor impersonal. It is history as narrative. A story initially told as the biography of a person sentenced to die, made relevant by the law that allows the broadest range of evidence in mitigation, becomes a story of incompetent defense counsel, corrupt prosecutors, inattentive judges, and ultimately of a society whose structures of inequality are made visible in the lives of those condemned to die. By using their lawyering skills to narrate structural injustice, death penalty lawyers politicize the work of representing individual clients.

According to one lawyer who practices in a public interest setting,

> The story you are trying to construct has a number of parts. As a narrative it could be told from any of several perspectives. There

is the life story of the client. Where did he come from, who was he as a child, and that includes what are the influences on him. Then there is the story of the crime. And retelling the story of the crime is really important because once an inept defense lawyer and a malicious prosecutor are done, the story of the crime is always of a cold, calculating, deliberate person, delighting in people's suffering. While the truth is that the crime is a culmination of neglect and abuse which the client himself has suffered. And this is a story of social injustice. The third part of the story is what happened at trial. Did his lawyer even bother to interview any witnesses? Was the family contacted to find out about his background? Was the judge a racist who referred to all the black jurors as "coloreds." And this is a story of legal injustice.

At each stage in the construction of such complex narratives these lawyers seek to present their clients as victims of both society and the legal process itself. Because they co-opt the rhetoric of victimization and dilute its meaning, their work infuriates proponents of state killing. Moreover, their narratives take on special significance because "they become part of the public record," which means that they have "staying power," they "won't go away." Making such a record, this lawyer explained,

is our way of acting in the world, our way of struggling against the system. We create these papers that we write. They are not going anywhere. They will be in government document warehouses forever. And I think that someday somebody will look at this, maybe a hundred years from now, but someone will look and say "Oh my God, it was true that the death penalty was really just an engine of discrimination." Even if it seems fruitless now, it is worth doing because we are making a record of who is getting the death penalty, and it was just the people who were mentally ill and too poor for treatment who came from unhappy, broken families. And we did nothing to help these people, until they did something horrible so we could then get rid of them. We all—this is not just my perception, but I've talked with enough other people—describe this work as a witnessing sort of function.

What seems "fruitless" today takes on meaning when viewed in the long term. A society now unwilling to see the links between poverty, neglect, and the death penalty, may, "a hundred years from now" be more receptive to that structural narrative. Death penalty lawyering thus requires a concerted effort to write an enduring story, a story told to an audience present only in the imagination. While the language of "witnessing" is explicit in this account, what this lawyer says is as much about the recording of history as a narrative of social injustice as it is about being a witness in the present. This lawyer does not say just what happened; he constructs an explanation that focuses attention on mental illness and poverty, on social neglect and the unforgivable desire to "get rid of" people with problems rather than trying to fix those problems. He, and others like him, writes history by "claiming that they can give at least partial explanations of past events . . . that *in some sense* we may understand a particular event by locating it in narrative."[50]

This component of the work of death penalty lawyers is referred to, within that community, as "making a record." They not only describe the legal work of building a case on appeal but refer to the broader political work of putting history into narrative. By making a record they remember the future and insist that the future, if it is to be more just, must remember.

"Look, as a lawyer, every single act or omission that I am doing is calculated to make a record," one lawyer who practiced in a Resource Center explained.

> But not just the record on appeal. It is bigger than that. I think you are making a record above and beyond the immediate case. You are making a record such that even after you ultimately fail to save your client's life you show that he was a worthy human being, that there was an explanation for what he did which the legal system could not, or would not, hear. I know that because I know him in ways no one else does. And that there are other young men and women out there who can be helped if we learn from this case. You see what we do is we tell a story that would otherwise not be told, or remembered. There are lessons in the stories we tell, lessons

about poverty, abuse, and injustice. Maybe they can't be heard just yet, but maybe they will be heard sometime.

This lawyer first speaks as a witness, whose work testifies to the humanity of those condemned to die. Here he speaks as someone who has firsthand knowledge. "I know that," he says, "because I know him in ways no one else does." But he also talks about his work in the language of stories and storytelling. The stories told are the suppressed, virtually invisible narratives of the present, stories that "would not otherwise be told, or remembered."[51] These are stories of pattern and structure in which the injustice of executing this particular poor and, all-too-often, black man is given meaning in a narrative of larger forces of "poverty, abuse, and injustice."

Other death penalty lawyers talk about their work in similar terms, revealing their belief that the narratives they produce will one day have broad political effects.

> I just don't see it as if I'm fighting a battle that is already lost. I think that we are setting the record. We are telling stories of injustice, and those stories always have power. You see, in a biblical sense, I believe in redemption. We're now setting a record that will shape world opinion. I think every single day about how I can tell a story that will reach the world, that will get beyond the shackles of this country and spread the movement to end capital punishment from the world back home. So the record we are making, yes, it is very important. I feel strongly that we will not be forgotten in history. I know that I'm very conscious of the fact that what I do has great historical significance even though I don't really know who I am talking to or writing for.

The address to an indeterminate future, as well as to an audience beyond our borders, complicates the narrative task. All narratives are part of "a social transaction . . . [in which] any narrator's behavior will be constrained in part by various assumptions he will have made concerning his present or presumed audience's motives for listening to him."[52] Not knowing who one is talking

to, or writing for, makes the task of creating a compelling or persuasive narrative daunting. Because the power and persua-
siveness of narrative is always specific to the audience, one cannot rely on the available conventions with any confidence.
Narrative, Hayden White contends, is "a form of discourse pre-
eminently suited to mediate between alternative notions of what
the moral order should consist of." This, White continues, "offers
the prospect of accounting, at least in part, for changes in what
audiences regard as the appropriate modes of discourse as well as
the appropriate contents or referents of different modes of representation. One can find any number of meanings in a given genre
by imputing to real or imagined audiences a competence to do
with a text whatever it takes to make that text meaningful."[53]
Yet an indeterminate audience cannot be addressed with an indeterminate narrative. Writing for history is then always a historical shot in the dark.

In addition to the issue of the indeterminacy of the audience,
death penalty lawyers realize that the narratives they produce are
part of an adversarial process in which each story is met with a
counternarrative. In law narratives proliferate; the closure produced in one telling of events is challenged by an alternative account. Indeed, it is the distinctive job of death penalty lawyers to
mount alternative accounts, to resist narrative closure in order
to forestall the closure of their clients' lives. Yet precisely in this
process of reminding their audience that there is an alternative,
an as yet unheard account, death penalty lawyers play in the
genre of the realist tale. Events can always "be ordered otherwise,
in an order of narrative, that makes them, at one and the same
time, questionable as to their authenticity and susceptible to
being considered as tokens of reality."[54]

Death penalty lawyers disrupt the tight narrative of wrongdoing that leads to a conviction and death sentence by pointing out
disarticulations, oversights, simplifications, and partial truths in
that narrative.[55] This work undermines the satisfaction or reas-
surance narrative provides in the face of our existential predicament; its unsettles by taking advantage of the narrative-counter-

narrative structure of law. "Legal argument," Georgetown University law professor David Luban suggests, "is a struggle for the privilege of recounting the past. . . . When you control the power of recounting history, you have therefore won a legal argument, for a legal argument is nothing but the confluence of a political narrative . . . and a local narrative of events surrounding the lives of the litigants."[56]

The adversarial quality of legal narratives and the struggle to control the recounting of history that legal argument represents also propel death penalty lawyers in their roles as historians of the present. The record that they create serves as a corrective to the "official story" of the cases that they handle. "You can't let that stand," one lawyer stated. She continued,

> You can't let the future look back and only have the story as the state produces it. You have to get your side out. You have to make it more, much more, plausible as an account of the state of this society in the 1990s. I am always alive to the need to produce something that will be more compelling and more believable. If we are going to win this thing in the long haul we can't be lazy now. You have to do your job, and tell the story to compel attention, to shock the people who someday will look at all this stuff. We just can't roll over and let the fight for history go unfought.

Another lawyer noted,

> We are, in a sense, a kind of truth squad. We have to tell our stories, our clients' stories, to make sure that the truth gets told. It is important if for nothing else than for the record. It means that when we put together cases we have to think not just about what the court wants to hear, but about what they don't want to hear. We have to be willing to say what they would rather we not say, things that today will be called irrelevant or frivolous. We have to do this because at some point in time, even in cases we lose, we are not going to have the chance ten years from now to go back and complete the story. We have to do it now. We have to make sure that in the stories we tell there is also a saga of America in the eighties

and nineties, of our shortsightedness, of our insensitivity, of our willingness to respond to injustice with the cruelest injustice of them all, capital punishment. I think that the greatest service I can do for a client before he is executed is to be sure that they will not go anonymously, quietly, that they will be part of history. Breaking through that anonymity, that is what our work is all about.

The narrative strategy necessary to write a history of the present in the face of the counternarratives produced in the legal process requires a bold willingness to speak the unspeakable, to tell the story that no one now wants to hear in the hope that other audiences at other times will be more receptive.

Without assurance that any audience will ever hear or care about what they say, a few death penalty lawyers seem more frustrated than hopeful. "Sometimes we talk like we are making a record for posterity," one longtime practitioner told me, "I hate that. I hate the idea that we are making a record for history. You know people say that all the time. But," she asked, "who the hell is going to read it? Who are we making a record for, God?"

Yet, despite such frustration, belief in the importance of making a record remains pervasive. It is a belief grounded in a temporal consciousness that holds the future to be as important, if not more important, than the present, a consciousness that sustains political commitment in the face of political defeat. Making a record thus links lawyering for an individual client with the broader, political goal of ending state killing in an imagined future.[57]

Conclusion

All lawyers traffic in narrative, but narrative plays a particularly important role in the work of lawyers trying to end state killing. Narrative helps to make meaningful a world whose violence is sometimes overwhelming. It connects a bleak present to an image of justice that can be realized, if at all, only in the future. This function of narrative suggests that the current effort to limit appeals by those on death row is not simply an effort to move them more quickly to their death. It is also an effort to silence their stories, to foreclose and frustrate the strategies death penalty lawyers have developed to speak to the audiences of today and tomorrow, and to prevent courthouses from being turned into sites of memory from which the future might someday judge the injustices of our era.

As witnesses giving testimony and as historians of the present, death penalty lawyers use narrative to both remember the future and insist that the future remember.[58] They construct narratives first to humanize their clients and second to connect their clients' fates with broader social and political concerns. In so doing, they make a powerful political claim even in an era when the odds of ending capital punishment are so heavily stacked against them.

Their work is a form of what Cover called "redemptive constitutionalism." For death penalty lawyers, "redemption takes place within an eschatalogical schema that postulates: (1) the unredeemed character of reality as we know it, (2) the fundamentally different reality that should take its place, and (3) the replacement of one with the other." Cover uses the example of an abolitionist struggle of another era, namely antislavery activism in the midnineteenth century, to suggest that the work of "redemptive constitutionalism" reveals "a creative pulse that proliferates principle and precept, commentary and justification, even in the face of a state legal order less likely to hold slavery unconstitutional than to declare the imminent kingship of Jesus Christ on Earth."[59] In this view, the lawyer serving a losing cause speaks in a prophetic voice even as she supplies the argumentative and interpretive resources to bridge the gap between the violence of the present and the beckoning possibility of justice.

The lawyers' political claim and their address to the future are based on a "democratic optimism."[60] Here they take instruction from the late justice Thurgood Marshall, who, when confronted with evidence of widespread public endorsement of capital punishment, argued that "whether a punishment is cruel and unusual depends, not on whether its mere mention 'shocks the conscience and sense of justice of the people,' but on whether people who were fully informed as to the purposes of the penalty and its liabilities would find the penalty shocking, unjust, and unacceptable." If they were given such information, Marshall believed, "the great mass of citizens would conclude . . . that the death penalty is immoral and therefore unconstitutional."[61]

Telling life stories is for death penalty lawyers both the only meaningful way to help their clients in the legal process and their preferred method to inform, enlighten, and educate. Some death penalty lawyers argue, following Marshall, that the task of witnessing and writing the history of the present will indeed have such a predictable result. "Look at Blackmun," one lawyer said. "He is not so very different from the rest of the country. His evolution is very representative of what eventually this country will come to if we continue to do our work. We have to look a little longer down the road, beyond the present moment."[62]

Others, however, are more uncertain about the outcome of their work.

> What we do is try to tell good stories, you know, like anyone would. We are like journalists who investigate but then have to produce readable accounts. If we do what has to be done in telling those stories, then I don't think that the death penalty will exist X number of years from now. I don't know what X is, but I think at some point people are going to look back and think "Holey, moley, look at this. Look at what was going on there." We are gonna make sure that the truth gets out so that it gets put into a box somewhere so that fifty years from now when somebody opens it they'll be able to see the true horror of capital punishment and the damage that it does to everyone and to the country as a whole.

Such sentiments give law a life in and through time. Time is everything for death penalty lawyers. Buying time to keep their clients alive, holding on to time by addressing their work to an audience of the future, these are the key activities of the death penalty bar. Through narrative these lawyers wed language and time.[63] The narrative commitments of death penalty lawyers help frame the larger political dimensions of a style of lawyering that appears, at first glance, to be entirely focused on particularities of individual cases, and they help resist the temporal presence of state violence in the name of the deferred possibility of justice. In an era when saving the lives of those condemned to die is so difficult, saving their stories may be all the more valuable.

part

THE CULTURAL LIFE OF

three

CAPITAL PUNISHMENT

7

TO SEE OR NOT TO SEE:

ON TELEVISING EXECUTIONS

Punishment . . . [has] become the most hidden part of the penal pro-
cess. . . . We are far removed indeed from . . . accounts of the life
and misdeeds of the criminal in which he admitted his crimes, and
which recounted in detail the tortures of his execution. . . . It is ugly
to be punishable, but there is no glory in punishing. Hence . . . those
who carry out the penalty tend to become an autonomous sector;
justice is relieved of responsibility for it by a bureaucratic conceal-
ment of the penalty itself.
—Michel Foucault; *Discipline and Punish*

There is a difference between real and fictional murder, between
murder and execution, between innocence and guilt. It may be a
sign of humility and fellow-feeling to argue the fuzziness of the
boundaries in each case, but it is no service to justice or to the inno-
cent to erase them altogether.
—Wendy Steiner, "We Are All Murderers Now"

Television's principal compulsion and major attraction comes to us
as the relation to law.
—Avital Ronell, *Finitude's Score*

*I would be pleased to have an execution on the "Donahue Show."
What's wrong with it? Let's see future bad guys watch these people
fry right here on television.*—PHIL DONAHUE

One of the crucial decisions in Timothy McVeigh's trial was Judge Matsch's refusal to allow it to be televised. By issuing this prohibition, the judge reminded us that the right to see how the killing state operates is restricted. During a capital trial only those who can find a seat in the courtroom can claim a right to view the proceedings. The right to see the ultimate act of the killing state, execution, is even more severely controlled.

An execution, Wendy Lesser argues, is "a killing carried out in all our names, an act of the state in which we by proxy participate; it is also the only form of murder that directly implicates even the witness, the bystanders."[1] Beyond the corridors of justice or the walls of the execution chamber, state killing lives in culture as a set of images and imaginings, a sight unseen except in the most mediated way. To comprehend the impact of state killing on the American condition we must attend to those images and imaginings, asking, as we do so, what messages they convey, and whether we are better off in a world in which capital punishment is seen almost solely in fictive recreations.

Historically, public executions were occasions of public theater but also for the exercise of popular power, if not popular sovereignty. In Michel Foucault's words, "In the ceremonies of the public execution, the main character was the people."[2] On these occasions people could, and sometimes did, mass themselves against the punishment that was to be carried out before their eyes and in their presence. Their presence ensured that the act of execution itself, not just the judgment of death, always could be contested. Their presence insured that execution could not be reduced to a bland routine. "It was on this point," Foucault suggests, that the people, drawn to the spectacle intended to terrorize it, could express its rejection of the punitive power and sometimes revolt. Preventing an execution that was regarded as unjust, snatching a condemned man from the hands of the executioner, obtaining his pardon by force, possibly pursuing and assaulting the executioners, in any case abusing the judges and causing an uproar against the sentence—all of this formed part of the popular practices that invested, traversed and often overturned the ritual of public execution. . . . It was evident that the great spectacle of punishment ran the risk of being rejected by the very people to whom it was addressed.[3]

While executions have been removed from the public eye for more than fifty years, in most states capital punishment still must be witnessed by members of the public in order to be legal.[4] The witnesses, a small, select, and carefully controlled group, are provided a fleeting glimpse of the rituals of state-sponsored death as it is turned into a problem of administration. The chance of either disruption or rejection has been minimized. What was visible in the fullest and most complete sense is today mostly hidden from view. As Foucault notes,

> This has several consequences: . . . [punishment] leaves the domain of more or less everyday perception and enters that of abstract consciousness; its effectiveness is seen as resulting from its inevitability, not from its visible intensity; it is the certainty of being punished and not the horrifying spectacle of public punishment that must discourage crime. . . . As a result, justice no longer takes public responsibility for the violence that is bound up with its practice.[5]

Silencing the condemned and limiting the visibility of lawfully imposed death is part of the modern bureaucratization of capital punishment[6] and of the strategy for transforming execution from an arousing public spectacle of vengeance to a soothing matter of mere administration. "It . . . [was] as if this rite that 'concluded the crime' was," Foucault argues, "suspected of being in some undesirable way linked with it. It was as if the punishment was thought to equal, if not exceed, in savagery the crime itself . . . to make the executioner resemble a criminal, judges murderers."[7]

Despite the end of public executions, state killing still continues to be publicized: newspaper accounts and television news reports as well as appellate court decicions all attempt to describe and to show the act of execution. But still the question persists of how widely executions should be witnessed and viewed and what, if any, limits should be placed on the media? Should executions be televised? What would it mean for us and for our culture were citizens routinely turned into viewers of capital punishment?

I take up these questions in this chapter, engaging in a colloquy with Wendy Lesser's argument that executions should not be televised. Her book, *Pictures at an Execution*, is the most sustained previous examination of the issue of televising executions. However, like Moussorgsky's *Pictures at an Exhibition*, it proceeds less as a linear presentation of an argument than as a pastiche of readings, impressions, suggestions.[8] It roams far and wide to examine murder in canonical works of literature, detective fiction, popular culture, and film. It explores what Lesser calls the "increasingly blurry borderline between real murder and fictional murder, between murder as news and murder as art, between event and story."[9]

The thread of unity that runs throughout Lesser's book is supplied by her examination of a single case *KQED v. Vasquez*[10] in which a public television station in San Francisco sought permission to film and televise the execution, by lethal gas, of Robert Alton Harris. It claimed a First Amendment right to use the "tools of its trade to cover the execution," in particular video equipment. While KQED ultimately lost its lawsuit, Lesser uses this case not only to develop an argument about capital punishment but also to explore "the crucial connection between murder and theater—between death imposed on a human being by another human being and dramatic spectacle." For Lesser the case brought by KQED is an occasion for analyzing "execution and its real or potential witnesses" and for helping us "to understand why and how we identify with the various participants in a murder story."[11]

In the course of her analysis of this case Lesser makes an argument with which I take issue. She announces her opposition to state killing by boldly comparing it with murder, but then argues that executions should not be televised, that it would be indecent and voyeuristic to do so. In her view the citizenry, like the jurors described in chapter 5, should not be able to see the visual evidence of what happens when the state kills. In this chapter I take up Lesser's opposition to televising executions and suggest that, in contrast to her concerns for what I call the "manners of viewing," the problem of televising executions must be addressed in a more overtly political way. I suggest that the survival of capital punishment in America depends, in part, on its relative invisibility.

What the Eye Cannot See

On January 16 and 17, 1995, ABC's *Nightline* broadcast a two-part series focusing on a single execution in Texas.[12] On the first night the program introduced viewers to various inmates on Texas's death row, including Mario Marquez, the man scheduled to be executed. We saw the prison and its daunting architecture, met Marquez's lawyer as well as some of the people who would carry out the execution, and saw repeated views of the death chamber and the hospital gurney on which the condemned would be strapped to receive his lethal injection. At the end of the first night's broadcast, Ted Koppel made what was meant to be the dramatic announcement that he was going to witness the Marquez execution that very night. Koppel explained his decision to be a witness by saying that, "If we are going to live with capital punishment, we have to see it and know what it is about."

But note that he did not say that he was going to show the actual execution to his viewers. Koppel spoke of a "we" who were there, faintly echoing, while dramatically altering, Edward R.

Murrow's famous "You are there." Despite his insistence that executions have to be seen, he could not show them to us. He could only report on what *he* was going to see. And report he did the very next night.

In the second installment viewers again saw the death chamber, only this time we followed as the witnesses, including Koppel, were assembled, searched (to ensure they were carrying no recording equipment), and led to the witness room to see what we would not be allowed to see. In a voice over, Koppel calmly, and without comment, reminded his viewers, "We can't show it [the execution] to you, but we were there and we will tell you about it." Thus this television program had to rely on verbal descriptions of the execution itself and its effects on the condemned. Koppel told us that "there was a short explosion of breath. That is all there was to see." Another witness said that the execution was like "seeing a dog euthanized. He was gone the moment he gasped." These verbal descriptions could not help calling attention to the exclusion of television from the execution itself. It is remarkable that ABC would air a television program that dramatically calls attention to the fact that television was excluded from the very event that demanded to be seen. Television's act of "showing itself not showing" was even more remarkable because it was done with almost no comment.

Koppel's inability to show us what he saw is the result of a series of cases, *KQED v. Vasquez* being but one, in which courts have acknowledged the right of legislative and executive officials to regulate and control the conditions under which punishments are administered. These cases date back to 1890 when, in *Holden v. State of Minnesota*, the Supreme Court refused to invalidate a death sentence on the basis of certain alleged inconsistencies and procedural irregularities in state statutes and regulations. The first Justice Harlan, writing for the Court, accorded wide latitude to legislatures in setting the terms on which executions could be carried out. "Whether a convict sentenced to death," Harlan noted, "shall be executed before or after sunrise, or within or without the walls of the jail, or within or outside of some other inclosure, and whether the inclosure within which he is executed shall be higher than the gallows, thus excluding the view of persons outside, are regulations that do not affect his substantial rights. . . . These are regulations which the legislature, in its wisdom, and for the public good, could legally prescribe."[13]

Such authority allowed state legislatures to change execution from a public display to the semiprivate, bureaucratic event that now is found wherever the death penalty is used.[14] As part of this change, *Holden* allowed states to adopt regulations concerning the witnessing of executions and controlling press access. Legislatures could now closely regulate the prerogative to see an execution. In so doing, they could make executions less dangerous to sovereignty and to those who carry out those death-inflicting acts. The exclusion of the public means the exclusion of the court of last resort; no longer can the people rise up to save the condemned; no longer is the people's judgment truly the last word in state killing.

But the exclusion of the public does not solve the problem of spectatorship. Even within the prison's secret chamber, select press representatives, the warden, perhaps a few friends and family members, and the executioner watch the condemned man die. The structure of watching within the execution chamber reflects the effort of the state to minimize the fascination of looking by effecting death as mechanically and precisely as possible.[15] This structure is described by Susan Blaustein, a reporter who recently offered this account of witnessing an execution by lethal injection:

> Near Cook's head stood Warden Jones; near Cook's feet stood Reverend Pickett, his hands folded. Suddenly I saw movement in front of me and realized that on Cook's far side was a one-way mirror in which we all were reflected. It was our own movement, not that of the symmetrical threesome in the death chamber itself, that had been captured in the glass. The effect was eerie; not only would I witness an execution but I would witness myself witnessing it. Behind the mirror, in an adjacent room, stood the execu-

tioner (whether man or woman, or more than one, no one would tell me), who would, upon a signal from the warden, activate the death device.[16]

That one-way mirror marks the boundary between victim and executioner, physically separating them while allowing the executioner to control the gaze. Unseen and anonymous, the executioner loses all personality and virtually melds into the machinery itself.[17] The relationship between the condemned and the apparatus of death supplants the human relation between victim and executioner. As I argued in chapter 3, modern law strives for a death without a putting to death, an execution without an executioner.[18] The one-way mirror gives the executioner unrestricted sight while obscuring him (or her) from the gaze of the victim and the witnesses; it works like the one-way lens of the televising camera. It allows the executioner to be both the deadly instrument of the state and the one to whom the state reveals its deadly secret.

The execution chamber thus highlights the questions of who may see, who may be seen, and what may be shown. In this tightly controlled setting the camera would be a mechanical intruder, a stand-in and a channel for the unruly crowds that gathered at public executions. Rather than simply transmitting an image of solemn and dignified ceremony to an attentive outside world, the presence of the camera would signify the flood of thousands, or millions, of uncontrollable looks into the execution chamber. While Lesser believes that "modern videotape technology makes it possible to bring millions of 'witnesses' into the death chamber without noticeably altering the nature of the event,"[19] I believe that with those looks would come resistances, demands, assertions of power, some calling for more vengeful pain, some for the end of death imposed in the name of popular sovereignty. Just as jurors renarrate, rework, and supplement the stories presented to them, allowing citizens to view state killing would provide for their own creative and unpredictable interpretations of it.[20]

Judging Television

Prohibitions on televising executions have on several occasions in recent years been subject to, and survived, constitutional challenges. The first and most important of these cases, *Garrett v. Estelle*, arose when a television reporter in Texas sought permission to film and show the first execution in that state after the post-*Furman* hiatus in capital punishment. Claiming a violation of the First Amendment, he challenged the refusal of the State Department of Corrections to allow him to do so. The state countered that it had a compelling interest in regulating the procedures through which executions were to be conducted and that "the press has no greater right of access" than does the public, and "since the public has no right under the First Amendment to film executions, a member of the press has no such right."[21]

The Fifth Circuit Court of Appeals reversed a district court ruling in favor of the petitioner on the ground that "the First Amendment does not invalidate nondiscriminatory prison access regulations."[22] The court held that the bar on televising executions was a permissible restriction because it was based on "time and place" rather than "content." As Judge Ainsworth explained,

> In the present case . . ., access is provided except for one purpose, to film executions. In order to sustain Garrett's argument we would have to find that the moving picture of the actual execution possessed some quality giving it "content" beyond, for example, that possessed by a simulation of an execution. We discern no such quality from the record or from our inferences therein. Despite the unavailability of film of the actual execution the public can be fully informed; the free flow of ideas and information need not be inhibited.[23]

In this passage Ainsworth acts as media critic as he assesses the visual representation of violence and the power, significance, and special qualities of the moving image, only to hold that they have no special qualities at all. His opinion contains an implicit theory of representation in which television is by no means superior to a "simulation of an execution," and in which he assures the public that its capacity to be informed about what transpired would not be impeded by exclusion of the camera. Yet even Lesser contends that "there is a difference between planning to watch a real, scheduled murder taking place on television, and watching either a simulated execution or a real but unscheduled murder."[24]

In Ainsworth's approving references to "simulation," he seems to concede the special power of the visual to convey information even as he claims that the "unavailability of film of the actual execution" does not inhibit "the free flow of ideas and information."[25] The court's decision turns on this problematic passage. To sustain the Texas prohibition on televising executions, Ainsworth argues that no privilege can be given to a video representation of a real execution as opposed to an imaginative reconstruction; a film of a real execution is no more real than that execution's dramatic reenactment.

Ainsworth goes on to note that "there is no effort here to conceal conditions at the prison or inhibit press investigations of those conditions."[26] It is not that something real exists that the state is hiding, but instead there is simply nothing "real" to be seen. Like Lesser, then, Ainsworth suggests that we can never truly understand executions.[27] By refusing to privilege the film of an actual execution, Ainsworth implies that the death penalty has neither fixed meaning nor singular significance, but may be represented, interpreted, or recast in a number of different, and equally plausible, ways.[28]

Ainsworth found nothing indecent or unacceptable about allowing some people actually to witness execution. Thus members of the press, like Ted Koppel, could be present and could report on what they had seen. In his view, however, the camera added nothing, and, as a result, nothing would be lost by its exclusion. Rejecting the maxim that "one picture is worth a thousand words," Ainsworth contended that film did not make anything available that could not be conveyed by words or reenactments, a position that paradoxically derives support from Koppel's recent television program. Moreover, the judge contended that "televising an execution would amount to conducting a public execution" and would thus frustrate the policy that Texas has followed since 1920 of forbidding public executions.[29]

Ainsworth did not pause to consider what makes an execution public. But surely there is more to the question of whether execution is public than whether it is made available through a particular representational medium. An execution is public by its very nature. Executions are public in the sense that they are a state-imposed punishment for an offense against the law. They are public in the sense that their conduct can be and is regulated by public norms. And they are public enough that they can and must be witnessed.

In *Garrett*, Ainsworth not only fails to acknowledge the public nature of state killing, he ignores the distinction between witnessing an actual execution and watching an execution on film. While Lesser argues that the dynamic of spectatorship is quite different when viewers are isolated, watching alone or in small groups,[30] Ainsworth suggests that the act of televising alone, by making the image available to a mass audience, threatens to transform the execution, however solemn and dignified its procedures, into an event linked to a history of blood, cruelty, and sadism that marks public execution.[31] He is right to suggest such an association. It is this linkage, and the political issue of who, in the final analysis, will control capital punishment, that should be at the heart of the debate about televising executions.

Like Ainsworth, Lesser opposes televising executions. However, she misses the crucial political questions that must be addressed as we think about television, capital punishment, and state violence. Lesser's opposition is based, in part, in her own judgment of the medium and its representational capacities, a judgment with which I tend to agree. Like Ainsworth, she does not oppose the representation of execution in literature, art, or film. Television is singled out for special attention. But unlike

Ainsworth, who thinks that television adds nothing to the way we would know or understand execution, Lesser thinks television actually gets in the way.

Televised executions, she contends, turn death into a "pure spectacle, unmediated by the understanding and knowledge that convert spectacle into experience. Far from 'being there' with the condemned man, we would be completely outside him, viewing him as an easily liquidatable object."[32] Television gets in the way by pretending to a false objectivity. "KQED's special case for television," Lesser says,

> focused heavily on the idea of the camera's objectivity. In so doing, the plaintiff's side appeared to confuse two different senses of the word: on the one hand, our sense that an objective report is disinterested, honest, reliable, impartial; and, on the other hand, the sense that only something which is not subjective—which does not partake of the individual human viewpoint—can be fully objective, neutrally conveying things and events that are out in the world without the distorting coloration of human consciousness. A good newspaper reporter can be objective in the first sense . . ., but only a machine like a television camera could possibly be objective in that second sense. And even that possibility seems remote . . . for in order to become a functional picture of reality, even television's images need to be absorbed by our particular minds. The picture itself can have no meaning until viewers make something of it.[33]

Television is, in Lesser's view, a barrier, not an aide, to understanding. This is because the only way to know murder or death is through imagination. She argues that "the television news camera, purporting to give us unmediated reality, all the while leaves out something crucial." To make this point Lesser quotes anti–death penalty activist and lawyer David Bruck who says that "The truth of the matter is that the public's imagination of what this must be like—and I say this having seen two of these executions take place—the public's imagination is much truer than what they would see on TV." She contends that the murder story (and executions are always murder stories) "is about what must

be imagined, what can't actually be seen—what can't, in any veri-
fiable way, be known." The journalistic television camera, Lesser
notes, "has no projective imagination."[34]

Rather than exploring, as she promises at the outset, the "increasingly blurry borderline between real murder and fictional
murder," Lesser's arguments against televising executions erect
strict boundaries between the real and the fictional, testimony
and literature, knowledge and imagination, boundaries that
should, in fact, be blurred. And, having erected such boundaries,
Lesser consistently favors literary representations of murder over
their allegedly nonfiction counterparts. In her view art gives
meaning and sense to the otherwise elusive and terrifyingly inexplicable murder. "The murders rendered in art," she writes, "are
reassuringly not our own: we can't experience murder, and we
don't wish to. . . . [Yet] the game of art won't work if we don't at
least partially believe in the reality of the fictional deaths being
described to us. . . . We may be least likely to believe in, in the
sense of caring about and being frightened by, those murders
which are the most newsworthy. For the newsworthy, the real, is
quite often unexplainable." Thus, "art about murder tends to be
about the search for structure and meaning in an apparently random existence."[35]

Lesser ultimately argues that televising executions not only
provides a "bad story" but involves a moral violation.[36] Rather
than offering a richly shaped and authorially controlled murder
tale, the camera would purport to show murder itself to an audi
ence that has put nothing at risk.[37] Television, in her view, is a
poor substitute for other media precisely because it fools us into
thinking that we understand what is in truth inaccessible.

What Lesser labels the most "profound objection" to televising
executions was again first made by Bruck, who she reports "challenged the truth of what the camera would show."[38] For Bruck,
televising executions would give a false and misleading picture
of the damage and suffering that is necessarily part of the capital
punishment process—for example, the years on death row, the
damage to the families of the condemned. Viewers of the
Nightline programs certainly may have come away thinking that

they understood the suffering that is part of capital punishment and, like Koppel, may have been ready to conclude that "life in prison seems more devastating than this death [death by lethal injection]." If so, they would confirm Bruck's concern that television would be false precisely because it would not convey enough. But is this an argument against televising executions, or instead for a more searching media scrutiny of the entire process of execution?

While only two courts have ever been willing to order the televising of an execution,[39] Lesser's skepticism about television's ability to convey useful knowledge is not fully shared by the judiciary. In several cases having nothing to do with televising executions, courts have spoken about the special virtues of television as a carrier of information about important public issues. Thus in *Houchins v. KQED* the Supreme Court upheld the refusal by local officials to allow a television station to inspect and take photographs of the portion of a local jail where a prisoner's suicide reportedly had occurred. Yet Justice Stewart, while he concurred in the result, advocated a flexible approach in deciding when and with what restrictions the press could be granted access to penal institutions. Stewart noted that our society "depends heavily on the press" for the information upon which enlightened political choices are made. Moreover, he argued that the Constitution requires special sensitivity to the unique role and needs of the press. "A person touring Santa Rita jail," Stewart continued,

> can grasp its reality with his own eyes and ears. But if a television reporter is to convey the jail's sights and sounds to those who cannot visit the place, he must use cameras and sound equipment. In short, terms of access that be reasonably imposed on individual members of the public may, if they impede effective reporting without sufficient justification, be unreasonable as applied to journalists who are there to convey to the general public what visitors see.[40]

Here Stewart links "effective" reporting to the ability of cameras and sound equipment to capture and covey "sights and sounds." For him the unique capacity of film to convey information must be recognized; not all representations are alike.[41]

A similar view, though in a very different context, was expressed by Judge Evans of the Federal District Court for the Northern District of Georgia in a decision concerning a suit by CNN challenging an action by the White House Press Office, which allegedly gave favored status to ABC, CBS, and NBC in certain "limited coverage" events. Judge Evans granted a temporary injunction against the restrictions imposed by the White House and suggested that the

> interest of the public in having the television media present at "limited coverage" White House events while not overwhelming cannot be denominated as insubstantial. . . . it cannot be denied that television news coverage plays an increasingly prominent part in informing the public at large of the workings of government. Many citizens likely rely on television as their sole source of news. Further, visual impressions can and do sometimes add a material dimension to one's impression of particular news events. Television coverage of the news provides a comprehensive visual element and an immediacy, or simultaneous aspect, not found in print media.[42]

For Evans, unlike Lesser, there is something irreplaceable about the images conveyed by television. And, as Justice Powell suggested in his dissent in *Zacchini v. Scripps-Howard Broadcasting*, the "public is . . . the loser" when news coverage of "clearly newsworthy events" is confined to "watered-down verbal reporting, perhaps with an occasional still picture."[43]

Indeed, in an ironic twist to the Harris execution, which was the subject of the KQED suit about which Lesser writes, after one federal district judge upheld the state's prohibition on the media's use of television cameras to film the execution, another judge ordered that the execution be videotaped so that she could use the tape in a subsequent suit to help determine whether execution by lethal gas violated the Eighth Amendment. Emphasizing the unique value of film, Judge Patel found that videotaping would provide "evidence critical to . . . [the] claim that execution by gas is torturous, painful and cruel." She noted that crucial evidence would be "irretrievably lost unless the impending execution is videotape recorded."[44]

In addition, a district court judge in Maryland, ruling in a suit alleging that the use of lethal gas as a method of execution violated the Eighth Amendment, similarly ordered the videotaping of an execution of an inmate who had given his consent so that the tape might be used in a suit by a person condemned to die at a later date. A crucial issue in this case was "the length of time a person remains conscious after the introduction of lethal gas into the chamber." The court noted, without comment, that "the State's expert witness criticized the lay eyewitness accounts of lethal gas executions provided by Thomas' counsel as unscientific, anecdotal, and too 'emotionally' charged to be relied upon." The state argued that the request to videotape should be denied because, among other things, "the Warden maintains a privilege in the area of the gas chamber during the execution of the death sentence [and because] the request is not likely to produce relevant evidence."[45]

The court rejected these contentions and ordered the videotaping "in the name of fairness, judicial economy and simple common sense, [of] relevant evanescent evidence capable of preservation [that] should be preserved so that arguments and decisions can be made with reference to the best and fullest evidence available." The court further recognized that "technological advances" could capture new types of evidence that could be and were relevant to the venerable question of whether a particular means of execution violated the "evolving standards of decency" that are central to Eighth Amendment adjudication. Yet, while noting the unique ability of film to provide the "best and fullest" evidence on a crucial matter of constitutional concern, the court also observed that the petitioner did not "seek permission to televise Mr. Thomas' execution, or in any way to make a public spectacle of it."[46]

What if he did? Why should the "best and fullest" evidence concerning a matter of substantial public concern—namely whether the state should be allowed to execute its citizens—be available solely in the limited confines of the courtroom, and not to the public at large? The orders by Judge Patel in California and Judge Garbis in Maryland testify to what they see as the power of television to capture and convey the nature of capital punishment.[47] In their view, film, tape, or live pictures may reveal death by gas, by electricity, by rope, or by injection to be painful, tortuous, or indecent like "euthanizing a dog." While by no means objective or beyond interpretation, the camera is indeed its own kind of witness.[48] It and only it can present the sight and sound of the modern execution and, in so doing, possibly disrupt the version of the legitimacy of state killing.

Were television images let loose, they might "prove" too powerful to be contained.[49] Thus, just as execution is obscured from view by the enclosures of the prison, so the videotape must be contained *in camera*, in the judges chamber. Patel's and Garbis's decisions, allowing filming of executions solely for evidentiary purposes in constitutional challenges, suggest that it is not the nature of film itself that is at the heart of the debate about televising executions. Instead, what is at stake are certain assumptions about the imagined audience and its capacities, dispositions, and inclinations as viewers, and about its prerogatives to make judgments about capital punishment.

What Decent People Should Not See

Lesser's analysis depends on these assumptions about the audience even as it obscures more pressing political concerns about who controls executions. While she expresses doubt, a doubt that I share, about the objectivity of the camera and a belief that death is to be imagined, not known, most of her argument against televising executions goes to the "manners of viewing"—namely, to how a mass audience would use and consume images of execution. "The most persuasive reason I can think of not to televise executions," she writes, "like the most persuasive reason not to have executions, has to do with the effect on us. . . . I'm thinking of what it would mean about us, the audience, if we allowed someone's actual murder to become our Theater of Cruelty." Thus she argues that the "danger of a TV execution is that we would not take it personally." She suggests that the medium would invite "coldness" in our reception of capital punishment. "It is possible," she says, "that instead of making the killing more real to us, the sight of a condemned person dying on TV might only acclimate us further to such violent images."[50] Yet the effects of televising executions on a mass audience are not likely to be so fixed and predictable; instead, they are likely to be diverse and indeterminate.

Lesser's analysis reflects the widely shared assumption that the medium of television itself connects us "to a network of assumptions, moving us into a tract of time where our inclination to war can be satisfied without our needing to feel its most unpleasant effects, the blood, the pain, the smell of death."[51] But it is not as if we can ever have an unmediated relation to those effects. It is true that being there would be better, but if we cannot be there like Ted Koppel, are we better off relying on his eyes and ears and his reconstruction?

And if there is a critique to be made of televising executions, isn't it to be found in the invitation that television provides not to watch at all? Because television acclimates us to violence, it poses the danger that we will barely notice televised executions at all in the continuous flow of images.[52] Thus, televising executions might produce "corpses that need not be mourned because, in part, of the persistence of surviving that is shown."[53]

But televising executions, in Lesser's view, is not just an invitation to a certain kind of unseemly desensitization. It is an invitation to be rude, to see things that we have no right to see, and to get an "abnormal 'inside' view, seeing things from which we would normally be excluded."[54] In this seeing we would display bad manners. Here *Pictures at an Execution* seeks to mark "real and symbolic distances between respectable and vulgar purlieus."[55] The former would not watch an execution; in addition, they have an obligation to prevent the latter from indulging its indecent curiosity. Moreover, Lesser argues:

> Our death, which is intended for us alone, is the one experience in our life we can't directly experience. . . . We can have access to the event only indirectly, by extrapolating from the experience of

others. . . . With a fictional character, this dying-through-another seems a reasonable solution. With a real person, it seems nothing short of ghoulish, as in sharing among ourselves the dying man's singular fate we make it less singular, less his own. This is why our collective presence at a condemned man's execution would be such a violation.[56]

Watching a televised execution would on Lesser's account be "a new kind of voyeurism. We, from the invisibility of our private living rooms, are given the opportunity to peer into the most inti mate event in someone else's life: his death." Such peering, Lesser contends, would be in "extremely bad taste."[57] But execution is hardly an "intimate," or private event. There is nothing intimate about being strapped into an electric chair or onto a hospital gurney against one's will, by prison officials, before witnesses, and made to die. Lesser just gets it wrong.

Ghoulish or not, the public is always present at an execution. It is present as a juridical fiction, but as more than a fiction, as an authorizing audience unseeing and unseen, but present nonetheless. This is the haunting reality of state killing in a constitutional democracy. So long as there is capital punishment in the United States, the only question is the terms of our presence. Are we able to see what we do? For if execution, as Lesser argues, is murder, then aren't we the murderers? The death of a condemned is in no sense just his own death. And the question of whether executions should be televised is more than just a question of manners.

Control over vision is, as I see it, a question of control over execution itself. This was not coincidentally the primary argument made by the state in *KQED v. Vasquez*.[58] Executions are, in this view, properly just bureaucratic events that must be left in the hands of the professionals. Excluding television is but one way of maintaining control. The decline of public executions was the result not of humanistic movements or the dawn of a new sensibility but of a reconfiguration of power relations involving punishment.[59] "In attempting to civilize society, private execution laws had the perverse effect of degrading America's democracy. . . . they often attempted to suppress public debate about the death penalty itself."[60] Modern power fosters and regulates life through a multiplicity of local institutions and everyday practices, rather than by threatening death in spectacular but sporadic displays.[61] In a society that has replaced public punishment and torture with the penitentiary, state killing appears anachronistic, a practice to which the state has an apprehensive, uneasy relationship.

> As soon as power gave itself the function of administering life, its reason for being and the logic of its exercise—and not the wakening of humanitarian feelings—made it more and more difficult to apply the death penalty. How could power exercise its highest prerogatives by putting people to death, when its main role was to ensure, sustain, and multiply life, to put this life in order? For such a power, execution was at the same time a limit, a scandal, and a contradiction.[62]

Maintaining state killing in the face of this "limit," "scandal," and "contradiction" has required dramatic changes in its form. To survive it had to be transformed from a public to a private affair, from an affair of politics to a matter of administration, and the visual field into which it would be projected had to be circumscribed. Opposing this circumscription of vision may be, as Lesser would have it, an exercise in bad manners. But it is also a resistance to execution itself.

The solidity and impenetrability of the prison wall create a space where the killing of a person may be explained and justified by reassurances of procedural safeguards, theories of retribution, claims of just deserts, and stories of the criminal's dangerousness and brutality. These legitimating gestures are particularly crucial for the imposition of the death penalty, because execution, even execution by lethal injection, seems rudely out of place, a throwback to earlier, more savage times; at the point of execution, state violence and extralegal violence approach each other. Televising execution would mean changing the terms of control, removing state killing from the bureaucratic domain, and recognizing its political configuration.

Conclusion

Pictures at an Execution provides a bracing reminder of the place of murder and capital punishment in the popular imagination. However, the legal prohibition of televised executions goes well beyond the issues of decorum that preoccupy Lesser. It is rooted in a set of beliefs about the political threat of particular types of representation, beliefs that sustain the very possibility of capital punishment. Barring the camera and eliminating the public audience are like the quest to find a painless method of killing, ways in which law tries to purify state killing, creating an uninteresting, nonsadistic, administrative death. Thus if television is to be kept out of the death chamber we must be clear that it is not a worry about bad taste that merits or explains the exclusion.

The drama of state killing, the battle between sovereign and criminal, that animated public executions is intentionally displaced in the modern, bureaucratic form with its intense policing of who can and cannot view. While public execution made it possible for the public to challenge state killing, bureaucratization smooths the way from the authorizing words to the violent act itself. The very uncontrollability of the gaze and the indeterminacy of its political effects are what make televising executions so threatening to the survival of capital punishment. While televising executions could not again make the possibility of contest part of the risk the state runs when it conducts an execution, it would provide one way of contesting the bureaucratic cover-up.

As in capital trials, the elision of the visual helps state killing to appear different from violence outside of law. In going along with the banning of visual representations of the death penalty, law has silenced one particularly powerful avenue for generating alternative interpretations of execution and provided a safe space for our own legitimating narratives. The camera, however, threatens to render the prison wall transparent, revealing the object that the law has tried to obscure. "Photography's inimitable feature . . . ," Roland Barthes writes, "is that someone has seen the referent . . . in flesh and blood, or again in person." "The photograph," he continues, "is literally an emanation of the referent. From a real body, which was there, proceed radiations which ultimately touch me, who am here."[63] As a result, "The image has great power over us: it is often feared, avoided, hidden."[64]

The power of film and photography is precisely in its *seeming* transparency, its appearance as fact rather than interpretation. But the transparency is always only "seeming." Rather than presenting us with death stripped to its essentials, however, the camera threatens to reconjure the linkage between sadism, spectatorship, and popular power explicitly displayed in the terrible executions of the ancien regime. As a result, televising executions has the potential to disrupt the effort of modern law to make us forget that we are killing. "Clearly televised coverage of executions may," law professors Jef Richards and R. Bruce Easter explain, "create feelings of unrest and anger in some viewers. In so doing, however, these broadcasts probably will promote debate on an issue of high public importance—the death penalty. Thus, the public debate that television access likely will cause is precisely the reason that the government must allow it."[65] This is what Lesser herself fails to see and fails to come to terms with.

Televising executions would disrupt the attempt to dignify state killing and to reduce it from political spectacle to administrative act. Even in the secrecy of the execution chamber, however, death cannot be sanitized or purified, for, in executing, the state manifests, even if only to the executioner, its dark desire to see a person die.[66] Foucault is right to suggest that "in modern justice and on the part of those who dispense it there is a shame in punishing, which does not always preclude zeal."[67] Making both this shame and this zeal visible to a mass audience would as likely reveal the sadism that is at the heart of the state's tenacious attachment to capital punishment as reveal and invite the "bad taste" of its viewers. For me the possibility of the former is well worth the risk of the latter.

8

STATE KILLING IN POPULAR CULTURE:

RESPONSIBILITY AND REPRESENTATION

IN *DEAD MAN WALKING, LAST DANCE,*

AND *THE GREEN MILE*

For death must be somewhere in a society; if it is no longer (or less intensely) in religion, it must be elsewhere; perhaps in this image which produces Death while trying to preserve life.
—ROLAND BARTHES, *Camera Lucida*

Every death agony expresses a certain truth. . . . Hence the insatiable curiosity that drove spectators to the scaffold to witness the spectacle of sufferings truly endured; there one could decipher crime and innocence, the past and the future, the here below and the eternal. It was a moment of truth that all the spectators questioned: each word, each cry, the duration of the agony, the resisting body, the life that clung desperately to it, all this constituted a sign.
—MICHEL FOUCAULT, *Discipline and Punish*

Punishment, as Friedrich Nietzsche reminds us, helps make us who we are and constitutes us as particular kinds of people. The person so constituted is watchful, on guard, fearful, even if never directly subject to the pains of state-imposed punishment. One of the primary achievements of punishment, to use Nietzsche's vivid phrase, "is to breed an animal with the right to make promises," that is, to induce in us a sense of responsibility, a desire and an ability to discharge properly our social obligations.[1] Dutiful individuals, guilt-ridden, morally burdened—these are the creatures that punishment demands, creatures worthy of being punished.

Punishment helps make us who we are through the complex juridical mechanisms that put it in motion as well as the moral tenets and legal doctrines that legitimate it.[2] Here too we can see the centrality of responsibility.[3] The state will only punish persons whose "deviant" acts can be said to be a product of consciousness and will, persons who "could have done otherwise." As the famous jurist William Blackstone put it, "to constitute a crime against human laws, there must be, first, a vicious will, and, secondly, an unlawful act consequent upon such vicious will."[4] Thus the apparatus of punishment depends on a belief in individual responsibility and conceptions of will that represses or forgets its "uncertain, divided, and opaque" character.[5]

In addition, because most citizens are never directly subjected to the state's penal apparatus, punishment creates a challenge for representation that is deepened to the point of crisis when the punishment is death. Punishment lives in images conveyed, in lessons taught, in repressed memories, in horrible imaginings. Some of its horror and controlling power is, in fact, a result of its fearful invisibility. It may very well be, however, that the more punishment is hidden, the more power it has to invade our imaginative life. We watch; we seek an image of punishment; we become particular kinds of spectators, anticipating a glimpse, at least a partial uncovering of the apparatus of state discipline. Thus public fascination with "crime and criminal justice never flags."[6]

What is true of all punishment is particularly true when death is a punishment. Here we confront the question of who decides what can and cannot be seen and of the adequacy of particular representations in conveying the "reality" of the pain on which the penal apparatus depends. Capital punishment is an occasion for rich symbolization, for the production of public images of evil or of unruly freedom, and for fictive re-creations of the scene of death. This is true in films such as the James Cagney and Pat O'Brien classic, *Angels with Dirty Faces* (1938), the Oscar-winning *I Want to Live* (1958), *The Chamber* (1996), and Clint Eastwood's forgettable *True Crime* (1999), which provide most of us with our only way of "seeing" what happens when the state kills.

In this chapter I examine the cultural life of capital punishment through a reading of three of the many films about capital punishment: *Dead Man Walking* (1996), *Last Dance* (1996), and *The Green Mile* (1999).' These films all appeared in the late 1990s and, with the star power of Susan Sarandon, Sean Penn, Sharon Stone, and Tom Hanks, they were clearly intended to reach a mass audience. They came out at a time of deepening public support for capital punishment and increasing impatience with the delays that frequently attend the movement from death sentences to executions. *Dead Man Walking*, *Last Dance*, and *The Green Mile* are important interventions in the debate about capital punishment, but, as I argue, they are strictly limited in the questions they raise and more important for what they reveal about certain of our most significant culture of beliefs.

I am interested in the cultural politics of these films and the way they convey knowledge of capital punishment. How do they portray the death penalty and what connections do they forge among death, spectatorship, and the American condition? What do they suggest about the legitimacy of state killing?

To answer these questions, I analyze the way these films speak to two of the basic cultural categories that help to organize our politics and our responses to state killing. The first of these is individual responsibility and its utility in explaining the causes of, as well as directing our responses to, crime. *Dead Man Walk-*

ing, Last Dance, and *The Green Mile* do not explore the social structural factors that some believe must be addressed in responding to crime[8] and that defense lawyers often highlight in the penalty phase of a capital trial. Instead, they are preoccupied with the question of personal character and responsibility. To the extent these films contain an explanation of crime and a justification for punishment, they locate it in the autonomous choices of particular people.

Moreover, like the victims' rights movement, the films wrestle with the question of whether criminals can and should be accorded the status of victims. Their dramatic work thus depends upon the politics of sentimental identification. While building dramatic tension around whether their hero or heroine deserves the death penalty, these films convey a powerful double message: first, citizens can, and will, be held responsible for their acts; second, they can, and should, internalize and *accept* responsibility.

Each of these films highlights categories—agency, will, and responsibility—the meaning of which is at issue in contemporary culture wars.[9] Rather than engaging the doubt that some now feel about the adequacy of those categories, these films are grounded on the notion of a responsible person as the proper object of punishment, someone who, as Nietzsche would have it, has the "right to make promises," someone caught up in simplifying narratives of good and evil. They suggest that there is, and should be, a tight link between crime and punishment such that those personally responsible for the former can be legitimately subject to the latter.

The second issue to which this chapter speaks is the manner in which film presents state killing to us and the cultural politics of those presentations. While *Dead Man Walking, Last Dance,* and, to a lesser extent, *The Green Mile* initially appear to deploy complex representational practices that call attention to the partiality and limits of all representations,[10] in the end they depend on the kind of realism criticized by Lesser in her argument against televising executions.[11] They allow their viewers to think that they can know the reality of the crimes for which death is a punishment and of the death penalty itself. Instead of inviting us to *imagine* the scene of death and its significance, they seek to inspire confidence that their viewers can "know" the truth about capital punishment through their "You are there" representations of execution.

Yet, I contend, the death penalty plays an uncanny role in film, pointing as it does to the limits of our ability to "know" death and, as a result, to our inability to be sure whether state killing is an appropriate, proportional response to the deaths that appear to justify it. Whenever and however death is present in film, it reminds us that seeing in this domain is not, and cannot be, knowing.[12]

In the way they address questions of responsibility and in the representational practices on which they depend, *Dead Man Walking*, *Last Dance*, and *The Green Mile*, whatever the intentions of those who made them, enact and depend on a conservative cultural politics[13] in which large questions about what state killing does to our law, politics, and our culture are set aside and in which viewers are positioned as jurors, like those in the Connors case discussed in chapter 5, deliberating solely on whether a particular person merits death.[14] While they raise questions about the calculus of desert that justifies the death penalty in particular cases, they shore up the conceptual foundations of state killing and help to legitimate it.

The Scene of the Crime and the Construction of Responsibility

As we saw in the McVeigh, Brooks, and Connors cases, every story about punishment is inevitably a story about crime, about its causes and the process of assigning responsibility for it. How we think about punishment, whether death or something less severe, is, partly, a function of what we know and think about the crimes that give rise to it.[15] Conventional wisdom holds that the severity of punishment should be proportional to the seriousness of the crime and that punishment should only be deployed against free and moral agents, persons capable of knowing right from wrong and choosing to do one or the other. Former Supreme

Court justice Robert Jackson once explained that "the contention that injury can amount to crime only when inflicted by intention is no provincial or transient notion. It is as universal and persistent in mature systems of law as belief in freedom of the human will and a consequent ability and duty of the normal individual to choose between good and evil."[16]

This is another instance of what law professor Stephen Carter calls "bilateral individualism,"[17] a response to crime that ignores or brackets the difficult question of what kinds of social conditions breed crime. In this vision the legitimacy of punishment depends on a relatively precise moral calculus in which punishment is a measured and proportionate response to crime. Linking crime and punishment is the supposed reality of individual responsibility.

A second explanation for crime complicates the calculus of punishment, Carter notes, by altering this straightforward story of responsibility. It does so by pointing away from individual agency toward the sweep of history and the unequal positions of the social groups from which criminals (and often their victims) come.[18] This "enterprise takes the form of a search for explanations rather than a search for villainous agents and attributions of blame; the remedial enterprise is directed to altering institutions, systems, and incentives rather than to exacting punishment."[19] This approach is based less on carefully reconstructing the crime and assigning personal responsibility than on using the fact of crime to highlight the need to alter social structures.

In the cultural life of capital punishment, at least as it is exemplified in the films I am discussing, Carter's bilateral individualism dominates. Because stories of the lives and deeds of particular persons have much more dramatic appeal than stories in which causation is impersonal and the source of crime is located in social structure,[20] it is not surprising that these films provide narratives of crime and punishment that focus on describing what a particular person did and on fixing responsibility on that person.

In popular culture the link between crime and punishment is frequently made visual. This is certainly the case in the films under consideration. *Dead Man Walking* and *Last Dance* focus on someone already condemned to death, living on death row, about whose legal guilt there is little doubt, someone whose crime is graphically, and repeatedly, presented to us. Both are tales of persons coming to terms with their responsibility for gruesome crimes. *The Green Mile* is a story about a person convicted of a crime he did not commit, in which much of the dramatic action of the film depends on the gradual unfolding of the truth of that crime.

In *Dead Man Walking*, Matthew Poncelet (played by Sean Penn) has been sentenced for his part in a double murder in which a classically clean-cut boy and girl are accosted while parking in the woods. They are led off into a clearing, where the girl is raped and repeatedly stabbed. Both ultimately are shot execution style. In *Last Dance*, Cindy Liggitt (Sharon Stone) is on death row for killing two people with a crow bar during a burglary of their home. In *The Green Mile*, John Coffey, a seven-foot-tall African American (played by Michael Clarke Duncan) awaits execution for the rape and murder of a pair of nine-year-old twin sisters. In this film we also meet three other death row inmates, including one, "Wild Bill" Wharton, who turns out to be the twins' real killer.

Each of these films asks how one human being can take the life of another. What forces propel such "evil" deeds? They inquire about the capacity of spectators to recognize a shared humanity, to empathize, and to care for or about the condemned. They do so through the pairing of the condemned with a cinematic "buddy."[21] Each shows the relationship with the condemned of one significant other person—a nun, a lawyer, a prison guard— who becomes the stand-in for the film's viewers. Can we have as much understanding, compassion as that person? Should we? Should it matter to us whether either Cindy Liggitt or Matthew Poncelet accepts responsibility for crimes for which each has already been found legally responsible? Can we be as generous in seeing the humanity of society's outcasts as is the death-row guard played by Tom Hanks in *The Green Mile*?

In *Dead Man Walking*, *Last Dance*, and *The Green Mile* images of the crime play a large role in suggesting how those questions should be answered. The crime appears in a variety of ways and is reenacted repeatedly throughout the first two films in a duet with the impending execution. In *The Green Mile* we see two images of the crime, one used to explain how John Coffey came to be accused, the second to reveal the true killer in all his cold-hearted brutality. Here the viewer never sees the actual crime as it is committed. We first see the immediate aftermath of the crime; later we see the events leading up to the rape and the murder. Nonetheless, in this film as well as the others visual equivalences are created, and the viewer alternatively is positioned as crime scene investigator, juror, omnipotent truth seeker, voyeur.

Through their preoccupations with the scene of criminality, these films establish the background conditions against which responsibility and blameworthiness can be fixed and punishment ultimately assessed. Each focuses a "who-did-what-to-whom" logic on criminal and victim, ignoring questions about history and structure that would complicate the assignment of responsibility and the assessment of punishment. Additionally, by repeatedly presenting incomplete reenactments of the crime, in which the "truth" of what happened only gradually unfolds, these films seem to highlight the partiality and problematics of viewing, of seeing and knowing. Yet this suggestion unravels in climatic scenes in which the viewer ultimately is reassured that the whole truth has been revealed.

Although the reimagining of the crime puts us at the scene as both potential victim and killer, we see the crime most often from the perspective of the killer, first approaching the victim and then acting out a murderous passion. What criminologist and cultural critic Alison Young says about *Psycho* and *Silence of the Lambs* is also true for *Dead Man Walking*, *Last Dance*, and *The Green Mile*: "While offered temporarily the experience of identifying with the victim, the spectator is incorporated into the film much more significantly as an accomplice of the killer. . . . This . . . identificatory relation is achieved through an association of the spectator's look with the gaze of the cinematic apparatus."[22] We are powerless to stop the violence that unfolds before us and cinematically reminded of that powerlessness because we see crimes already committed and for which the murderer is already in the custody of the state. So we are safe; the deed is done; we cannot rewrite history. As in sentimental literature, these films put the viewer in a situation in which innocent victims suffer and in which "it is too late to act or to intervene."[23]

In *Last Dance* the crime is presented in various ways—through photographic stills seen by different characters and in moving images presented in flashbacks. Each of these techniques has particular significance in focusing the viewer's attention on issues of responsibility and representation. Thus when we first see the crime in the form of photographs glimpsed over the shoulder of Rick Hayes, lawyer, ne'er-do-well brother of the governor's chief of staff, and new employee of the state clemency board, the camera gives us but a brief view of the bloodied body of a man laying on the floor, a fleeting suggestion of what happened. Then it pans quickly to Rick and pauses as his face, now shot in close-up, registers the horror of what he sees. This register marks one dimension of the responsible person, someone who identifies with the victim and knows, at the deepest level, that they are incapable of doing such gruesome deeds.

We see more of the crime scene when Rick's first romantic interest in the film, Jill, knocks over a file in his apartment spilling its contents onto the floor. Again there is a quick shot of the bloody photos, now strewn on the floor as if in a photo array presented to a court. This time the camera pans to Jill to catch the same distressed and disgusted look that had marked Rick's first sight of the photographs, the same reminder of the way "respectability" depends on just the right combination of responsibility and inhibition.

The looks on the faces of Rick and Jill are "our" looks. They establish a shared understanding of the horror of a sudden, murderous death, and they represent our reaction to the horrible violence that lurks just beyond law's boundary. Responsible people are repelled by the kind of violence depicted in the photographic representation of Cindy Liggitt's crime.

The baseline of responsibility established by Rick's and Jill's innocent gaze does two things. First, it provides a standard for viewers to judge Cindy as she later relives the crime in flashback. It also sets up an argument that Rick makes later in the film, namely that those who respond to murder with state killing are no different from those they condemn. As he puts it talking to the governor about Cindy, "We never gave her a chance to become like us. Now we've become like her."[24]

This is a key moment in *Last Dance*. It provides another example of the appropriation of the language of victimization on behalf of perpetrators of crime and a glimpse of what a structuralist response to crime would look like in popular culture. In Rick's line, responsibility is temporarily shifted from the criminal to those who occupy respectable positions in society; "we" are responsible for not giving Cindy the chance to be respectable. Moreover, those who use capital punishment as their way of responding to murder become murderers themselves.[25]

Yet, as *Last Dance* proceeds, the structuralist critique fades. Rick becomes preoccupied with his own romantic attraction to Cindy, an attraction signaled by the film's title. More important, Cindy herself counters Rick's initial structuralist response by her own insistence on taking responsibility.

At the level of the film's representational practices, the photographic stills through which we first see the crime in *Last Dance* present it as an evidentiary matter. We see the evidence as a jury would have seen it, indeed as the jurors in the Connors case discussed in chapter 5 saw the evidence of his crime. The still photographs present death through the most graphic representations of the wounds inflicted (see Figure 6). Yet they also serve as a reminder that when we see motion pictures of the crime we are being given a privileged viewing available to us only in our access to the memories of the film's central characters. Motion pictures serve as the revealed truth of the crime; they fix our gaze as coextensive with Cindy's recollection of the crime.

We see the crime through Cindy's eyes twice, once as she looks through an art book at a dark and evocative painting of a woman being tormented for her sins, the other in a dream that disturbs and awakens her. In these scenes her insistence on the appropriateness of the logic of free will, agency, and responsibility become clear. The first time we get an abbreviated look as she bludgeons one of her victims—Matt McQuire—and sends him hurtling through a glass door. In this moment of murder she appears to be in a trance, until finally interrupted by her accomplice's call to stop. The second time we get a more complete picture, a picture not available to the crime's victims or the jury, as we see Cindy and her accomplice driving toward the house where the crime will occur, both of them getting high smoking crack cocaine.[26] We watch the entry into the house and helplessly follow Cindy as she goes into the bedroom where Debbie Hunt, the murder victim, awakens, recognizes Cindy, and yells, "It's you, you fucking whore. Get out of my house." Cindy silences her with a blow to the skull.

In Cindy's deeply troubled reactions to these graphic recollections the narrative of responsibility unfolds. These reactions both connect her with Rick and Jill and, through them, with us. They serve as a point of critical engagement with Rick's assertion that "we" are somehow to blame. Although she is a murderer, she is disturbed, indeed haunted, by what she has done. While Rick, the lawyer and clemency investigator, is eager to see her as a victim and to forgive her crime, or to attribute responsibility to her troubled childhood and the fact that she was high on crack at the time of the killing, Cindy, who has already been found legally responsible, insists on *taking* responsibility (see Figure 7). As she explains to Rick, "That night [the night of the killing] is inside me like a giant shadow. I hated everything I didn't have and Debbie Hunt used to rub my nose in it. All that hate blew everything apart. I killed them. I killed myself. I know what I did. I can't change that. I can only change myself. I guess there are some things that can't be forgiven." In an odd foretelling of the drama that would unfold around Karla Faye Tucker,[27] and in a recapitulation of Carter's bilateral individualism, Cindy focuses attention on an "I" who acted; she insists that no one is to blame but herself.[28]

This insistence on taking responsibility marks a change that has already occurred in Cindy, reminding us that she, like us, is an agent capable of being held responsible. That she is guilt-ridden and morally burdened makes her an icon of modernist subjectivity, a person fully embracing the burden of her will put to "evil" purposes. Moreover, it establishes the dramatic question that haunts the film: Does she *really* deserve to die for her crime?

In *Dead Man Walking* the drama of responsibility unfolds in a more conventional way. Instead of the criminal resisting the structuralist analysis of his interlocutor, it is the latter who, in this film, speaks the language of responsibility against the evasions and deflections of the condemned. This film fixes the viewer's attention on a gradual unfolding of the "truth" of the crime against which responsibility can be measured and punishment fixed.

We see the crime primarily through the imagination of the main character, Sister Helen Prejean. As in *Last Dance*, the scene of the crime provides a recurring dramatic frame within which the film poses the question of whether Matthew Poncelet deserves to die. The repeated reenactment of the crime in a series of flashbacks spread throughout the film is key to the construction of Poncelet's character. It delineates the difference between *being* responsible and *taking* responsibility.

As to the question of innocence and guilt, the law is indifferent to the distinction between *being* responsible and *taking* responsibility. The Fifth Amendment protects the accused from being forced to take responsibility, in part because being "forced" to take responsibility undercuts whatever moral significance such a gesture would have.[29] While under current Supreme Court doctrine being an accessory is sufficient to create culpability for first-degree murder and eligibility for the death penalty, the assumption that taking responsibility has enormous significance in constituting the moral quality of a person is as crucial to the dramatic unfolding of *Dead Man Walking* as it is in *Last Dance*.

Will Matthew Poncelet confess? Will he admit his true involvement and genuine culpability for the murders for which he was sentenced? Or will he go to his death still insisting that he was only an accessory swept up in the evil deeds of another? These questions rather than any broader effort to understand the society of which his crime is a part, or the ongoing political and legal problems with the death penalty, provide the dramatic frame of the film.[30]

Dead Man Walking is more concerned with Sister Helen Prejean's ability to tame the savage beast in Matthew Poncelet, a heroic effort in the face of death, than about the question of whether state killing is compatible with our Constitution and our commitments as a political and legal community. As the spiritual counselor to Poncelet, Sister Helen insists that legal responsibility is not enough to heal the wounds inflicted, or to mark a soul that is to be saved. Thus she informs the parents of one of Poncelet's victims, "I want him to take responsibility for what he did."

Whereas in *Last Dance* the lawyer tries to diminish the responsibility of the condemned, even as Cindy Liggitt insists that she is responsible for her crime, in *Dead Man Walking* Sister Helen works to constitute Matthew Poncelet as fully responsible. She does so, in part, by imaginatively reconstructing the crime—trying to figure out exactly what he did, if not why he did it. This chronology of imaginative reconstructions gives us the opportunity to assess responsibility and serves as a continual reminder who did what to whom.

Dead Man Walking begins the visual reconstruction of the crime after Sister Helen has heard a verbal description of Poncelet's deeds[31] from the jaded prison chaplain who warns her, "There is no romance here, sister. This ain't no Jimmy Cagney 'I've been wrongly accused. If only I had someone who believed in me' nonsense. They [the men on death row] are all con men and they will take advantage of you every way they can." This is a warning to the viewer as well. Be wary. Don't be taken in. Remember who we are about to meet and why he is on death row. Unlike in *Last Dance* where Cindy Liggitt is presented as torturing herself into responsible personhood, Poncelet is the unrepentant con man.

As Sister Helen leaves the chaplain and walks into the prison for her first meeting with Poncelet, the film moves back and forth between her observation of the strange world she is about to enter and scenes of the crime, set off in black-and-white. We approach a car parked in the woods; we see the barrel of a rifle; we see a shot fired, followed by the legs of someone laying face down, then a twisted and bruised arm, and finally a knife raised in slow motion in three repeated sequences and one dramatic, *Psycho*-like stabbing gesture. But in none of these scenes do we see the faces of the killers; we know something horrible has happened but we cannot yet fix responsibility. The anonymity of the criminal and the lack of narrative cohesion in this scene serve both to keep our gaze fixed on the horror of the act that is presented to us and to warn us that we, like Sister Helen herself, are not yet in a position to judge or to assign blame.

After each of the images of the unfolding crime, the camera cuts back to Sister Helen's increasingly disturbed facial expression, a kind of "what am I doing here, what have I gotten myself into" look. What is left undecided is whether her distress is the register of her image of the crime, or the prospect of meeting the killer face-to-face, or both. But it is nonetheless important to note that at this point Sister Helen has not yet imagined the actual killing or the bloody bodies.

The camera's move to black-and-white and slow motion does the job of suggesting that it is a fantasy we are seeing. Yet it is an incomplete fantasy, though one already filled with dread even as it avoids the most visually horrible image of the crime. Without its most graphic detail, the scene of the crime is registered on Sister Helen's face as it would be on ours. Like Rick and Jill in *Last Dance*, hers is the face of a responsible person responding to horror.

In its gradual and partial reconstructions of the crime, *Dead Man Walking* also seems to highlight the problems of viewing and of representation. Perspective is everything; nothing is complete or certain. Thus we see the crime sometimes only briefly as when, during a hearing of the pardon board, we look over the shoulders of its members as they listen to arguments about whether they should recommend clemency for Poncelet. The prosecutor arguing against clemency hands crime-scene photos to each of the board members. We see parts of several of the photos, shown in color to mark their status as representations of the real, as the camera moves behind the row of chairs on which the board members sit. When the camera moves to the front we see them going through the photos, but the wide angle of the shot makes it hard to discern their facial expressions. Finally, we return to a position behind the pardon board and get a close-up of a single photo of the naked body of a young woman bloodied by multiple stab wounds (see Figure 8).

This is the very image that Sister Helen was unable or unwilling to conjure as she walked to her first encounter with Poncelet, and it provides a devastating moment in the film, a suggestion that only by refusing, at least initially, to contemplate the full horror of the crime can Sister Helen, or we, muster any compassion for someone who did what Matthew Poncelet did. The photo of the young, dead woman demands a response from the film's viewers, just as the prosecutor hoped it would demand a response from the pardon board. Who did this? More precisely, what kind of person could do such a thing? The photo works to narrow consideration, to keep the question of responsibility at the center of our thoughts. In its vividness and its horror it blots out almost everything else.

A similar effect occurs when, later in the film, the parents of one of the victims, Hope Percy, retell the story of the discovery of their daughter's body to Sister Helen. We see Hope's body with stab wounds clearly visible, again in color, suggesting that what we see is an accurate re-creation, not Sister Helen's incomplete imagining. "My daughter's body," Hope's mother recounts, "was found nude, spread eagled. . . . The police wouldn't let us go down to the morgue to identify the body. They said it would be too traumatic." Sister Helen listens intently, caught up in the narrative logic of sentimentality, tears welling up in her eyes.[32] This time we see the crime from the perspective of the surviving, grieving parents, their pain retold as if in a victim impact statement, recounting the gruesome way their daughter died and the consequences for their life.

Vision threatens; all reconstructions of horrible crimes astonish their viewers. As William Connolly notes, "The desire to punish crystallizes at that point where the shocking, vicious character of a case blocks inquiry into its conditions."[33] A structuralist explanation, in which the perpetrator himself appears as a kind of victim, seems morally inappropriate when confronted with the crime's horror; only bilateral individualism supplies the stuff out of which blame and punishment can be forged.

This reconstruction of the crime is based on the Percys' assumption that Sister Helen has come to share their belief that Poncelet is an "animal" who deserves to be executed for his crime. Their characterization of Poncelet contains two dissonant elements. To believe that crime merits commensurate punishment they must hold Poncelet responsible, even if he doesn't take responsibility. He must be treated as a free agent who could have and should have made a different choice. At the same time, the anger that drives punishment expresses itself in the view that Poncelet is unlike us, an animal, a monster. Here *Dead Man Walking* captures something close to the heart of the desire that always fuels punishment. Punishment, as noted earlier, involves imagining the object of vengeance to be a responsible person who deserves whatever he gets, and, at the same time, a dangerous monster with whom we must deal.[34]

When we next are brought back to Sister Helen's imagining of the crime, the question of responsible agency begins to emerge more clearly. The signal is a return to black-and-white footage. She revisits the crime as she is driven through the prison grounds to the special holding cells where inmates are kept in the days immediately before their execution. The crime appears as a series of scenes interspersed with her observations of the prison.

On this occasion her view is somewhat more detailed than in her first imagining. We see more than weapons and legs and arms; we are now able to identify the assailants and to see what they do. It is from this reconstruction of the crime that a tale of responsibility can be built. At this point, however, we must be wary because Sister Helen's reconstruction is based on replaying what she has heard from the Percys.

Yet she adds important details; she imagines Poncelet holding a rifle on Walter Delacroix, while his accomplice rapes Hope Percy. In her image Poncelet is surprised by his accomplice's brutality, scared and spooked when his accomplice comes over, grabs the rifle, and shoots Walter. This imagining is faithful to the story that Poncelet has told Sister Helen throughout the film. It is a version of events that maintains some distance between him and the burden of full moral responsibility. That she believes it is testimony to her willingness to take things on the terms on which they present themselves, the very trait about which she was warned by the prison chaplain. As Sister Helen later says to Poncelet, "You watched while two kids were murdered." Throughout Poncelet insists that he is "innocent," having neither raped nor murdered anyone. While his claim of innocence is not legally tenable, if it were true it would diminish his moral responsibility and invite a reappraisal of the appropriateness of his impending punishment.

Late in the film, on the day of the execution, we finally get an apparently complete, authoritative, visual reconstruction of the crime. This reconstruction serves to fix responsibility at the same time that it allays any doubt that we can know the truth of the crime. Representational realism underwrites the narration of responsible agency. This double gesture comes in response to Sister Helen's suggestion that Poncelet "talk about what happened. Let's talk about that night." The responding narrative is highlighted in its claim to truth because it is again accompanied by color photography of the crime scene. We follow Poncelet and his accomplice as they come upon Walter and Hope kissing in their car. The criminals force them out of the car by claiming that they are trespassing on private property.

Dead Man Walking fully reveals its conservative cultural sensibility when Sister Helen demands that Poncelet take responsibility for these acts. "What possessed you," she asks, "to be in the woods that night?" "I told you I was stoned," Poncelet responds. "Don't blame the drugs. You could have walked away," Sister Helen says, fully embracing the language of agency, will, and bilateral individualism. Echoing themes in the classic individualist tradition, Sister Helen insists that the responsible person makes choices and must accept responsibility for those choices (see Figure 9). "Don't blame [your accomplice]. You blame him. You blame drugs. You blame the government. You blame blacks. You blame the Percys. You blame the kids for being there. What about

Matthew Poncelet? Is he just an innocent, a victim?" The language of responsibility directs attention away from the legal and political issues surrounding state killing just as it refuses to accept social structure, accident, or conspiracy as justifications for actions. It insists that whatever the external factors that made an act possible, it is the choice to act that is crucial.

The ultimate unfolding of responsibility for the crimes in *Dead Man Walking* comes in a telling just before we see the completion of this "truest," and most complete, reenactment of the crime.[35] After his last call to his family Poncelet says to Sister Helen, "It was something you said. I could have walked away. I didn't. I was a victim. I was a fucking chicken. He was older and tough as hell. I was boozing up trying to be as tough as him. I didn't have the guts to stand up to him. I told my momma I was yellow. She kept saying 'It wasn't you. It wasn't you, Matt' [pause]. The boy, Walter, I killed him." In this moment Poncelet takes responsibility in just the way Sister Helen has been urging him to. Ultimately Sister Helen puts the question directly. "Do you take responsibility," she asks, "for both of their deaths [referring to Walter and Hope]?" "Yes ma'am," Poncelet responds. The construction of the responsible subject is completed as complex, uncertain causation is banished by a narrowly focused question and a simple response.

Sister Helen's question and Poncelet's response play out one of the key conventions of the sentimental story, namely a "deathbed" confession, which sets the stage for an act of contrition.[36] His assumption of responsibility is enacted as religious ritual, and the constitution of responsibility is only completed through the intervention of spiritual necessity. The admission of guilt that law could not secure is finally obtained. Free will and responsibility are affirmed because "sentimental fiction disintegrates whenever extenuating circumstances muddy the moral field on which its pure victims and fiendish oppressors must perform."[37] *Dead Man Walking*, like the prosecutors in the McVeigh, Brooks, and Connors cases, helps its viewers see through and beyond any such circumstances in the life of this fictive criminal. Poncelet's "voluntary" assumption of responsibility reassures *Dead Man Walking*'s viewers of the validity of bilateral individualism by suggesting that behind every narrative of social responsibility for crime is a deep, authentic truth about choice and voluntary, if misguided, action.

The assumption of responsibility in *Dead Man Walking* takes place as a journey in which the responsible person comes to acknowledge that he could have acted differently; he could have "walked away," but he chose not to. "Subjects, we say, are 'free.' They are not bound by the determined. They could always have done 'more' or done other than what they did. This is the basis on which we as legal subjects can be held legally responsible."[38] Yet, while the language of responsibility insists on autonomy, the process through which Poncelet comes to take responsibility emphasizes his relationship to Sister Helen. "It was something you said," he tells her. It is this relationship, with its promise that confession leads to forgiveness, that enables Poncelet to do what law, with its promise of punishment, was unable to get him to do. However, as literary critic Peter Brooks has recently argued,

> The problem may be that the very act of confessing will so often be the product of a situation, a set of physical conditions, a psychological state that do not conduce to the fullest expression of human autonomy. . . . the search for the true confession, the moment of the baring of the soul, may uncover that moment as one of human abjection. Telling the shameful truth may reap all sorts of psychosocial benefits . . . but it does not necessarily promote an image of human autonomy and dignity. On the contrary it reveals pathetic dependency and a kind of infantile groveling. . . . Even the most indisputable "voluntary" confession may arise from a state of dependency, shame, and the need for punishment, a condition that casts some doubt on the law's language of autonomy and free choice.[39]

The ultimate product of his confession is Poncelet's public acknowledgment of responsibility in the ritual of the condemned's last words, uttered while strapped to a gurney elevated with Poncelet in a Christ-like pose facing Walter's and Hope's families; "I ask your forgiveness. It was a terrible thing I did taking your son away from you. I hope my death gives you some relief" (see Figure 10).

It is only as Poncelet is himself being executed that the "complete truth" of the crime is presented visually. In this presentation we move from the scene of the execution back and forth to the scene of the crime. This quite literal effort to raise the question of whether execution is a just and proportionate response to murder shows Poncelet raping Hope and shooting Walter. The question is further precipitated by the use of parallel images shot from above of Walter and Hope laying face down, arms and legs spread in the woods, and then of Poncelet laying face up, as if crucified. Are these the same acts, the film seems to ask? Does *Dead Man Walking* condemn state killing, as Poncelet does when he says at the time of his execution "I think killing is wrong no matter who does it, whether it is me, or y'all, or your government," or does it provide the strongest justification for it by refusing to let us forget the nature and brutality of the crime to which it is a response? The film is rigorously indeterminate in its answers to these questions.[40] It is not, however, indeterminate in its presentation of responsibility. Like *Last Dance*, it affirms the perspective of bilateral individualism against a more structural account of crime.

This affirmation provides, although not in a straightforward way, a backdrop for the unfolding narrative of responsibility in *The Green Mile*. This film is presented as a flashback in which Paul Edgecomb, long retired from his job on death row, retells the events leading up to and surrounding the execution of an inmate, John Coffey, sixty years earlier. Coffey is a black man, unjustly condemned for the rape and murder of two little girls in the south in the 1930s. Through its deployment of this racialized story the film nods toward a structuralist explanation of crime and punishment. But it is little more than a nod. *The Green Mile* depends on a conventional melodramatic narrative. The world is divided into people who possess good characters, or at least who have redeeming human qualities, and those who are unredeemingly evil. Bad people do bad things, *The Green Mile* suggests, steering clear of the question of whether any of the causes of brutality may be found in the arrangement of social institutions or in the circumstances that shape human character.

This film depends on a kind of mirroring to produce its melodramatic tale. It turns out that evil exists in some of those who are condemned to die and as well as in some of those who condemn them. While being a good person provides no armor against either ordinary human suffering or gross injustice, evil cannot escape judgment and punishment. This mirroring is worked out in the characterization of the five guards who walk "the green mile," as Cold Mountain Penitentiary's death row was called, and of the inmates on the row. Four of the guards, most of all Tom Hanks's Paul Edgecomb, exhibit extraordinary human decency to the men who are awaiting execution. One, Percy Wetmore, is cruel, sadistic, and brutal, taking every opportunity to torment those he guards. In the four inmates we see this same distribution of good versus evil. John Coffey (JC) is not only an innocent man, he has been touched by the divine, blessed with the capacity to heal the sick, bring the dead back to life, and see into people's hearts and into the future. Two others are clearly guilty of the crimes they committed, but are presented in such a way as to suggest that their evil deed is but one aspect of their character. The fourth, "Wild Bill" Wharton, is Wetmore's double, equal in his cruelty, sadism, and brutality.

The film focuses in particular on Paul's relationship to John, a not subtle reference to the Apostle Paul and Jesus Christ. In this religious allegory Paul's faith, his belief in the possibility of miracles, his willingness to accept and embrace what he cannot fully understand, is tested and ultimately vindicated. He comes to know not only that John is innocent but that he is graced. In addition, it is through John that Paul and we learn the truth about the rape and the murder of the two girls. It is through John, though he himself is ultimately executed, that justice is done.

In *The Green Mile*, as in *Last Dance* and *Dead Man Walking*, the revelation of the truth of the crime is crucial to the film's insistence that responsibility can and should be assigned and that responsible people can and should be punished. So important is the crime that the film opens with a scene of men in a field, carrying guns, hurrying, obviously searching for someone. We see a man picking up a patch of cloth torn off on a branch. He holds it as if it were a clue. At first, in part because of the presence of the weapons, this seems to be a manhunt for a criminal on the run. Later in the film this scene is revisited. By that point we know it to be a search for two girls who are missing from home, and we know that the man who finds the cloth is their father.

This scene is revisited as a flashback within a flashback as Paul looks through the file of the newly arrived inmate John Coffey. As he reads the transcript of the trial, the film takes us to a farmhouse where we see tranquil scenes of domesticity. The tranquillity is shattered when the little girls do not come down for breakfast. The frantic yelling and anguished calling of parents who cannot find their children provide vivid reminders that no one is ever really safe, that in the 1930s, as in the age of Polly Klaas and Megan Kanka,[41] at any moment children can be taken from their homes to be coldly abused. We watch as the father and son grab their guns and rush out of the house and later appear in a reprise of the scene with which the scene opens. We first register the discovery of the missing children, covered in blood in John Coffey's arms, through the eyes of their father. As the search party approaches, Coffey stammers, "I couldn't help it. I tried to take it back, but it was too late."

"I couldn't help it" seems to be both an admission of guilt and an excuse, a plea for mercy from someone responsible for a heinous crime. But as we eventually come to know, it is, in fact, neither. It is instead a true account of Coffey's earnest but failed efforts to help the girls whose bodies he had apparently discovered abandoned in a field near their home. We come to know the truth of this account as we, like Paul, see instances of John's gifts (one of which involves bringing a dead mouse back to life). But in order for John to bring the dead back to life he must act in a timely manner; they must not have been dead very long. In addition, John has the capacity to take the sources of suffering from someone's body onto himself. After he heals an infection which has left Paul in great pain he says, "I just wanted to help. I just took it back, that's all."

As Paul gets to know John Coffey, and to see his divine gift as well as his gentle character, he gradually comes to believe in his innocence. As he says to the cynical, racist lawyer who had "defended" John, "There doesn't seem to be any violence in him." Eventually he reveals his view to several of his fellow guards. "I don't think he did it at all. God wouldn't put a gift like that in a man who killed a child."

But, late in the film, the story of the innocent man being held responsible for a crime he did not commit takes an unexpected turn when John turns Percy into a killer, using his miraculous power in a way that leads him to shoot Wharton, his cinematic double. At this point the viewer feels that a kind of justice has been done, the sadistic guard executes the sadistic prisoner and is then driven crazy, such that we see him being taken to the very same mental hospital where we are first introduced to Wharton. The justice of this execution and its connection to the idea of responsibility is, in a sense, played out for viewers in a reverse of the way it would have been in a legal trial. Through his conduct on death row Wharton shows that he has no redeeming human qualities, nothing that might point toward mitigation, and we know that he is on death row for killing three people in a hold up. Still the question arises, Why would the nonviolent, divinely inspired John cause Wharton's death?

"I've punished them bad men [Percy and Wharton]," Coffey explains to Paul. He then offers to "give you [Paul] the gift so you can see for yourself" why he made Percy turn on Wharton. In yet another flashback we see the tranquil domestic scene from which the twin sisters were abducted. We see Wharton working as a farmhand salaciously eyeing them. We watch Wharton break into the farmhouse late at night, cutting through a screen and then lifting a latch. We see him telling first one of the twins and then the other "If you yell I'll kill her [pointing to one of the sisters]. If you yell, I'll kill her [pointing to the other]" (see Figure 11).

Guilt is determined, responsibility is assigned, punishment is carried out. Some among us are simply unredeemable. Evil people do evil things for which they can and should be held responsible. The explanation for the violence that Wharton does to his victims or John does to Wharton is reduced to a simple morality tale. Revealing its own cultural conservatism, it is as if the film uses this narrative about guilt, responsibility, and punishment to justify state killing so long as it is used rarely and wisely.

There is, of course, the important twist in *The Green Mile* having to do with John's own impending execution. Here the film draws on another genre of death penalty films, the race to save the innocent. Will John be saved? How can this story of guilt and responsibility cohere if guilty and innocent alike are executed? What should Paul do?

For the resolution of these questions, the film turns to a conversation in which an anguished Paul goes to John and says, "We are coming down to it in a couple days. . . . Tell me what you want me to do. Do you want me to let you go?" John answers that he does not want to go on living, that he is "tired of it all . . . tired of people being ugly to each other, like pieces of glass in my head" (see Figure 12). John dies for our sins, assuming responsibility for the heartless acts of mere mortals in a world in which all too often they refuse to assume the responsibility that is properly theirs. Explaining the meaning of Wharton's killing in a way that provides an explanation for his own death, John tells Paul, "He killed them with their love. They loved each other. That's the way it is everyday, all over the world." John too will be killed because of his love, a love manifest in an acceptance of responsibility.

Although in different ways, *The Green Mile* joins *Last Dance* and *Dead Man Walking* in providing cultural affirmation of the social necessity of responsibility against those who would blur the distinction between criminals and victims or those who would ask us to attend seriously to the conditions that breed crime. They refute broad narratives of responsibility that would implicate us all in the circumstances that produce crime and would undermine the moral and legal scaffolding on which the apparatus of punishment is built.

Seeing the Technology of State Killing and the Representation of Death

At first glance, two of the three films I am discussing (*Last Dance* and *Dead Man Walking*) seem to question certain critical assumptions about our ability to know and represent crime. They do so through a series of visual reenactments, the first of which is partial or incomplete. Yet eventually both films give us views of the crime that are identified as full and accurate through the use of specific visual techniques. However, no such movement from doubt to certainty, from the partial to the complete, afflicts the films' presentation of the scene of punishment. Indeed, these films, as well as *The Green Mile*, are unusually preoccupied with the techniques and technologies of execution, showing, often in minute detail, how those technologies work and what their effects are on the body of the condemned. Nothing is left to the imagination as the camera zeroes in on the apparatus of death. Realist detail is put in the service of sentimental narration.

These films play off the contemporary legal prohibitions surrounding the sight (and the site) of execution that I discussed in the previous chapter.[42] It is as if they are trying to provide a rendering of reality "made more real by the use of aesthetic device."[43] Yet this effort runs into certain problems because of the presence in the films of witnesses to the executions. These films try to tell us what it means to see an execution by letting us watch others watch, by alternatively merging our gaze with the witnesses depicted in the films and then separating the gaze of the viewer from that of the witnesses (see Figure 13).

The presence of witnesses marks a difference the films insist on, namely the difference between those who "really" see an execution and those who have access only to its representations. All three do this by giving the viewer a closer look than is available to the witnesses. We get behind-the-scenes views of the "death work" that precedes an execution, close-up, slow-motion views of the technology—lethal injection and electrocution—in action. We see switches being thrown, jolts of electricity firing through the body or vials of lethal chemicals methodically emptying, fluid passing through tubes into the veins of the condemned. We are close-up spectators to something that few are "privileged" to see.

We are made aware of our privilege because we can see the filmic witnesses in their tightly controlled, more limited viewing. We watch them; we are voyeurs at someone else's voyeurism. The act of witnessing is then held up as a mirror in which the viewer is herself captured. Unlike the witnesses to an execution, however, who are there to be seen by the condemned just as they are to see him,[44] the viewer of death penalty films sits at a safe remove, hidden from the condemned's gaze, "real or fictive." That gaze is, of course, the gaze of death itself; we escape it and, do not think ourselves implicated in the fictive death that takes place before our eyes.[45]

Nonetheless, we are invited through the detailed, close-up images that *Last Dance, Dead Man Walking,* and *The Green Mile* present to believe that we have seen what an execution is "really like."[46] In *Last Dance* and *The Green Mile*, there is a deep and unambiguous investment in the believability of the image of the execution. *Dead Man Walking*, in contrast, uses a more complicated representational strategy.

In *Dead Man Walking*, as I have already noted, the scene of execution is interspersed with flashbacks to the crime, and, at the moment when Poncelet dies we see the faces of Walter and Hope reflected in the glass window that separates the witnesses from the death chamber (see Figure 14). These devices partially undercut the film's "realism." They do so by multiplying images and specters of death, showing how Poncelet's death is inseparable from the deaths that he caused, and bringing Hope and Walter to the site of the execution itself. *The Green Mile* uses a more conventional strategy to bring us close to the instruments of state killing, showing its viewers the death by electrocution of three different men, culminating with the execution of John Coffey.

In *Last Dance* our witnessing begins as Cindy Liggitt is transported from the women's prison to the death house in the state's male correctional institution. From the high-tech, modern, clean confines of the former, she descends into the archaic, fortresslike place where death is done by the state. There we wait with her as the time set for her execution approaches. As in many death penalty films, this one is literally preoccupied with time, flashing scenes of clocks on the wall, marking the inexorable process of life's march toward death.

But juxtaposed with the seemingly inexorable movement of time—the clock on the wall—is the prospect of last-minute legal, or executive, intervention. Set against time is law itself, death-doing but also potentially life-saving.[47] Thus for every clock, there is a telephone, the silence of which affirms the stillness of death, but which may, at any moment, come alive to end that stillness.

As Cindy waits in the special holding cell, caught between the clock and the telephone, the visual fetishizing of the technology of death and the marking off of the difference between the thing itself and its filmic representations begin. We see the backstage work of filling vials with lethal substances and close-ups of the vials being fitted into the machinery that will mechanically do the job that no human is authorized to do, of delivering those lethal substances to the body of the condemned (see Figure 15). When she is "escorted" into the room where she will be put to death, we again see what the witnesses cannot see, namely the condemned managed with military-like precision, strapped down, an intravenous needle inserted into an outstretched arm. Through these close-ups and backstage scenes viewers are invited to believe that this is what an execution is "really like,"[48] even as we are reminded that it is not a real execution that we will see. We are brought behind the scenes so we can see, and in our seeing know, what the death penalty is and how it operates.

It is only when the curtain separating the room where the witnesses sit from the death chamber opens that our view merges with the view of the witnesses. But we quickly concentrate on the exchange of looks between Cindy and Rick. The privileged, almost omniscient, view of a moment earlier dissolves, replaced by the gaze of intimacy, the gaze of love. Can that look be our

look? Can the viewer move from engagement with the bureaucratic and technological details of state-administered death to
embrace and identify the look of love? *Last Dance* works visually
to shift us from one register of spectatorship to another, from almost clinical detachment to loving engagement. This move
allows no other visual space. There is no possibility that we can
view the execution either as bureaucrats or as intimates. The
space of citizenship, the juridical posture that this film otherwise
seeks to cultivate, evaporates in the moment of execution.

In *Last Dance*, however, the phone does ring, and in hurried
response the execution is halted, as the warden shouts "Stand
down! Stand down!" Here two things come together. First, a les-
son emerges about the difference between state killing and murder, namely that the former is subject to the continuing normative standards and control of the community. As Cover notes, the
last-minute stay of execution reminds us that "the violence of
the warden and the execution . . . [is] linked to the judge's deliber-
ative act of understanding. The stay of execution, the special line
open, permits, or more accurately, requires the inference to be
drawn from the failure of the stay of execution. . . . In short, it is
the stay, the drama of the possibility of the stay, that renders the
execution constitutional violence."[49]

Second, the intervention of law ends the privilege of viewing,
but only for the witnesses. Quickly the curtains close, but we
neither terminate nor avert our gaze. We see Cindy, once un-
strapped and removed from the table, collapse and scream, as if in
a rage against her reprieve. The responsible person having taken
responsibility is turned into the victim of a legal process whose
obsession with technical legalisms, some now believe, obscures
issues of responsibility, justice, and punishment. Cindy becomes
the shrieking stand-in for a judiciary and public increasingly out-
raged by such obsessions.[50] Having been ready to die in the consolation of Rick's gaze, she is wrenched back into life by a legal
process that neither she, nor we, respect.

It is, of course, Rick's frantic efforts to find the one sympathetic
judge who might grant a stay that led to the excruciating agony
of Cindy's last-minute rescue. She screams because she knows

what the ultimate outcome will be, that she and we will return
to the death chamber. But before her return, before the stay is
lifted, Cindy talks about the redeeming power of the gaze, of a
certain form of spectatorship. "I saw you," she says to Rick, "I
could feel your eyes on me. I wasn't scared." After the stay is
lifted she says "You have got to let me go now. Please. . . . Don't
take your eyes off of me." What redeems is that the spectator can
himself be seen, that his gaze can be returned. Such a redeeming
power is not available to us. We are reminded, as if we need reminding, of our distance, our safe disengagement, of the limits of
our power and role as spectators.[51]

When Cindy is subsequently returned to the death chamber
there is no last-minute reprieve. The execution resumes as does
our encounter with the machinery of death. We are given another
extreme close-up as the procedure for dispensing the lethal chemicals proceeds. First one vial, then another is emptied in a slow-
motion sequence that echoes the tempo of our two views of the
scene of the crime. But unlike the violence that Cindy dispensed,
the violence done to her seems bloodless, antiseptic.[52] No human
hand is seen. Death comes through the automatic operation of a
machine. We are again brought to a scene of death, given the illusion of seeing what is generally forbidden and, through that
seeing, of knowing death.

In this scene viewers are positioned as seekers of unattainable
knowledge, knowledge of death itself. What Lesser says about the
desire to see an execution is the desire that *Last Dance's* seeks to
satisfy. "We want . . . [the condemned] to enact something *for* us;
we want to live the terror of death through him [or her], and then
be able to leave it safely behind."[53] Yet the realistic presentation
of the execution promises a knowledge it cannot produce. "Death
remains ever beyond us."[54] Seeing an image of the technology in
action cannot produce for us the experience of the death that the
technology produces.

Like *Last Dance*, *The Green Mile* fetishizes the technology of
death, but, set as it is in 1935, the technology is electrocution and
not lethal injection. While the guards await the first execution in
the film, we watch as, the day before, they fuss over the chair,

polishing its stern wooden arms and checking the straps. We see an initial backstage view as they conduct an elaborate dress rehearsal, walking a stand-in for the condemned man from his cell to the electric chair in the nearby room, strapping him in, pronouncing the death sentence, asking him if he has any last words, putting a hood over his head, wetting a sponge and putting it on his head, securing the electrodes through which the current will pass, and issuing the command to a guard seated behind a screen to throw the switch.

We watch as the witnesses assemble, not shielded by a glass partition, seating themselves on folding wooden chairs inside the death chamber. We see the execution as they see it: the signal is given; the executioner throws the switch and sets loose a surge of current; the body jerks upward, and finally slumps over. As if to remind us of the imperfections in the state's tools of death, a doctor comes forward to determine if the condemned is dead. Finding he is not, the camera takes us behind the screen where the executioner sits to show him throwing the switch again. We see the denouement through Percy's eyes, as, totally attentive to the scene before him, he stands next to the executioner. But the effort to make this first encounter with state killing seem adequate in conveying the reality of capital punishment is carried to its conclusion when, in the next scene, we see the guards in the prison basement preparing the executed man's body to be removed. It is as if *The Green Mile* seeks to assure its viewers that they have seen all there is to see, as if it wants to convey a confident comprehensiveness in its depiction of the process of state killing.

The presentation of the second execution seems to proceed along the same path, with a detailed rehearsal, made all the more detailed by the fact that Percy is now being taught what he needs to know so that he can take charge of the death squad. Through this dramatic device, we are given yet another close-up view of what real witnesses do not see, of men working to perfect and routinize state killing. But as the second electrocution goes forward it is hardly perfect or routine. As the second inmate to be executed in *The Green Mile*, an eccentric old Cajun named Eduard "Del" Delacroix, is brought to the electric chair, the camera again at first connects our view to the assembled witnesses. But the privilege of film spectatorship allows viewers to see what they cannot, namely Percy taunting him, calling him a "faggot." We watch as Percy leads the strap-down team through its paces and get a close-up view as he surreptitiously torpedoes the execution. Instead of dipping the sponge in water, which is necessary to ensure that the electrical current is efficiently conducted to the brain, he puts a dry sponge under the electrode that is strapped to Del's head. Following Percy's order to throw the switch, the camera again gives up a close-up view of the executioner doing his job behind a screen.

In a scene reminiscent of the botched electrocution of Pedro Medina, discussed in chapter 3, flames leap out from Del's head (see Figure 16). Paul glances at the bucket of water, quickly grasping what Percy has done. But there is nothing he can do except watch. As the fire engulfing Del intensifies, one of the witnesses asks her companion whether this is the way executions always happen. This question reminds the film's viewers of their privilege. We have seen the first execution, and know the answer to her question. Soon, however, the witnesses flee from the gruesome sight before them, a man burning to death. Yet, in their flight from *this* execution, the film seems to suggest that there is nothing that decent people should find offensive or gruesome about a "normal" electrocution.

Our third trip to the scene of state killing again is replete with close-up shots of the electric chair, of the behind-the-scene switches that activate it, of lights dimming as the switch is thrown, and of witnesses assembled—this time to see the electrocution of a man who we, but not they, know to be innocent, namely John Coffey. As the proceedings begin, Coffey and the guards try to comfort each other, the former saying "It'll be all right, fellas," and the latter assuring him "We don't hate you. Can you feel that?" Yet it is hatred that Coffey hears as the dead girls father yells, "Kill him twice," and as the mother asks "Does it hurt yet. I hope it does. I hope it hurts like hell."

Because John does not want the black hood put over his head, this execution allows viewers to see death etch itself on his face.

But John's is not the only face we see. The camera pans to the guards who stand with tears streaming down their faces, tears indicating their own inability to rescue John from legal injustice and their spiritual distress at the sacrifice of a blessed person. As John dies, the lights in the death chamber explode, creating a shower of light. Through this visual effect the film seems again to ask, "Is this the way electrocutions always end?" or "Is this the light of angels welcoming John to heaven?" The film thus allows us to imagine that we can know the ins and outs of state killing, down to its most minute technical details, while momentarily marking the distance between the scene of state killing and the sanctity of a place of eternal life.

Marking this distance is also part of the work done by the representational realism of *Dead Man Walking*. It too uses the extreme close-up of the machinery of death to bring us behind the scenes at an execution. Unlike in *The Green Mile*, we see only one execution. Unlike *Last Dance*, the representational strategy is more unsettling to the viewer. We are brought to and then away from the execution and, through that gesture, not allowed to forget the fictive quality of what we see. In contrast to both of the other films, what we see of the preparations for the execution initially comes only through the eyes of the cinematic buddy of the condemned, Sister Helen; we get no privileged preview. We watch as she catches a glimpse of the death squad practicing its drill and sees preparations being made to feed the witnesses before the execution. We see the distress on her face later when she sees them eating, distress that registers the cruel juxtaposition of their preoccupation with life's necessities even as they are about to see the end of life. We follow as she is led into the witness room. It is only then that our gaze parts from hers.

In this moment of separation the privileged position of the film's viewer is reasserted. We see Poncelet strapped to the table and a nurse searching for a vein into which she inserts the intravenous tube that will soon carry substances that will end his life. Over her shoulder we catch a brief glimpse of the vials containing those substances. But from here our gaze now fixes on the witnesses, as the camera pans from Sister Helen to the faces of the families of the victims. For a moment it seems as if our choice is to see the scene of execution through one or another of these sets of eyes. But in the back row we can see an unidentified, impassive female face. In her anonymity and distance the viewer is reminded of his or her position, poised, looking at the execution from farther away than either Sister Helen, Mr. Delacroix, or the Percys. We are again made aware of the fact that executions are today, as they always have been, about a particular form of spectatorship. We are again invited to believe that we will see and, through our seeing, come to know more than those whose witnessing is so tightly controlled.

But the camera shifts, fixing its gaze on the eyes first of Poncelet and then of Sister Helen. They stare into each others eyes; as in *Last Dance* and *The Green Mile* the truest connection between the condemned and those who have come to know his character is expressed in what they see. But Poncelet also fixes his gaze on us. He watches and in his look seems to ask how we will see him.

Finally, as in *Last Dance*, we see one close-up, then an even more intense view, of the vials from which will flow the lethal substances that mark the latest of the state's technologies for taking life. The camera follows the fluids as they leave the vials and travel through the tube into Poncelet's arm and, finally, to his head. We follow as if we too could enter his consciousness and know, in the last minutes in which knowing is possible, what it is like to lose consciousness forever. The visual device is stark in its invitation to exchange positions, if only for a minute, with the condemned in order to possess and bring back a knowledge forbidden to the living. Poncelet dies quietly. Only in this moment is his gaze ended and ours released.

In both *Last Dance* and *Dead Man Walking*, the scenes of state killing, of an execution presented as if the act of a machine, are stripped of grandeur or horror. How far have we come, these films seem to ask, from the awe-inspiring majesty of the scaffold or terror of an electrocution gone bad? There is, in fact, now almost nothing to see. Death comes quickly; it leaves no visible mark on the body of the condemned. We are invited to see that there is

nothing to see in what I have previously described as the bureaucratization and medicalization of death.

Yet, as noted in chapter 7, the sight of execution is always a
moment of transgression. In this transgression there is a mixture
of fear and fascination, of what we know and what we cannot
know. This is especially true when we see more than the carefully
controlled visual field of the witnesses; such sight involves a
fleeting refusal to acquiesce in the state's definition of the death
that it dispenses and in its determined effort to regulate the privilege of seeing. In addition, the presentation of death in films like
Last Dance, *The Green Mile*, and *Dead Man Walking* reminds us
that we too will die and that our death may be as untimely and
gruesome as the deaths we are shown; as film viewers, however,
we confront death from a distance and are allowed to walk away
unscathed.

As in *Last Dance* and *The Green Mile*, the preoccupation with
the act of witnessing and the focus on the gaze in *Dead Man
Walking* suggest that even a bureaucratized, medicalized execution "is—as Foucault already implies—more of a show, spectacle,
and theater than a closed structure."[55] Show, spectacle, theater,
these representational media are central to the rituals of state
killing. But by focusing on the act of watching and by fetishizing
the technologies of death, these films play out the limits of representation itself, limits imposed by law (the prohibition of televising executions) and life (the unknowability of death). These films
want to give us what life itself will not allow. They domesticate
state killing and allow us to believe that we can know what the
state does in our name, that we can measure the effects of capital
punishment and in that act precisely fix the balance of pains necessary to make the punishment fit the crime.

Conclusion

Last Dance, *The Green Mile*, and *Dead Man Walking*, I have argued, are exemplary cultural reflections on responsibility and representation. They juxtapose crime and punishment as a figura-

tion of law's commitment to proportionality and affirm bilateral individualism against more radical, structuralist accounts of crime. They make clear the distinction between *being* legally responsible and *taking* responsibility. In this distinction they chart a space in which all citizens can be said to reside, a space of individual autonomy, choice, and desert, a space in which those who take responsibility are accorded "the right to make promises." Despite their "transgressive" efforts to represent visually the site and processes of execution, they redeem their central characters—Liggitt, Coffey, and Poncelet—through the conventional high moralist discourse of a believing world. In this sense they speak to the American condition by embodying a conservative cultural politics, one reluctant to explore the instability of the very categories on which the modern apparatus of punishment depends.

What I am calling the conservative cultural politics of these films also manifests itself in the way they imagine the viewer and in the consequences of that imagining. While viewers are positioned in several different ways in both films—as investigators, truth seekers, voyeurs, as adventurers into the world of mystery and miracles—the basic structure of viewing is juridical. Although none of these films takes us into a courtroom, they invite the spectator to judge as if they were making a life-and-death decision.[56] The juridical role offered to the spectator of these films is, however, not the role of adjudicator of guilt or innocence; instead, we sit as if on a jury in the penalty phase of a capital trial deciding who deserves to die and who does not.

In *Last Dance* and *Dead Man Walking* the brief reconstructions of the lives of the condemned and the reasons for their acts play out as evidence in mitigation presented by the defense lawyer in cases like those of McVeigh, Brooks, and Connors. Through their extensive focus on the brutality of the crime and the suffering of those left behind, we see the kind of aggravating factors that made those cases so excruciatingly painful. If Liggitt and Poncelet take responsibility for their brutal acts, the films seem to ask, are they worthy of mercy? Or, is the only mercy that can and should be provided God's mercy, not ours? In *The Green Mile*, does Wharton's refusal to accept responsibility mark him as unworthy of that mercy and therefore deserving of execution?

The consequence of this juridical role is to distract us from, or to derogate, broader questions about the legitimacy and meaning of state killing and to focus our attention on the particularities of a single case. This is typical of the way state killing appears to us in popular culture, and it is recognizable in certain silences in both films as well as in the way they portray the political and legal controversy surrounding capital punishment. Toward the end of *Last Dance* the political controversy surrounding the legality or morality of capital punishment appears in a series of scenes focusing on the gathering of pro– and anti–capital punishment groups outside the prison where Cindy Liggitt is to be executed. Those scenes suggest the simultaneous routinization and irrationality that lies at the heart of all such gatherings—routinization in the sense that they are part of the ritual and "ceremony" surrounding every execution and irrationality when they erupt into angry shouting.[57]

In *Dead Man Walking* the gathering of demonstrators plays a similar role as a figure for the controversy surrounding capital punishment. We are shown a brief scene of Sister Helen in a candlelight vigil at the execution immediately preceding Poncelet's (see Figure 17); there we also see the parents of his victims strongly defending the right of the state to use the death penalty. "It is the only way we can ensure that they won't kill again," says Mr. Delacroix during a television interview outside the prison. "These people are mad dogs, maniacs," adds Hope's father. In contrast the clearest political message against capital punishment is delivered by the least credible speaker, Matthew Poncelet, when, before his execution, he says, "I think killing is wrong no matter who does it, me, y'all, or your government."

The scenes of demonstrators seem jarring, out of place in films that focus so intently on the question of whether a single person deserves to die for his crimes and on the simplifying effort to distinguish evil from good, the redeemable from those who cannot be saved. That focus invites the viewer to accept, in a spirit of resignation if not celebration, the legal and political status quo.

Thus cultural conservatism ends up serving the cause of legal and political conservatism. In all three of the films discussed in this chapter, "the basic categories through which we judge murderers and assess penalties are themselves treated as stable and unshakable. The harsh childhood of the killer, for instance, is taken to 'mitigate' the crime or to provide 'extenuating' circumstances; but these experiences are not treated as elements that may enter into the very formation of the perpetrator's will itself."[58] *Last Dance*, *The Green Mile*, and *Dead Man Walking* legitimate state killing, even as they point out some of its operational failures, by insisting that all that counts is the question of character and responsibility and by trying to convince their viewers that they can know the reality of the death penalty and, as a result, assess its proportionality.[59]

As I have argued, death, whatever its cause, marks the limits of representation. Films can neither capture death nor help us know what cannot be known. We can and do watch others die without being able to capture death's meaning or significance. Yet *Last Dance*, *The Green Mile*, and *Dead Man Walking* do not acknowledge that "both death and film are negotiations with absence, and that the representation of violent death in film constitutes a special crisis of believability, a threshold of realism and its own critique."[60] In the end, whatever our particular judgments about whether their main characters are justifiably or unjustifiably condemned to death, these films invite us to embrace the conceptual categories of responsibility and representation that, in a deep sense, justify the apparatus of criminal punishment and keep the machinery of state killing in place and operating.

9

CONCLUSION:

TOWARD A NEW ABOLITIONISM

The death penalty . . . corrupts the integrity of the criminal law and the criminal process that seeks its enforcement.
—FRANKLIN ZIMRING, "The Executioner's Dissonant Song"

Before our government takes the life of even one more citizen, it has a solemn responsibility to every American to prove that its actions are consistent with our nation's fundamental principles of justice, equality, and due process.
—SENATOR RUSSELL FEINGOLD, Statement on the Introduction of the National Death Penalty Moratorium Act of 2000

From this day forward I no longer shall tinker with the machinery of death.—JUSTICE HARRY BLACKMUN, *Callins v. Collins*

The Timothy McVeighs of the world pose a dramatic challenge for all of us. In the face of such demonstrable evil how can we respond without becoming evildoers ourselves? Can we respond to those who kill on our terms, not theirs? And what will those terms be? All too often the answer to these questions is anything but clear.

What I have tried to show in this book is that state killing is a distraction or, worse, a force that makes our society neither safer nor saner. At its best, capital punishment may give some temporary satisfaction to the legitimate personal anger of those whose loved ones are killed in senseless acts. But state killing is part of a strategy of governance that makes us fearful and dependent on the illusion of state protection, that divides rather than unites, that promises simple solutions to complex problems.[1] State killing is, in addition, caught up in the contemporary cultural preoccupation with identifying and paying homage to *real* victims while challenging claims that criminals can be victims too. So powerful is this preoccupation that there seems little space to imagine another vocabulary for thinking about the American condition and yet it is precisely such a vocabulary that we need.[2]

In today's America capital punishment has become a major front in the culture war. As Connolly rightly notes, state killing

> mobilizes political divisions between one set of partisans, who seek to return to a fictive world in which the responsible individual, retributive punishment, the market economy, the sovereign state, and the nation coalesced, and another set, who seek to respond in more generous ways to new experiences of the cultural contingency of identity, the pluralization of culture, the problematical character of traditional conceptions of agency and responsibility, and the role of the state in a new world order.[3]

Connolly cites William Bennett's *The Devaluing of America: The Fight for Our Culture and Our Children* as an example of the way the embrace of state killing works in a cultural contest. In his book, Bennett describes part of an interview he did on *Larry King Live* in which a caller pressed him as follows, "Why build prisons? Get tough like [Saudi] Arabia. Behead the damned drug dealers. We're just too damned soft." Bennett responded by saying,

> "One of the things that I think is a problem is that we are not doing enough that is morally proportional to the nature of the offense. I mean, what the caller suggests is morally plausible. Legally, it's difficult."

"Behead?" King asks.

"Yeah. Morally, I don't have anything wrong with it. . . . I mean ask most Americans if they saw somebody out on the streets selling drugs to their kid what they would feel morally justified in doing—tear them limb from limb. . . . What we need to do is find some constitutional and legally permissible way to do what the caller suggests, not literally to behead, but to make the punishment fit the crime. And the crime is horrible."

"During the program," Bennett explains, "I strongly rejected calls for drug legalization and endorsed capital punishment for major drug dealers."[4]

Reading this exchange, I feel the overwhelming gravitational force of an argument for state killing with its appeal to personal tragedy and justifiable anger.[5] I am reminded of the moment when, in the second presidential debate in 1988, Bernard Shaw asked Michael Dukakis what he would do if someone raped and murderer his wife, Kitty. Dukakis responded by saying, "Bernie, you know that I'm against the death penalty" and by changing the subject. At the moment I wished for a different response, the same kind of response that one might have hoped that Bennett might have given to his caller. It might have gone like this.

> Of course, I would want anyone who did such a thing to someone I loved to be made to suffer. Indeed, if I got my hands on him I'd tear him limb from limb. But the death penalty is something different. What my love and anger propels me to do is not what our government should do. It should help heal my pain, but also find ways to punish that do more than exact the most primitive kind of vengeance.

There is, of course, much more to the argument against state killing than this straightforward separation of private desire and public justice. Connolly comments on the Bennett exchange by saying that the repeated invocation of what is "morally proportional," "morally plausible," and what feels "morally justifiable" invests intense feelings of outrage and vengeance in the blue-chip stock of morality, covertly debasing the latter until it becomes a container into which selective energies of revenge can be poured. . . . Public objections by liberals miss the point unless we are able to change the line of associations between morality, simplicity, revenge, and death. Until we do, the agents of the culture war will succeed in using our opposition to associate us with moral softness toward murderers, drug dealers, welfare cheats, and pornographers.[6]

Until we do we will spend too much time answering the question, If Timothy McVeigh doesn't deserve to die, who does?

In the United States opposition to the death penalty traditionally has been expressed in several guises. Some have opposed the death penalty in the name of the sanctity of life.[7] Even the most heinous criminals, so this argument goes, are entitled to be treated with dignity.[8] In this view, there is nothing that anyone can do to forfeit the "right to have rights."[9] Others have emphasized the moral horror, the "evil," of the state willfully taking the lives of any of its citizens.[10] Still others believe that death as a punishment is always cruel and, as such, is incompatible with the Eighth Amendment.[11]

Each of these arguments has been associated with, and is an expression of, humanist liberalism, political radicalism, or religious doctrine. Each represents a frontal assault on the simple and appealing retributivist rationale for capital punishment.[12] Each puts opponents of the death penalty on the side of society's most despised and notorious criminals; to be against the death penalty one has had to defend the life of Timothy McVeigh.

Those who oppose state killing cannot, and should not, take on the political burden of explaining the acts of McVeigh, or Brooks, or Connors. It is hard enough to do this work in the carefully controlled environment of a capital trial or an appellate argument. It is impossible to do so in the hurly-burly of political contest. Thus it is not surprising that while traditional abolitionist arguments have been raised repeatedly in philosophical commentary, political debate, and legal cases, none has ever carried the day in the debate about capital punishment in the United States.

Yet today many who oppose the death penalty continue to try to carry on the struggle by pursuing traditional abolitionist strategies. To take but one example, the Italian clothing company Benetton published, in January 2000, a glossy catalog called *We, On Death Row*. Benetton hoped to prompt a rethinking of America's attachment to capital punishment by giving those condemned to die a human face. Staring out from the pages of its catalog are about thirty people who await execution. Posed in their cells, learning against freshly painted cinder block walls, or walking down deserted corridors, these men and women give Americans a close-up look at those we would put to death. The catalog also contains short interviews in which inmates tell about their families, the lives they led outside prison, their dreams, and their fears about execution.[13]

The Benetton catalog, whatever its intentions, misses the mark. As we think about capital punishment, the faces we should be looking at are our own. The question to be asked about state killing is not what it does for us, but what it does *to* us. In asking this question we need not think of ourselves as yet another category of victims. Indeed this question points beyond the logic of victimization and the sentimental narrative on which it depends toward an examination of the cost of state killing to our law, our politics, our culture. In my judgment the cost is great.

State killing diminishes us by damaging our democracy, legitimating vengeance, intensifying racial divisions, and distracting us from the challenges that the new century poses for America. It promises simple solutions to complex problems and offers up moral simplicity in a morally ambiguous world.[14] We need a new abolitionism that leaves McVeigh, Brooks, and Connors, as well as the Benetton catalog, behind, and assesses the injuries that state killing does to those who love America and its political and legal institutions, that allows and encourages more nuanced views of moral responsibility and of political action, and offers new narrative possibilities in the conversation about state killing.

The abolitionism I have in mind is, however, less new than it might seem. Glimpses of it can be found in the words of those in the death penalty bar whose story I told in chapter 6. And it also can be glimpsed in the Supreme Court's assessment of the constitutionality of capital punishment found first in *Furman v. Georgia*. In that assessment opposition to state killing no longer takes the form of a frontal assault on the morality of state killing. Instead, arguments against the death penalty occur in the name of constitutional rights other than the Eighth Amendment, in particular due process and equal protection. Abolitionists today argue against the death penalty, claiming that it has not been, and cannot be, administered in a manner that is compatible with our legal system's fundamental commitments to fair and equal treatment. This new abolitionism is seen most vividly in two places, one an opinion by former Justice Harry Blackmun, the other a resolution by the American Bar Association.

A Constitutional Conundrum

As I noted in chapter 3, in February 1994, Justice Harry Blackmun of the Supreme Court announced, "From this day forward I no longer shall tinker with the machinery of death."[15] This dramatic proclamation capped his evolution from longtime supporter of the death penalty to tinkerer with various procedural schemes and devices designed to rationalize death sentences to outright abolitionist. Twenty-two years before his abolitionist announcement, he dissented in *Furman v. Georgia*, refusing to join the majority of his colleagues in what he labeled the "legislative" act of finding execution, as then administered, cruel and unusual punishment.[16] Four years after *Furman* he joined the majority in *Gregg v. Georgia*, deciding to reinstate the death penalty in the United States.

However, by the time of his abolitionist conversion, Blackmun had left a trail of judicial opinions moving gradually, but inexorably, away from this early embrace of death as a constitutionally legitimate punishment.[17] As a result, the denunciation of capital punishment which he offered in 1994 was as categorical as it was vivid: "I no longer shall tinker with the machinery of death." It was most significant as a moment in the transformation of abolitionist politics, as an example of abolition as a kind of legal and political conservatism, and as an indicator of the anxiety that abolitionists seek to cultivate in the face of the increased popularity of state violence.

Blackmun's abolitionism found its locus in neither liberal humanism nor radicalism nor religious doctrine, nor in the defense of the most indefensible among us. It is, instead, firmly rooted in the mainstream legal values of due process and equal protection and in a deep concern with what state killing does to the condition of America. Blackmun did not reject the death penalty because of its violence, argue against its appropriateness as a response to heinous criminals, or criticize its futility as a tool in the war against crime. Instead, he shifted the rhetorical grounds.

Harkening back to *Furman*, as if rewriting his opinion in that case, he focused on the procedures through which death sentences are decided.[18] "Despite the efforts of the States and the courts," Blackmun noted, "to devise legal formulas and procedural rules . . ., the death penalty remains fraught with arbitrariness, discrimination, caprice, and mistake. . . . Experience has taught us that the constitutional goal of eliminating arbitrariness and discrimination from the administration of death . . . can never be achieved without compromising an equally essential component of fundamental fairness—individualized sentencing."[19]

Two things stand out in Blackmun's argument. First he acknowledges law's effort to purge death sentences of any taint of procedural irregularity. As he sees it, the main implication of *Furman* is that a death penalty is constitutional only if it *can be* administered in a manner compatible with the guarantees of due process and equal protection. Here Blackmun moves the debate away from the question of whether capital punishment is cruel or whether it can be reconciled with society's evolving standards of decency. Second, Blackmun identified a constitutional conundrum in which consistency and individualization—the twin commands of the Supreme Court's post-*Furman* death penalty jurisprudence—could not be achieved simultaneously. As a result, Blackmun concluded that "the death penalty cannot be administered in accord with our Constitution."[20] His language is unequivocal; after more than twenty years of effort Blackmun says, in essence, "enough is enough."

The new abolitionism that Blackmun championed presents itself as a reluctant abolitionism, one rooted in an acknowledgment of the damage that capital punishment does to central legal values and to the legitimacy of the law itself. It finds its home in an embrace, not a critique, of those values. Those who love the law, in Blackmun's view, must hate the death penalty for the damage that it does to the object of that love. "Rather than continue to coddle the Court's delusion that the desired level of fairness has been achieved . . .," Blackmun stated, "I feel morally and intellectually obligated simply to concede that the death penalty experiment has failed. It is virtually self-evident to me now that no combination of procedural rules or substantive regulations ever can save the death penalty from its inherent constitutional deficiencies."[21] In this admonition we again see Blackmun's categorical conclusion that nothing can "save" capital punishment, a conclusion spoken both from within history, as a report of the result of an "experiment," but also from an Archimedean point in which the failure of the death penalty is "self-evident" and permanent.

The new abolitionism provides an important contemporary avenue for engagement in the political struggle against capital punishment, providing abolitionists a position of political respectability while simultaneously allowing them to change the subject from the legitimacy of execution to the imperatives of due process, from the philosophical merits of killing the killers to the sociological question of the impact of state killing on our politics, law, and culture. Blackmun's rhetoric enables opponents of state killing to respond to the overwhelming political consensus in favor of death as a punishment; they no longer have to take on that consensus frontally. They can say that the most important issue in the debate about capital punishment is one of fairness, not one of sympathy for murderers; concern for the law abiding, not for the criminal. We should not let our central democratic and legal values be eroded just so we can execute evildoers. One can, abolitionists now are able to concede, believe in the retributive or deterrence-based rationalizations for the death penalty and yet still be against the death penalty; one can be as tough on crime as the next person yet still reject state killing. All that is required to generate opposition to execution is a commitment to democracy, the rule of law, and a mature engagement in responding to society's most severe social problems.

A Moratorium

The new abolitionism was also articulated in a resolution calling for a moratorium on state killing passed in February 1997 by the American Bar Association (ABA). Taking us back to *Furman's* condemnation of the death penalty as "then administered," the ABA resolution proclaimed that the death penalty as "currently administered" is not compatible with central values of our Constitution. Since *Furman* the effort to produce a constitutionally acceptable death penalty has, in the view of the ABA, been to no avail. Thus the ABA "calls upon each jurisdiction that imposes capital punishment not to carry out the death penalty until the jurisdiction implements policies and procedures . . . intended to (1) ensure that death penalty cases are administered fairly and impartially, in accordance with due process, and (2) minimize the risk that innocent people may be executed."[22]

However, the language of the ABA resolution, unlike Blackmun in *Callins*, seems conditional and contingent in its condemnation of death as a punishment. Even as it calls for a cessation of executions it appears to hold out hope for a process of reform in which the death penalty can be brought within constitutionally acceptable norms. As if to leave little doubt of its intention, the ABA resolution concludes by stating that the association "takes no position on the death penalty."[23]

Some might argue that the ABA recommendations, qualified as they seem to be, remain deeply invested in a sentimental narrative—that all we need to do is to stop victimizing those convicted criminals with poor counsel, the erosion of postconviction protections, and racism in order to purify state killing. However, the

ABA resolution, despite its explicit refusal to take a position on the ultimate question of the constitutionality of capital punishment, amounts to a call for the abolition, not merely the cessation, of capital punishment. It does the work of the new abolition without Blackmun's overt and categorical renunciation. If one takes seriously the conclusions of the report accompanying the ABA's recommendation, then the largest association of lawyers in the country is asking us to save further damage to America by ending the death penalty. In so doing the ABA provides a striking response to the continuing anxiety that attends the embrace of the state's ultimate violence. Just as rushing a fresh contingent of troops into a battle going badly may reinvigorate those grown weary in battle even if ultimately it does not stem the tide, so too the ABA's action provides an important vehicle for thinking about capital punishment and the American condition.

The ABA report provides three reasons for a moratorium on executions, each a crucial component of the new abolitionism. First is the failure of most states to guarantee competent counsel in capital cases. Because most states have no regular public defender systems, they are frequently assigned to indigent capital defendants lawyers with no interest, or experience, in capital litigation.[24] The result often is incompetent defense lawyering, lawyering that has become all the more damaging in light of new rules requiring that defenses cannot be raised on appeal or in habeas proceedings if they are not raised, or if they are waived, at trial.[25] The ABA itself calls for the appointment of "two experienced attorneys at each stage of a capital case."[26] While, in theory, individual states could provide competent counsel in death cases, and while there is ample evidence to suggest the value of skilled lawyers in preventing the imposition of death sentences, the political climate in the United States as it touches on the crime problem suggests that there is, in fact, little prospect for a widespread embrace of the ABA's call for competent counsel.

The second basis for the ABA's recommended moratorium is the recent erosion in postconviction protections for capital defendants. While the ABA notes that "the federal courts should consider claims that were not properly raised in state court if the reason for the default was counsel's ignorance or neglect and that a prisoner should be permitted to file a second or successive federal petition if it raises a new claim that undermines confidence in his or her guilt or the appropriateness of the death sentence,"[27] the direction of legal change is, as I already have noted, in the opposite direction. Today courts in the United States are prepared to accept that some innocent people, or some defendants who do not deserve death, will be executed.[28] As Justice Rehnquist observed in *Herrera v. Collins*, "due process does not require that every conceivable step be taken, at whatever cost, to eliminate the possibility of convicting an innocent person."[29]

For Rehnquist, what is true in the general run of criminal cases is also true in death cases. If a few errors are made, a few innocent lives taken, that is simply the price of a system that is able to execute anyone at all. In Rehnquist's view finality in capital cases is more important than an extended, and extremely frustrating, quest for justice.[30] For him, and others like him, the apparent impotence of the state, its inability to turn death sentences into executions, is more threatening to its legitimacy than a few erroneous, undeserved deaths at the hands of the state. Here again what the ABA asks for, namely a restoration of some of the previously available habeas remedies, is theoretically conceivable. Yet like efforts to improve the quality of defense counsel in capital cases, it is hardly a likely or near-term possibility.

The third reason for the ABA's call for a moratorium is the "longstanding patterns of racial discrimination . . . in courts around the country,"[31] patterns of discrimination that have repeatedly been called to the attention of the judiciary and cited by anti–death penalty lawyers as reasons why the death penalty violates the Fourteenth Amendment guarantee of equal protection. The ABA report cites research showing that defendants are more likely to receive a death sentence if their victim is white rather than black,[32] and that in some jurisdictions African Americans tend to receive the death penalty more than do white defendants.[33] The report calls for the development of "effective mechanisms" to eliminate racial prejudice in capital cases, yet does not identify what such mechanisms would be.[34] Indeed, it is not clear that there are any such mechanisms.

The pernicious effects of race in capital sentencing are a function of the persistence of racial prejudice throughout the society combined with the wide degree of discretion necessary to afford individualized justice in capital prosecutions and capital trials. Prosecutors with limited resources may be inclined to allocate resources to cases that attract the greatest public attention, which often will mean cases where the victim was white and his or her assailant black. Participants in the legal system—whether white or black—demonize young black males, seeing them as more deserving of death as a punishment because of their perceived danger. These cultural effects are not remediable in the near term, not so long as we live in a killing state. As Blackmun noted in *Callins*, "we may not be capable of devising procedural or substantive rules to prevent the more subtle and often unconscious forms of racism from creeping into the system. . . . discrimination and arbitrariness could not be purged from the administration of capital punishment without sacrificing the equally essential component of fairness-individualized sentencing."[35]

Conclusion

Today the new abolitionism promoted by Blackmun and the ABA seems to be gaining a little momentum. While public opinion polls continue to register the support of the overwhelming majority of Americans for capital punishment, the June 12, 2000, issue of *Newsweek* reported that "For the first time in a generation, the death penalty itself is in the dock—on the defensive at home and especially abroad for being too arbitrary and too prone to error."[36] About the same time, the *New York Times* proclaimed the coming of "the new death penalty politics" saying that "heightened public concern over the fallibility of the criminal justice system [has caused] a dramatic shift in the national debate over capital punishment."[37]

Growing evidence of failures in that system revealed by the increased availability of DNA testing has been particularly consequential in bringing about this new situation.[38] Indeed since 1972, eighty-seven people have been freed from death row because they were proved innocent after their trials and appeals were completed, an error rate of about one innocent person for every 7 persons executed. This has made it possible for politicians seeking to remain in the mainstream to embrace the new abolitionism.

A remarkable moment for the new abolitionism occurred when, on January 31, 2000, Governor George Ryan of Illinois, a longtime supporter of capital punishment, announced plans to block all executions in that state by granting stays before any scheduled legal injections are administered. His act effectively imposed a moratorium on the death penalty, the first time this had been done in any state. Ryan said that he was convinced that the death penalty system in Illinois was "fraught with errors" and "broken" and that it should be suspended until thoroughly investigated.[39] Subsequently, Governor Ryan stated that until he can be given a "100% guarantee" against mistaken convictions, he would authorize no more executions.[40]

Following Ryan's announcement, the U.S. Department of Justice initiated its own review "to determine whether the federal death penalty system unfairly discriminates against racial minorities."[41] Moreover, legislation has been introduced in Congress to lessen the chance of unfairness and deadly error by making DNA testing available to both state and federal inmates, and by setting national standards to ensure that competent lawyers are appointed for capital defendants.[42] Other legislation would suspend all executions at the federal and state levels while a national blue-ribbon commission reviews the administration of the death penalty.[43]

In May 2000 the New Hampshire legislature became the first to vote for repeal of the death penalty in more than two decades.[44] While this legislation was subsequently vetoed by Governor

Jeanne Shaheen, much of its support reflected new abolitionist sentiment. Thus one Republican representative, who like Illinois Governor Ryan had been a longtime supporter of capital punishment, explained his vote for repeal by saying, "There are no millionaires on death row. Can you honestly say that you're going to get equal justice under the law when, if you've got the money, you are going to get away with it."[45]

New and unexpected voices—including such prominent conservatives as the Reverend Pat Robertson and newspaper columnist George Will—have spoken out against what they see as inequality and racial discrimination in the administration of state killing and in favor of a moratorium. A National Committee to Prevent Wrongful Executions, whose members include death penalty supporters such as William S. Sessions, former Texas judge and FBI director in the Reagan and Bush administrations, has called for a reexamination of the process that leads to wrongful death sentences. If all this were not enough to signal the growing significance of the new abolitionism as a force in American politics, George W. Bush in June 2000 used his power as Texas governor to grant his first stay of execution after more than five years in office and after more than 130 people had been executed during his tenure. He did so in order to allow for DNA testing of evidence that linked a condemned man, Ricky McGinn, to the rape of his alleged victim. The news media were quick to note the symbolic significance of this gesture by contrasting it with one provided by Arkansas Governor Bill Clinton when, in January 1992, he interrupted his presidential campaign to return home to preside over the execution of Ricky Ray Rector, a mentally impaired black man convicted of killing a police officer.[46]

Despite these encouraging developments the new abolitionism is still a long way from bringing an end to capital punishment. Yet what its supporters have succeeded in doing is calling our attention to the condition of American, its laws, its culture, its commitments as a way of framing the debate about state killing. They remind us that the post-*Furman* effort to rationalize death sentences has utterly failed and has been replaced by a policy that favors execution while trimming away procedural protection for capital defendants. This situation only exacerbates the incompatibility of state killing and legality. As U.S. Senator Russ Feingold of Wisconsin noted, "At the end of 1999, as we enter a new millennium, our society is still far from fully just. The continued use of the death penalty demeans us. The death penalty is at odds with our best traditions. . . . And it's not just a matter of morality. . . . the continued viability of our justice system as a truly just system requires that we do so."[47] For Senator Feingold, as for Justice Blackmun, the ABA, Governor Ryan, and others, the rejection of the death penalty takes the form of an effort to prevent the erosion of the boundaries between state violence and its extralegal counterpart.

This effort, while speaking to some of the most pressing issues facing today's capital punishment system, also captures the spirit of *Furman*. It calls us back to *Furman*'s critique of the practices of capital punishment, to its doubts about whether those practices could be squared with the law's requirements. Yet it radicalizes *Furman* by reminding all Americans of this country's continuing inability, now almost thirty years later, to get state killing right. It reminds us of the spirit of vengeance and cultural division that attends the death penalty and calls on us to embrace the new abolitionism in the spirit of addressing our most pressing social problems so that our future might be better than our past. It offers us the chance to escape the compulsion to think only about victimization, to cast problems of crime and punishment in morally simplistic terms, and to reconsider what this society wishes to be.

In the end, the new abolitionism calls on America to stop one line of killing that we have within our power to stop, namely capital punishment. It asks us to do so to preserve what we value in our legal institutions. It asks us to do so in order that we might begin the work of healing the divisions in our culture. It asks us to do so in the hope that our present embrace of the killing state is the result of fear rather than venality, misunderstanding rather than clear-headed commitment.

NOTES

CHAPTER 1
INTRODUCTION

1. Emily Bernstein, "Terror in Oklahoma: Islam in Oklahoma: Fear about Retaliation among Muslim Groups," *New York Times*, April 20, 1995, A26.

2. "Terror in Oklahoma City: Official Response: Statements by the President and Attorney General," *New York Times*, April 20, 1995, B12.

3. Ibid.

4. David Johnston, "Lawyers Want Reno Barred from Death-Penalty Decision in Bombing," *New York Times*, July 25, 1995, A10.

5. Edward Walsh, "Once Arraigned, Two Undergo Questioning in Bombing as Death Toll Climbs," *Washington Post*, April 22, 1995, A1, A13.

6. Richard Willing and Kevin Johnson, "Will McVeigh Try to Save Himself?" *USA Today*, June 3, 1997, 1A.

7. Charles Linder, "A Political Verdict: McVeigh: When Death Is Not Enough," *Los Angeles Times*, June 8, 1997, M1, M3.

8. Robert Jackson, "The McVeigh Verdict," *Los Angeles Times*, June 3, 1997, A23, A24.

9. "Guilty on All Counts; Jury to Consider Death Penalty; McVeigh Convicted in Deaths of 8 in Oklahoma Bombing," *St. Louis Post Dispatch*, June 3, 1997, A1.

10. Michael Fleeman, "McVeigh: Guilty on All Counts, Death Penalty Eyed for Oklahoma Blast," *Toronto Star*, June 3, 1997, A1.

11. Tom Kenworthy and Lois Romano, "McVeigh Judge Limits Penalty Evidence," *Washington Post*, June 4, 1997, A1, A12. It is now relatively common for judges to allow videotaped presentations, pictures,

letters, stories, diary entries, even poetry as forms of victim impact evidence. See Wayne Logan, "Through the Past Darkly: A Survey of the Uses and Abuses of Victim Impact in Capital Trials," *Arizona Law Review* 41 (1999): 153.

12. Quoted in Eric Pooley, "Death or Life?" *Time*, June 16, 1997, 38.

13. Ibid.

14. "Judge Vows to Avoid McVeigh 'Lynching': Some Evidence to Be Barred from Sentence Hearing," *Toronto Star*, June 4, 1997, A3.

15. For a discussion of the effect of this testimony, see *U.S. v. McVeigh*, 153 F. 3d 1166, 1216–1221 (1998). As Judge Ebel put it in upholding the use of victim impact testimony in this case,

> The bombing of the Murrah Building was the deadliest act of domestic terrorism in the history of the United States. The magnitude of the crime cannot be ignored. It would be fundamentally unfair to shield a defendant from testimony describing the full effects of his deeds simply because he committed such an outrageous crime. The sheer number of actual victims and the horrific things done to them necessarily allows for the introduction of a greater amount of victim impact testimony in order for the government to show the "harm" caused by the crime. In addition, the jury could not have been shocked to learn that some victims had exemplary backgrounds and poignant family relationships, nor that they left behind grief-stricken loved ones.

16. "Prosecutor Urges Death for McVeigh," *Buffalo News*, June 4, 1997, 1A.

17. Ibid.

18. *U.S. v. McVeigh*, Reporter's Transcript, vol. 136, June 6, 1997, 12357.

19. Ibid., 12358.

20. The subsequent quotations from the trial's penalty phase are from Karen Roebuck, "Defense Tries to Spare McVeigh," *Houston Chronicle*, June 7, 1997, A1.

21. Rowland Nethaway, "Bombing Trial Produces Temporary Convert to Capital Punishment," *Tampa Tribune*, June 16, 1997, A7.

22. Sara Mehltretter, "In the Case of Timothy McVeigh, Death Was the Only Answer," *Buffalo News*, July 8, 1997, 5N.

23. Death Penalty Information Center, Washington, D.C., "Facts about the Death Penalty," April 30, 1999, 2.

24. See, for example, Michel Foucault, *Discipline and Punish: The Birth of the Prison*, trans. Alan Sheridan (New York: Vintage Books,

1977), and Norbert Elias, *The Civilizing Process*, trans. Edmund Jephcott (New York: Pantheon Books, 1982).

25. Abraham McLaughlin, "Across the U.S., New Doubts Surface on Death Penalty," *Christian Science Monitor*, February 24, 1999, 1. Also "The New Death Penalty Politics," *New York Times*, June 7, 2000, A22. Important examples of this reawakening include a February 1997 resolution of the American Bar Association calling for a moratorium on executions in the United States, a moratorium declared by the governor of Illinois (Dirk Johnson, "Illinois, Citing Faulty Verdicts, Bars Executions," *New York Times*, February 1, 2000, A1), opposition to state killing by important religious leaders (see Frank Bruni, "Cardinal Tells Police Officers of Perils of the Death Penalty," *New York Times*, March 25, 1996, City, B1, and Gustav Neibuhr, "Catholic Bishops Seek End to Death Penalty," *New York Times*, April 3, 1999, A1), and increased criticism from abroad (David Cole, "Defying World Law in the Angel Breard Case," *Legal Times*, April 27, 1998, 24, and John Goshko, "U.N. Panel Calls on U.S. to Halt Death Penalty," *Washington Post*, April 4, 1998, A2).

26. "Support for the death penalty is overwhelming, but recent Gallup polls have shown it slipping, from a peak of 80 percent in 1994, to 66 percent, its lowest point since 1978, when it was at 62 percent." Fox Butterfield, "Death Sentences Being Overturned in 2 of 3 Appeals," *New York Times*, June 12, 2000, A1. See Samuel Gross, "Update: American Public Opinion on the Death Penalty—It's Getting Personal," *Cornell Law Review* 83 (1998): 1448.

27. Phoebe Ellsworth and Samuel Gross, "Hardening of Attitudes: Americans' Views on the Death Penalty," *Journal of Social Issues* 50 (1994): 29.

28. Jonathan Simon, "Violence, Vengeance and Risk: Capital Punishment in the Neo-Liberal State" (unpublished manuscript, University of Miami, Miami, Fla., 1997), 13.

29. Stuart Banner, "Dangling between Heaven and Earth: A History of Capital Punishment in the United States" (unpublished prospectus, Washington University, St. Louis., Mo., 1999), 5.

30. See Barry Scheck, Peter Neufeld, and Jim Dwyer, *Actual Innocence* (New York: Doubleday, 2000). Also Butterfield, "Death Sentences Being Overturned in 2 of 3 Appeals."

31. On the nature of the criticism in the international arena, see Elizabeth Olson, "Good Friends Join Enemies to Criticize U.S. on Rights," *New York Times*, March 28, 1999, A1, and Kevin Cullen, " 'This Man

Must Not Die,' " *Boston Globe*, July 23, 2000, E1. On the persistence of state killing in America, see Franklin Zimring and Gordon Hawkins, *Capital Punishment and the American Agenda* (Cambridge: Cambridge University Press, 1986).

32. *Gregg v. Georgia*, 428 U.S. 153 (1976).

33. Robert Weisberg, "Deregulating Death," *Supreme Court Review* (1983): 305.

34. Samuel Gross, "The Romance of Revenge: Capital Punishment in America," *Studies in Law, Politics & Society* 13 (1993): 71. A recent newspaper article told of efforts by judges in the United States Court of Appeals for the Eleventh Circuit to remove some of the procedural barriers that defendants have used to slow down executions. See David Firestone, "Judges Criticized over Death-Penalty Conference," *New York Times*, August 19, 1999, National, A16.

35. The number of executions per year multiplied considerably during the 1990s, going from a low of fourteen in 1991 to a high of ninety-eight in 1999.

36. Sam Howe Verhovek, "As Texas Executions Mount, They Grow Routine," *New York Times*, May 25, 1997, A1.

37. See Michael Radelet and Hugo Adam Bedau, "The Execution of the Innocent," *Law and Contemporary Problems* 61 (Autumn 1998): 105. Also Samuel Gross, "Lost Lives: Miscarriages of Justice in Capital Cases," *Law and Contemporary Problems* 61 (Autumn 1998): 125. It is, of course, important to note that in a series of recent cases a number of death row inmates have had their convictions overturned on the basis of new DNA evidence. Leigh Bienen, "The Quality of Justice in Capital Cases: Illinois as a Case Study," *Law and Contemporary Problems* 61 (Autumn 1998): 193. Also Caitlin Lovinger, "Death Row's Living Alumni," *New York Times*, August 22, 1999, Sec. 4, p. 1.

38. Minow argues that, "Victim talk tends to invite more victim talk." See Martha Minow, "Surviving Victim Talk," *UCLA Law Review* 40 (1993): 1429.

39. "Characteristically the melodramatic plot . . . progressed through a struggle for clear moral identification of all protagonists and is finally resolved by public recognition of where guilt and innocence really lie." See Christine Gledhill, "The Melodramatic Field: An Investigation," in *Home Is Where the Heart Is: Studies in Melodrama and the Woman's Film*, ed. Christine Gledhill (London: British Film Institute, 1987), 30.

40. Minow, "Surviving Victim Talk," 1430.

41. See William Lyons and Stuart Scheingold, "The Politics of Crime and Punishment" (unpublished manuscript, University of Washington, Seattle, 1999), 23–24.

42. For the opposite case see Walter Berns, *For Capital Punishment: Crime and the Morality of the Death Penalty* (New York: Basic Books, 1979).

43. Reversibility is a procedural condition that itself reflects and posits a democratic vision of individuals as fallible.

44. Terry Aladjem, "Revenge and Consent: The Death Penalty and Lockean Principles of Democracy" (unpublished manuscript, Harvard University, Cambridge, Mass., 1990), 36. Robert Burt, "Democracy, Equality and the Death Penalty," in *The Rule of Law: Nomos XXXVI*, ed. Ian Shapiro (New York: New York University Press, 1994), 14.

45. Aladjem, "Revenge and Consent," 36. Also see Justice Brennan, in his concurring opinion in *Furman v. Georgia*, 408 U.S. 238, 270 (1972); Hugo Adam Bedau, "The Eighth Amendment, Dignity, and the Death Penalty," and, A. I. Meldren, "Dignity, Worth, and Rights," both in *The Constitution of Rights*, ed. Michael Meyer and William Parent (Ithaca: Cornell University Press, 1992), 145–77 and 29–46; and Jordan Paust, "Human Dignity as a Constitutional Right: A Jurisprudentially Based Inquiry into Criteria and Content," *Howard Law Journal* 27 (1984): 150.

46. Quoted in Louis Masur, *Rites of Execution. Capital Punishment and the Transformation of American Culture, 1776–1865* (New York: Oxford University Press, 1989), 65.

47. See Simon, "Violence, Vengeance, and Risk," 10. Also see Elaine Scarry, "The Declaration of War: Constitutional and Unconstitutional Violence," in *Law's Violence*, ed. Austin Sarat and Thomas R. Kearns (Ann Arbor: University of Michigan Press, 1992), 23–76, and Giorgio Agamben, *Homo Sacer: Sovereign Power and Bare Life*, trans. Daniel Heller-Roazen (Stanford: Stanford University Press, 1998), 142.

48. Jonathan Simon, "Governing through Crime," in *The Crime Conundrum: Essays on Criminal Justice*, ed. Lawrence Friedman and George Fisher (Boulder, Colo.: Westview Press, 1997), 171–90.

49. For a useful discussion of the politicization of capital punishment, see John Bessler, *Death in the Dark: Midnight Executions in America* (Boston: Northeastern University Press, 1997) chap. 6.

50. Simon, "Violence, Vengeance, and Risk," 1.

51. Michael Tonry, *Malign Neglect: Race, Crime, and Punishment in America* (New York: Oxford University Press, 1995).

52. John McAdams, "Racial Disparity and the Death Penalty," *Law and Contemporary Problems* 61 (Autumn 1998): 153. Also Stephen Carter, "When Victims Happen to Be Black," *Yale Law Journal* 97 (1988): 420.

53. Death Penalty Information Center, "Facts about the Death Penalty," April 30, 1999, 2.

54. Jonathan Simon, "Governing through Crime in a Democratic Society" (unpublished manuscript, School of Law, University of Miami, Miami, Fla., 1997), 15.

55. Habeas corpus literally translated means to produce the body. In law habeas proceedings allow constitutional challenges to be mounted even after someone has exhausted their procedural appeals.

56. Simon, "Violence, Vengeance, and Risk," 15–17. Also Nikolas Rose, *Powers of Freedom*. (Cambridge: Cambridge University Press, 1999), chap. 4.

57. As a result, we become what Berlant calls "infantile citizens." In this version of citizenship, "a citizen is defined as a person traumatized by some aspect of life in the United States. Portraits and stories of citizen-victims . . . now permeate the political public sphere." See Lauren Berlant, *The Queen of America Goes to Washington City: Essays on Sex and Citizenship* (Durham, N.C.: Duke University Press, 1997).

58. Quoted in Simon, "Violence, Vengeance, and Risk," 20.

59. See Judge Stephen Reinhardt, "The Supreme Court, the Death Penalty, and the *Harris* Case," *Yale Law Journal* 102 (1992): 205. Also Evan Caminker and Erwin Chemrinsky, "The Lawless Execution of Robert Alton Harris," *Yale Law Journal* 102 (1992): 225.

60. Beneath the headline "After Night of Court Battles, a California Execution" the April 22, 1992, edition of the *New York Times* (see A1) reported the tangled maze of last-minute legal maneuvers that immediately preceded Harris's death in California's gas chamber. As in many previous executions, the hope for clemency or the possibility of a stay of execution was pursued until the last minute.

61. The Court scolded Harris's lawyers for "abusive delay which has been compounded by last minute attempts to manipulate the judicial process" (*New York Times*, April 22, 1992, A1, A22). Rehnquist's interest in finality in the context of capital punishment displays a procedural disposition that is obviously quite at odds with the vision of reversibility that I have suggested is crucial in democratic politics. It is a vestige of an older, antidemocratic conception of sovereignty. For another statement of Rehnquist's position, see *Herrera v. Collins*, 506 U.S. 390 (1993).

62. For example, *Teague v. Lane*, 489 U.S. 288 (1989), and *Penry v. Lynaugh*, 492 U.S. 302 (1989).

63. Pub. L. No. 104–132, 110 Stat. 1214 (1996).

64. See Harvey Berkman, "Costs Mount for Indigent Defense," *National Law Journal* (August 7, 1995), A18.

65. The linguistic, representational violence of the law is inseparable from its literal, physical violence. For discussions of this claim, see Peter Fitzpatrick, "Violence and Legal Subjection" (unpublished manuscript, University of London, 1991), 1, and Robert Paul Wolff, "Violence and the Law," in *The Rule of Law*, ed. Robert Paul Wolff (New York: Simon and Schuster, 1971), 55.

66. Jacques Derrida, "The Force of Law: The 'Mystical Foundations of Authority,'" *Cardozo Law Review* 11 (1990): 927.

67. David Garland, "Punishment and Culture: The Symbolic Dimension of Criminal Justice," *Studies in Law, Politics & Society* 11 (1991): 191.

68. Ibid., 193, 195.

69. See Lawrence Friedman, *Crime and Punishment in American History* (New York: Basic Books, 1993), 445–48.

70. Michael Madow, "Forbidden Spectacle: Executions, the Public, and the Press in Nineteenth Century New York," *Buffalo Law Review* 43 (1995): 461.

71. Writing about the end of public executions in the mid-nineteenth century Masur notes that it "marked the triumph of a certain code of conduct and set of social attitudes among the middle and upper classes; it symbolized a broader trend toward social privatization and class segmentation; it turned the execution of criminals into an elite event centered around class and gender exclusion rather than communal instruction." See Masur, *Rites of Execution*, 6.

72. Lyons and Scheingold describe what they call a "top-down" explanation of the contemporary politics of punishment, with politicians precipitating, as much as responding to, anxieties about crime. See "The Politics of Crime and Punishment," 13.

73. Stuart Scheingold, Toska Olson, and Jana Pershing, "Sexual Violence, Victim Advocacy, and Republican Criminology: Washington State's Community Protection Act," *Law & Society Review* 28 (1994): 731. Also Kathleen Daly, "Men's Violence, Victim Advocacy, and Feminist Redress," *Law & Society Review* 28 (1994): 779.

74. For a useful discussion of sentimentality in narrative, see Jane Tompkins, *Sensational Designs: The Cultural Work of American Fic-*

tion, 1790–1860 (New York: Oxford University Press, 1985). The role of the sentimental story in criminal trials is described by Laura Hanft Korobkin, "The Maintenance of Mutual Confidence: Sentimental Strategies at the Adultery Trial of Henry Ward Beecher," *Yale Journal of Law & the Humanities* 7 (1995): 1. In making this argument about sentimentality as a basic mode of storytelling in capital trials, I agree with Korobkin that "Trial process as a whole . . . can never enact the unidimensional morality of sentimental fiction or melodrama, because it encompasses not only the necessarily opposing narratives of both parties, but the testimony of witnesses who often refuse to follow their lawyer-directed scripts" (45).

CHAPTER 2
THE RETURN OF REVENGE

1. See George Fletcher, *With Justice for Some: Victims' Rights in Criminal Trials* (Reading, Mass.: Addison-Wesley, 1995). Also Lois Forer, *Criminals and Victims* (New York: Norton, 1980).

2. "Hard on the heels of the civil rights movement, the women's liberation movement, and the movement to expand the rights of criminal suspects, the victims' rights movement burst on the scene in the early 1970s and quickly became a potent political force. Part backlash against what it considered the pro-defendant romanticism of the 1960s, the victims' rights movement was also a spiritual heir to the '60s ethos. With its suspicion of bureaucratic government and its concern for the disempowered, the victims' rights movement spoke for the 'forgotten' men and women of the criminal justice system." See Stephen Schulhofer, "The Trouble with Trials: The Trouble with Us," *Yale Law Journal* 105 (1995): 825. Also David Roland, "Progress in the Victim Reform Movement: No Longer the 'Forgotten Victim,' " *Pepperdine Law Review* 17 (1989): 35, and Stuart Scheingold, Toska Olson, and Jana Pershing, "Sexual Violence, Victim Advocacy, and Republican Criminology: Washington State's Community Protection Act," *Law & Society Review* 28 (1994): 736.

3. In 1981 President Reagan proclaimed the week of April 19 the first "National Victims' Rights Week." See Proclamation No. 4831, 3 C.F.R. 18 (1982). The president has proclaimed a Crime Victims Week annually since. Legislation now exists that grants victims a role in the plea bar-

gaining process and in sentencing decisions as well as a right to be notified about the release of the offenders who victimized them. See Leroy Lamborn, "Victim Participation in the Criminal Justice Process: The Proposal for a Constitutional Amendment," *Wayne Law Review* 34 (1987): 125. Moreover, "Today, the constitutions of at least 20 states now contain 'victim's rights amendments,' and similar legislation has been introduced at the federal level." Wayne Logan, "Through the Past Darkly: A Survey of the Uses and Abuses of Victim Impact in Capital Trials," *Arizona Law Review* 41 (1999): 144, n. 4. See also Maureen McLoed, "Victim Participation at Sentencing," *Criminal Law Bulletin* 22 (1986): 501; Frank Carrington and George Nicholson, "The Victims' Movement: An Idea Whose Time Has Come," *Pepperdine Law Review* 11 (1984): 1; and Lynne Henderson, "The Wrongs of Victim's Rights," *Stanford Law Review* 37 (1985): 937.

4. Nowhere was this fact more apparent than in prosecutor Marcia Clark's closing argument in the murder trial of O. J. Simpson. "Usually," Clark said in one of the most watched events in the history of the American legal system "I feel like I'm the only one left to speak for the victims. But in this case, Ron and Nicole, they're speaking to you. They're speaking to you. And they're telling you who murdered them. . . . And they both are telling you who did it with their hair, their clothes, their bodies, their blood. They tell you he did it. He did it. Mr. Simpson, Orenthal James Simpson, he did it. They told you in the only way they can. Will you hear them? Or will you ignore their plea for justice? Or as Nicole said to Detective Edwards, 'You never do anything about him.' Will you?"

5. Scheingold, Olson, and Pershing, "Sexual Violence, Victim Advocacy, and Republican Criminology," 734.

6. Wendy Kaminer, *It's All the Rage: Crime and Culture* (Reading, Mass.: Addison-Wesley, 1995). "To a victim," Kaminer writes, "the notion that crimes are committed against society, making the community the injured party, can seem both bizarre and insulting: it can make them feel invisible, unavenged, and unprotected" (75). See also Angela Harris, "The Jurisprudence of Victimhood," *Supreme Court Review* (1991): 77, and Susan Bandes, "Empathy, Narrative, and Victim Impact Statements," *University of Chicago Law Review* 63 (1996): 361.

7. Terry Aladjem, "Vengeance and Democratic Justice: American Culture and the Limits of Punishment" (unpublished manuscript, Harvard University, Cambridge, 1992), 3.

8. Jennifer Culbert, "The Body in *Payne*: The Rhetoric of Victims' Rights and the Predicament of Judgment" (paper presented to the 1995 annual meeting of the Law and Society Association, Toronto), 8.

9. Marianne Constable, "Reflections on Law as a Profession of Words," in *Justice and Power in Sociolegal Studies*, ed. Bryant Garth and Austin Sarat (Evanston: Northwestern University Press, 1998), 26.

10. *Payne v. Tennessee*, 501 U.S. 808.

11. Paul Gewirtz, "Victims and Voyeurs: Two Narrative Problems at the Criminal Trial," in *Law's Stories: Narrative and Rhetoric in the Law*, ed. Peter Brooks and Paul Gewirtz (New Haven: Yale University Press, 1996), 135–61. As Dubber observes, "In the past capital sentencing pitted the defendant against the State. . . . In the new paradigmatic sentencing hearing, the capital defendant now encounters an even more formidable opponent: the person whose death made her eligible for the death penalty, the capital victim." Markus Dubber, "Regulating the Tender Heart When the Axe Is Ready to Strike," *Buffalo Law Review* 41 (1993): 86.

12. *Booth v. Maryland*, 482 U.S. 496 (1987).

13. Scheingold, Olson, and Pershing, "Sexual Violence, Victim Advocacy, and Republican Criminology," 734.

14. As the cultural critic Lauren Berlant notes, the result is to produce a "special form of tyranny that makes citizens like children, infantilized, passive, and over dependent on the 'immense and tutelary power' of the state." Lauren Berlant, *The Queen of America Goes to Washington City: Essays on Sex and Citizenship* (Durham, N.C.: Duke University Press, 1997), 27.

15. In one sense it can be said that revenge never left the death penalty since state killing of its citizens, some would contend, is always vengeance pure and simple. Both critics and supporters agree that this is the case. Thus Camus says, "Let us call it by the name, for lack of any other nobility, will at least give the nobility of the truth, and let us recognize it for what it is essentially: a revenge. . . . It is a quasi-arithmetical reply made by society to whoever breaks its primordial law. That reply is as old as man; it is called the law of retaliation." Albert Camus, "Reflections on the Guillotine," in Albert Camus and Arthur Koestler, *Reflections on Capital Punishment* (Paris: Calmann-Levy, 1957), 236. Walter Berns, an ardent defender of the death penalty, notes, "Shakespeare shows us vengeful men because there is something in the souls of men— men then and men now—that requires . . . crimes to be revenged. Can we imagine a world that does not take its revenge on the man who kills

Macduff's wife and children?. . . Can we imagine a world that does not hate murderers?" Walter Berns, *For Capital Punishment: Crime and the Morality of the Death Penalty* (New York: Basic Books, 1979), 168.

16. *Furman v. Georgia*, 408 U.S. 238 (1972).

17. Margaret Radin, "Cruel Punishment and Respect for Persons: Super Due Process for Death," *Southern California Law Review* 53 (1980): 1143. In recent years, the Supreme Court has gradually cut back on super due process by restricting the availability of federal habeas corpus relief in death penalty cases. See Franklin Zimring, "Inheriting the Wind: The Supreme Court and Capital Punishment in the 1990s," *Florida State University Law Review* 20 (1992): 7.

So hostile have the courts become to extended litigation in capital cases that even new evidence of actual innocence has been found to be inadequate as the basis for challenging a death sentence. See *Herrera v. Collins*, 506 U.S. 390 (1993). In response to *Herrera*, Justice Blackmun charged the Court with coming "perilously close to murder." For the current Supreme Court "finality is more important than hearing every meritorious legal claim; there simply comes a point when legal proceedings must end and punishment must be imposed." See Evan Caminker and Erwin Chemrinsky, "The Lawless Execution of Robert Alton Harris," *Yale Law Journal* 102 (1992): 226: "The Court's desire to expedite the process of death . . . has now accrued a life of its own" (253). Also Joseph Hoffman, "Is Innocence Sufficient? An Essay on the United States Supreme Court's Continuing Problems with Federal Habeas Corpus and the Death Penalty," *Indiana Law Review* 68 (1993): 817.

18. "The official anti-vengeance discourse has a long history beginning with the Stoics, taken-up and elaborated by medieval churchmen, and later by the architects of state building. Revenge is still a kind of *eminence grise* in the 17th and 18th century classic texts of liberal moral and political philosophy." William Miller, "Clint Eastwood and Equity: The Virtues of Revenge and the Shortcomings of Law in Popular Culture," in *Law and the Domains of Culture*, ed. Austin Sarat and Thomas Kearns (Ann Arbor: University of Michigan Press, 1998), 161.

19. See Matthew Pauley, "The Jurisprudence of Crime and Punishment from Plato to Hegel," *American Journal of Jurisprudence* 39 (1994): 97.

20. See Susan Jacoby, *Wild Justice: The Evolution of Revenge* (New York: Harper & Row, 1983), 115.

21. Jacoby notes that, "Justice is a legitimate concept in the modern code of civilized behavior. Vengeance is not. We prefer to avert our eyes

from those who persist in reminding us of the wrongs they have suffered. . . . Such people are disturbers of the peace; we wish they would
take their memories away to a church, a cemetery, a psychotherapist's
office and allow us to return justice and vengeance to the separate com-
partments they supposedly occupy in twentieth-century life." Ibid. 2–
3. Also Francis Bacon, "Of Revenge," in *Selected Writings* (New York:
Modern Library, 1955).

22. See Jeffrie Murphy, "Getting Even: The Role of the Victim," *Social Philosophy and Policy* 7 (1990): 216. Also Jeffrie Murphy and Jean
Hampton, *Forgiveness and Mercy* (Cambridge: Cambridge University
Press, 1988). As St. Augustine put it, "We do not wish to have the sufferings of the servants of God avenged by the infliction of precisely similar
injuries in the way of retaliation. . . . our desire is that justice be satisfied. . . . who does not see that a restraint is put upon the boldness of
savage violence, and the remedies fitted to produce repentance are not
withdrawn, the discipline should be called a benefit rather than a vindictive punishment." St. Augustine, *The Writings of St. Augustine* (New
York: Fathers of the Church, 1947), 168–69.

23. See Miller, "Clint Eastwood and Equity," 162, 163.

24. Quoted in J. Ferrer, *Crimes and Punishments* (London: Chatto &
Windus, 1880), 190.

25. For a particularly interesting example, see Jon Elster, "Norms of
Revenge," *Ethics* 100 (1990): 862.

26. Jonathan Reider, "The Social Organization of Vengeance," in *Toward a General Theory of Social Control*, ed. Donald Black (New York:
Academic Press, 1984), 131–63. Also William Miller, *Bloodtaking and
Peacemaking: Feud, Law, and Society in Saga Iceland* (Chicago: University of Chicago Press, 1990), chap. 6.

27. Judith Shklar, *The Faces of Injustice* (New Haven: Yale University
Press, 1990), 93.

28. Ibid., 94.

29. See Robert Nozick, *Philosophical Explanations* (Cambridge: Harvard University Press, 1981). See also Hugo Adam Bedau, "Retribution
and the Theory of Punishment," *Journal of Philosophy* 75 (1978): 601;
John Cottingham, "Varieties of Retribution," *Philosophical Quarterly*
29 (1979): 241; and Joel Feinberg, *Doing and Deserving* (Princeton:
Princeton University Press, 1970).

30. Nozick, *Philosophical Explanations*, 366.

31. Miller, "Clint Eastwood and Equity," 166.

32. Nozick, *Philosophical Explanations*, 367.

33. Miller, "Clint Eastwood and Equity," 175.

34. Nozick, *Philosophical Explanations*, 367.

35. Ibid.

36. Ibid.

37. Ibid., 368.

38. Shklar, *The Faces of Injustice*, 93.

39. See William Connolly, *Identity/Difference: Democratic Negotiations of Political Paradox* (Ithaca: Cornell University Press, 1991), chap. 6.

40. Michel Foucault, *Power/Knowledge*, ed. Colin Gordon (New York: Pantheon, 1972), 80.

41. Aladjem, "Vengeance and Democratic Justice," 8. Robert Solomon contends that vengeance arises from "a primal sense of the moral sense and its boundaries. . . . Not to feel vengeance may therefore not be a sign of virtue but a symptom of callousness and withdrawal." *Passion for Justice: Emotions and the Origins of the Social Contract* (Reading, Mass.: Addison-Wesley, 1990), 41.

42. Culbert, "The Body in *Payne*," 3.

43. See Richard Murphy, "The Significance of Victim Harm: *Booth v. Maryland* and the Philosophy of Punishment in the Supreme Court," *University of Chicago Law Review* 55 (1988): 1303.

44. To some extent the full force of the victim impact statement is blunted when it is reported in a third-person account. To take but one contrasting example, the 1995 trial of Colin Ferguson for murdering commuters on the Long Island Railroad provides a more compelling version of the genre of the victim impact statement. "I know I have an impossible request, Your Honor. But given five minutes alone with Colin Ferguson, this coward would know the meaning of suffering. . . . (To Ferguson): Look at these eyes. You can't look at 'em, right? You can't. You remember these eyes. You're nothing but a piece of garbage. You're a (expletive) animal. Five minutes. That's all I need with you. Five minutes," said Robert Giugliano, who was one of Ferguson's victims. Quoted in Jeffrey Rosen, "Victims and the Interest of Justice," *San Diego Union-Tribune*, March 31, 1995, B5.

45. See *Booth*, 512.

46. Aladjem, "Vengeance and Democratic Justice," 26.

47. "Probably the most controversial type of information a victim could provide . . . is the victim's opinion of the defendant and what sentence the defendant should receive. . . . Victim opinion is probably the type of victim information that proponents of victim participation at

sentencing most want to be allowed in sentencing proceedings. Asking for a victim's opinion best recognizes his dignity and his role in the prosecution and punishment of the defendant. However, the victim's opinion may be the most inflammatory and prejudicial evidence the victim could provide." See Phillip Talbert, "The Relevance of Victim Impact Statements to the Criminal Sentencing Decision," *UCLA Law Review* 36 (1988): 210.

48. *Booth*, 504.

49. Ibid., 505.

50. Powell limited his holding to capital cases. He noted that "our disapproval of victim impact statements at the sentencing phase of a capital case does not mean, however, that this type of information will never be relevant . . . in a non-capital criminal trial. . . . We note . . . that our decision today is guided by the fact that death is a punishment different from all other sanctions . . . and that therefore the considerations that inform the sentencing decisions may be different from those that might be relevant to other liability or punishment determinations." Ibid., 507, 509, n. 10 and 12.

51. Ibid.

52. Ibid., 509, 508.

53. Ibid., 516, 518, 516.

54. Ibid., 517.

55. Ibid., 520. See also Steven Gey, "Justice Scalia's Death Penalty," *Florida State University Law Review* 20 (1992): 121.

56. *Booth*, 520.

57. Gey, "Justice Scalia's Death Penalty" 69.

58. *Payne*, 814–815.

59. Ibid., 815, 820, 825.

60. Ibid., 822, 825, 827.

61. Culbert, "The Body in *Payne*," 9–10.

62. *Payne*, 831.

63. Ibid., 832.

64. Ibid., 833, 834.

65. Gey, "Justice Scalia's Death Penalty," 125–26.

66. *Payne*, 837–38.

67. Ibid., 859, 864.

68. Ibid. 867. As Judge Cole put it in *Lodowski v. State*, 490 A. 2d, 1228, 1277 (1985), the very purpose of victim input seems to be to allow victims to plead for their "pound of flesh . . ., but the halls of justice

should not be the forum by which their cries for vengeance should be heard."

69. *Payne*, 861, 856.

70. Ibid., 834.

71. In Kaminer's view the call to hear the voice of the victim "partakes of a popular confusion of law and therapy and the substitution of feelings for facts. But if feelings are facts in a therapist's office . . . feelings are prejudices in a court of law. . . . Justice is not a form of therapy, meaning that what is helpful to a particular victim . . . is not necessarily just and what is just may not be therapeutic." See *It's All the Rage*, 84. See also Vivien Berger, "*Payne* and Suffering—A Personal Reflection and a Victim-Centered Critique," *Florida State University Law Review* 20 (1992): 59.

72. For a useful discussion of the difficulty of containing *Payne* and a careful assessment of the jurisprudence of victim impact statements post-*Payne*, see Logan, "Through the Past Darkly."

73. *Payne*, 844, 852, 856.

74. Rene Girard, *Violence and the Sacred* (Baltimore: Johns Hopkins University Press, 1989), 13–15.

75. Defending the use of victim impact evidence in capital trials, Paul Cassell claims that such evidence does not divert sentencers from their focus on the moral culpability of the offender and that without testimony from surviving family members judges and juries cannot adequately assess that culpability. See Paul Cassell, "Barbarians at the Gates? A Reply to the Critics of the Victims' Rights Amendment," *Utah Law Review* (1999): 479.

76. Oliver Wendell Holmes, *The Common Law* (Boston: Little, Brown, 1909), 45.

77 For a discussion of this belief, see Michael Tonry, *Malign Neglect: Race, Crime, and Punishment in America* (New York: Oxford University Press, 1995).

78. Martha Minow "Surviving Victim Talk, " *UCLA Law Review* 40 (1993): 1432.

79. Culbert, "The Body in *Payne*," 2.

80. See Judith Shklar, "The Liberalism of Fear," in *Liberalism and the Moral Life*, ed. Nancy Rosenblum (Cambridge: Harvard University Press, 1989), 21–38.

81. Holmes, *The Common Law*, 45.

82. As Dubber puts it, we now have a criminal justice system that "has thrown up its hands in frustration with its inability to accommo-

date all relevant interests within a framework of meaningful rules." See "Regulating the Tender Heart When the Axe Is Ready to Strike," 155.

83. See Cesare Beccaria-Bonesana, *An Essay on Crimes and Punishments*, trans. Edward Ingraham (Philadelphia: Philip H. Nicklin, 1819), 104–6.

84. *Payne*, 867.

CHAPTER 3
KILLING ME SOFTLY

1. See, for example, "Flames Erupt during Florida Execution: Gruesome Scene Renews Debate on Electrocutions," *USA Today*, March 26, 1997, A3.

2. "Flames Erupt in Electric Chair's Death Jolt; Execution: Fire Shoots from Florida Man's Head, Renewing Capital Punishment Debate," *Los Angeles Times*, March 26, 1997, A1.

3. "Retire 'Chair,' Use Lethal Injection," *Sun-Sentinel* (Ft. Lauderdale, Fla.), March 26, 1997, A22.

4. "Inmate Catches Fire in Florida Electric Chair: 'You Could Smell the Acrid Smoke'" *Houston Chronicle*, March 26, 1997, A6.

5. See *Jones v. Butterworth*, 701 So. 2d 76, 77 (1997).

6. "Inmate Catches Fire," A6.

7. "Retire 'Chair,' Use Lethal Injection," A22.

8. See "Botched, Gruesome Electrocutions Mandate Switch to Lethal Injections," *Sun-Sentinel*, June 30, 1997, A8. Prompted by a case brought to the United States Supreme Court challenging the constitutionality of electrocution, in January 2000 the Florida legislature made lethal injection the default method of execution in that state. As a result of the legislature's actions, the Supreme Court dismissed the case.

9. Ibid.

10. *Provenzano v. Moore*, Case No. 95, 973, Corrected Opinion (September 24, 1999), Supreme Court of Florida, 56.

11. Quoted in the dissenting opinion of Justice Shaw in *Provenzano v. Moore*, 57.

12. Electrocution will be used in Florida only on the written request of those condemned to die.

13. See Robert Johnson, *Death Work: A Study of the Modern Execution Process* (Pacific Grove, Calif.: Brooks/Cole Publishing, 1990).

14. There are, of course, some exceptions. Periodically controversy arises about the appropriateness or meaning of particular executions. Thus the very public discussion of the execution of Karla Faye Tucker, the first woman executed in the twentieth century in Texas, focused on the question of whether her apparently deep and sincere postconviction religious conversion should be considered in deciding whether to spare her life as well as on the question of why so few women are executed in the United States. See Rene Heberle, "Disciplining Gender: Or, Are Women Getting Away with Murder," *Signs* 24 (1999): 1103.

15. Abernathy argues that "contrary to what logic seems to dictate, the attempt over time has been to make the penalty of death gentle, hidden, and antiseptic." See Jonathan Abernathy, "The Methodology of Death: Reexamining the Deterrence Rationale," *Columbia Human Rights Law Review* 27 (1996): 422.

16. "Those Left Grief-Stricken by Bombing Cry for Vengeance," *St. Louis Post-Dispatch*, June 4, 1997, A1.

17. "The Executioner's Weapons: After a Man Is Burned Alive in Florida's Electric Chair, the 'New' Death Penalty Debate Focuses on the Manner in Which the Condemned Are Put to Death," *Buffalo News*, November 9, 1997, H1, quoting columnist Leonard Pitts.

18. Thomas Metzger, *Blood and Volts: Edison, Tesla, and the Electric Chair* (Brooklyn, N.Y. : Autonomedia, 1996).

19. See Allen Huang, "Hanging, Cyanide Gas, and the Evolving Standards of Decency: The Ninth Circuit's Misapplication of the Cruel and Unusual Clause of the Eighth Amendment," *Oregon Law Review* 74 (1995): 995.

20. Dissenting opinion by Justice Shaw in *Jones v. Butterworth*, 87.

21. Judge Reinhardt dissenting in *Campbell v. Wood*, 18 F. 3d 662, 701 (1994).

22. Michel Foucault, *Discipline and Punish: The Birth of the Prison*, trans. Alan Sheridan (New York: Vintage Books, 1977), 50.

23. Petrus Spierenburg, *The Spectacle of Suffering* (Cambridge: Cambridge University Press, 1984). Also V.A.C. Gatrell, *The Hanging Tree: Execution and the English People, 1770–1868* (New York: Oxford University Press, 1994), chap. 2.

24. Foucault, *Discipline and Punish*, 48–49.

25. Ibid., 58.

26. See Johnson, *Death Work*, 5. Also Susan Blaustein, "Witness to Another Execution," *Harper's*, May 1994, 53, and Richard Trombley,

The Execution Protocol: Inside America's Capital Punishment Industry (New York: Crown Publishers, 1992).

27. See Hugo Adam Bedau, *The Death Penalty in America* (New York: Oxford University Press, 1982), 13.

28. Michael Madow, "Forbidden Spectacle: Executions, the Public and the Press in Nineteenth-Century New York," *Buffalo Law Review* 43 (1995): 466, 469.

29. Huang, "Hanging, Cyanide Gas," 997.

30. Ian Gray, ed. *A Punishment in Search of a Crime: Americans Speak Out against the Death Sentence* (New York: Avon Books, 1989), 19–20.

31. The numbers add up to more than thirty-eight (the number of states using capital punishment) because statutes often permit more than one means of execution.

32. See *In re Kemmler*, 136 U.S. 436, 444 (1890).

33. Abernathy, "The Methodology of Death," 404.

34. William Bowers with Glenn L. Pierce and John F. McDevitt, *Legal Homicide: Death as Punishment in America, 1864–1982* (Boston: Northeastern University Press, 1984), 12.

35. See *Hill v. Lockhart*, 791 F. Supp. 1388, 1394 (1992). See also *Ex Parte Kenneth Granviel*, 561 S.W. 2d 503, 513 (1978). The court found that "The Texas Legislature substituted death by lethal injection as a means of execution in lieu of electrocution for the reason it would be a more humane and less spectacular form of execution." As Justice Anstead argued in *Provenzano*, "Just as electrocution may have been originally evaluated in comparison with hanging, we know today that the overwhelming majority of death penalty jurisdictions have long since rejected use of the electric chair and have turned to lethal injection as a more humane punishment" (70–71).

36. Kristina Beard, "Five under the Eighth: Methodology Review and the Cruel and Unusual Punishments Clause," *University of Miami Law Review* 51 (1997): 445.

37. *Wilkinson v. Utah*, 99 U.S. 130 (1878).

38. *In re Kemmler*, 136 U.S. 436 (1890).

39. Ibid., 447.

40. See Giorgio Agamben, *Homo Sacer: Sovereign Power and Bare Life*, trans. Daniel Heller-Roazen, (Stanford: Stanford University Press, 1998), 83. Also Peter Fitzpatrick, " 'Always More to Do': Capital Punishment and the (De)Composition of Law," in *The Killing State: Capital*

Punishment in Law, Politics, and Culture, ed. Austin Sarat (New York: Oxford University Press, 1999), 128–29.

41. *Francis v. Resweber*, 329 U.S. 459 (1947). For an interesting description of the case, see Arthur Miller and Jeffrey Bowman, *Death by Installments: The Ordeal of Willie Francis* (Westport, Conn.: Greenwood Press, 1988).

42. See *Francis*, 460, n. 12.

43. Francis also alleged that a second execution would violate the due process clause of the Fourteenth Amendment. Ibid., 462.

44. Indeed Willie Francis makes virtually no appearance in Reed's opinion. We learn little about him except that he was a "colored citizen of Louisiana." Ibid., 460. Neglect of the life experiences and feelings of the people whose fate is decided by law is characteristic of a wide range of legal decisions. See John Noonan, *Persons and Masks of the Law* (New York: Farrar, Straus and Giroux, 1976).

45. *Francis*, 464.

46. Ibid.

47. Ibid., 462, 464.

48. Ibid., 480, n. 2; 481 n. 2.

49. Ibid., 474.

50. See Alan Hyde, *Bodies of Law* (Princeton: Princeton University Press, 1997), chap. 11. Also Austin Sarat, ed., *Pain, Death, and the Law* (Ann Arbor: University of Michigan Press), forthcoming.

51. *Campbell*, 662.

52. *Fierro v. Gomez*, 865 F. Supp. 1387 (1994).

53. Case No. 95, 973, Corrected Opinion (September 24, 1999), Supreme Court of Florida.

54. *Campbell*, 682.

55. For a discussion of the hearing claiming that "the question of whether hanging is a form of cruel and unusual punishment is curiously absent," see Timothy Kaufman-Osborne, "The Metaphysics of the Hangman," *Studies in Law, Politics, and Society* 20 (2000): 35.

56. *Campbell*, 683.

57. Ibid., 683, 684, 687.

58. Ibid., 693.

59. Ibid., 701, 708.

60. Ibid., 702.

61. Ibid., 712.

62. *Fierro*, 1391, 1413, 1407.

63. Ibid., 1410–11, 1412.

64. Ibid., 1396, 1398.

65. Ibid., 1401.

66. Ibid., 1400.

67. Ibid., 1403, 1404.

68. This approach was recently followed in another case that found lethal gas to be unconstitutional in Arizona. See *LaGrand v. Stewart*, 173 F. 3d 1144 (1999).

69. Case No. 95, 973, Corrected Opinion (September 24, 1999), Supreme Court of Florida. This case is only one of a several recent cases in which Florida courts were confronted with challenges to electrocution. See, for example, *Jones* and *Buenoano v. State*, 565 So. 2d 309 (1990).

70. *Provenzano*, 3, 4.

71. Ibid., 34.

72. Ibid., 38, 43.

73. Ibid., 47, 51, 52.

74. As I will suggest later in the book (see especially chapters 7 and 8), turning to the visual does not resolve these problems. Indeed the seeming "transparency" of photographs of death creates its own difficulties.

75. Elaine Scarry, *The Body in Pain: The Making and Unmaking of the World* (New York: Oxford University Press, 1995), 3.

76. Ibid., 4. For an insightful criticism of Scarry's view of the nature of pain and its relation to language, see Timothy Kaufman-Osborn, "What the Law Must Not Hear: On Capital Punishment and the Voice of Pain," in Sarat, *Pain, Death, and the Law.*

77. Ibid., 6.

78. Ibid., 13, 15.

79. The movement from representing death to representing pain as the touchstone in judicial considerations of methods of executions may be less clear than I have so far made it out to be. Pain, as Scarry reminds us, is frequently used as a "symbolic substitute for death." Ibid., 31. She argues that the world-destroying experience of physical pain is an imaginative substitute for "what is unfeelable in death." Pain and death are, she suggests, "the most intense forms of negation, the purest expression of the anti-human, of annihilation, of total aversiveness, though one is an absence and the other a felt presence." In her view, then, when the courts speak about pain, they are neither eliding nor displacing the

subject of death. They are speaking to, and about it, in one of the most powerful ways available to human language.

80. Hyde, *Bodies of Law*, 192, 193, 194.

81. As Abernathy puts it, "the shifts from public to private executions and toward more humane means of killing have been designed to comfort the punisher, not the condemned" ("The Methodology of Death," 423). Alternatively they may be explained as efforts to reduce administrative inconveniences associated with continued use of methods of state killing not at the cutting edge of technologies for taking life. As Judge Harding noted when he called on the Florida legislature to authorize lethal injection, "Florida death row inmates almost routinely challenge electrocution as a cruel and unusual punishment. . . . Such challenges consume an inordinate amount of the time and resources expended by inmates' counsel, State counsel, and judicial personnel. Furthermore, each time an execution is carried out, the courts wait in dread anticipation of some 'unforeseeable accident' that will set in motion a frenzy of inmate petitions and other filings." *Provenzano*, 9, 10.

82. *Callins v. Collins*, 510 U.S. 1141, 1145, 1142 (1994).

83. *Provenzano*, 65.

84. Walter Benjamin, "Critique of Violence," *Reflections: Essays, Aphorisms and Autobiographical Writing*, trans. Edmund Jephcott (New York: Schocken Books, 1986).

CHAPTER 4
CAPITAL TRIALS AND THE ORDINARY WORLD OF STATE KILLING

1. For another description of the Brooks case, see William McFeely, *Proximity to Death* (New York: Norton, 1999).

2. In trials, Korobkin argues, "Lawyers inevitably, and often unconsciously, draw on the story-forms most familiar and powerful within the culture at the time. They do so, moreover, not just to make their clients' claims neatly coherent and thus 'tellable,' but to evoke the specific and predictable responses that jurors will have already learned to make *as readers* to stock characters and situations in familiar romances, farces, or sentimental tragedies." Laura Hanft Korobkin, "The Maintenance of Mutual Confidence: Sentimental Strategies at the Adultery Trial of Henry Ward Beecher," *Yale Journal of Law & the Humanities* 7 (1995): 13.

3. Robert Cover, "Violence and the Word," *Yale Law Journal* 95 (1986): 1601.

4. On the nature of this doubt see Walter Benjamin, "Critique of Violence," in Walter Benjamin, *Reflections: Essays, Aphorisms and Autobiographical Writing*, trans. Edmund Jepchott (New York: Schocken Books, 1986) and Jacques Derrida, "Force of Law: The 'Mystical Foundation of Authority,' " *Cardozo Law Review* 11 (1990): 925.

5. This argument is developed by Stephen Bright, "Counsel for the Poor: The Death Sentence Not for the Worst Crime but for the Worst Lawyer," *Yale Law Journal* 103 (1994): 1835.

6. Elaine Scarry, *The Body in Pain: The Making and Unmaking of the World* (New York: Oxford University Press, 1995), 10.

7. Ibid.

8. Cover, "Violence and the Word," 1622–23. As Cover suggests, "Because in capital punishment the action or deed is extreme and irrevocable, there is pressure placed on the word—the interpretation that establishes the legal justification for the act. At the same time, the fact that capital punishment constitutes the most plain, the most deliberate, and the most thoughtful manifestation of legal interpretation as violence makes the imposition of the sentence an especially powerful test of the faith and commitment of the interpreters. . . . Capital cases, thus, disclose far more of the structure of judicial interpretation than do other cases."

9. Albert Camus, "Reflections on the Guillotine," in Albert Camus and Arthur Koestler, *Reflections on Capital Punishment* (Paris: Calmann-Levy, 1957), 127–238 contends that there is no real difference between capital punishment and murder.

10. Robert Paul Wolf, "Violence and the Law," in *The Rule of Law*, ed. Robert Paul Wolff (New York: Simon and Schuster, 1971), 59. Friedenberg contends that, "the police often slay; but they are seldom socially defined as murderers. Students who block the entrances to buildings or occupy a vacant lot and attempt to build a park in it are defined as not merely being disorderly but violent; the law enforcement officials who gas and club them into submission are perceived as restorers of order, as, indeed, they are of the *status quo ante* which was orderly by definition." Edgar Friedenberg, "The Side Effects of the Legal Process," in *The Rule of Law*, ed. Robert Paul Wolff (New York: Simon and Schuster, 1971), 43.

11. In addition to my observation of the Brooks trial I read the trial transcripts of twelve other capital cases that reached the penalty phase.

The themes of race, law, and violence that are so vividly exemplified in the Brooks trial are found in most of those other trials as well. One important difference was the quality of Brooks's defense team. Brooks's lawyers were highly regarded death penalty specialists. Throughout this chapter I refer to the lead counsel as Brooks's lawyer.

12. See Charles Lawrence, "The Id, the Ego and Equal Protection: Reckoning with Unconscious Racism," *Stanford Law Review* 39 (1987): 317, and Patricia Williams, *The Alchemy of Race and Rights* (Cambridge: Harvard University Press, 1991). According to Omolade, "For the West, the mythic power of skin color determines good and evil, guilt and innocence, ignorance and knowledge in the real lives of black and white people." Barbara Omolade, "Black Codes: Then and Now: The Central Park Jogger Case and Multiple Representations" (unpublished manuscript, City University of New York, 1991), 6.

13. Omolade, "Black Codes," 16. Here, of course, the first trial of the police officers who beat Rodney King provides a vivid example of the way state violence is portrayed as an acceptable tool in a racial struggle. See Patricia Williams, "The Rules of the Game," *Village Voice*, August 11, 1992, 32.

14. For a discussion of the importance of the victim's "innocence" in trials of sexual assault charges see Kristin Bumiller, "Fallen Angels: The Representation of Violence against Women in Legal Culture," *International Journal of the Sociology of Law* 18 (1990): 125.

15. But Heddie's testimony is equally potent in conveying an image of Janine's effort to distance her mother from danger and to calm her: "I'll be back. Don't worry." The daughter, in her own moment of danger, heroically becomes the mother to her mother. Fisher contends that in sentimental narratives such images of family life play key roles. See Philip Fisher, *Hard Facts: Setting and Form in the American Novel* (New York: Oxford University Press, 1985), 102.

16. For a vivid exemplification of the fear of such an attack, see *McQuirter v. State*, 63 So. 2d 388 (1953).

17. That affirmation came in the testimony of the medical examiner who had conducted the autopsy on Janine. It was his testimony that Janine "was a virgin prior to the attack."

18. Scarry, *The Body in Pain*, 10. As Korobkin reminds us, "The trial's structural embrace of multiplicity makes it difficult for either party to remain untarnished; even a verdict in one party's favor at the trial's end cannot wholly erase the shadows thrown on the victor's story by the

insistent adversariality of the process." Korobkin, "The Maintenance of Mutual Confidence," 45.

19. After the trial, Bright told me that "I think one of the classic mistakes that people make is to try to keep denying the statement or challenging the voluntariness of it even when it is clear that it is coming in. When they had Brooks admitting to the rape and the robbery and admitting to every other evil, criminal thing that he did and then they wanted to say he was just trying to explain it away. As you know, my argument was that if we accepted everything else we should credit the statement in its entirety. Lawyers should find ways to turn statements like the one Brooks gave to their own advantage. That is what we were trying to do."

20. In our discussions Bright also accused the prosecution of rhetorical excess, of making a terrible thing seem needlessly worse than it was. "Part of this process is integrity. Things are bad enough. Some of these things were embellished. Things are bad enough. They don't need to be embellished."

21. See Wayne Booth, *The Rhetoric of Fiction*, 2nd ed. (Chicago: University of Chicago Press, 1983).

22. Robin West, "Narrative, Responsibility and Death: A Comment on the Death Penalty Cases from the 1989 Term," *Maryland Journal of Contemporary Legal Issues* 1 (1990): 11.

23. Ibid.

24. Garfinkel, in his famous discussion of the "conditions of successful degradation ceremonies," gives us a way of seeing how William Brooks and his heinous act can be accommodated to a general scheme of preferences and values. Both Brooks and his act are treated as instances of a "type." The prosecutor's denunciation of Brooks as the type who would use another human being for his pleasure and then dispose of her invites the jury to identify with a "dialectical counterpart." Harold Garfinkel, "Conditions of Successful Degradation Ceremonies," *American Sociological Review* 61 (1956): 422. It is only, as Garfinkel argues, by the reference "it bears to its opposite" that the "profanity of an occurrence . . . is clarified." Indeed Garfinkel makes explicit reference to murder trials as examples of degradation ceremonies. "The features of the mad-dog murderer," he argues, "reverse the features of the peaceful citizen" (423).

25. West, "Narrative, Responsibility and Death," 15.

26. Stephen Carter, "When Victims Happen to Be Black," *Yale Law Journal* 97 (1988): 421.

27. Ibid., 426–27. The construction of this narrative is made all the more complex when, as in the Brooks case, the defense lawyer argues that the defendant did not do what he is accused of doing (malice murder) in the guilt or innocence phase of the trial, and then, in the penalty phase, shifts the frame to the alternative conception of violence and victimization in order to explain *why* the defendant did what the jury found him guilty of doing.

28. Robert Weisberg, "Deregulating Death," *Supreme Court Review* (1983): 361. Also James Doyle, "The Lawyers' Art: 'Representation' in Capital Cases," *Yale Journal of Law & the Humanities* 8 (1996): 417.

29. Fisher, *Hard Facts*, 121.

30. West, "Narrative, Responsibility and Death," 14.

31. For a general discussion of the nature of mercy, see Jeffrie Murphy and Jean Hampton, *Forgiveness and Mercy* (Cambridge: Cambridge University Press, 1988).

32. Weisberg, "Deregulating Death," 362.

33. Garfinkel, "Conditions of Successful Degradation Ceremonies," 423.

34. As Minow reminds us, the tendency to turn to narratives of victimization in criminal trials invites defendants to respond in kind. "In each instance," she says, "the claim that 'I'm a victim, and I'm not responsible' triggers a rejoinder, 'I'm a victim, and *I'm* not responsible." See Martha Minow, "Surviving Victim Talk," *UCLA Law Review* 40 (1993): 1429. This rejoinder in turn, fuels the efforts of the victims' rights movement discussed in chapter 2.

35. I arrived in Georgia in time to watch the jury being selected for the Brooks trial. Immediately the specter of state killing took center stage as the presiding judge, Judge Lawson, a stout, balding, serious-looking man, conducted voir dire. Lawson provided each potential juror with a brief overview of the procedure to be followed in the case.

> The defendant is charged with one count of malice murder and if he is convicted the state will seek the death penalty. This trial will take place in two stages. In the first phase guilt and innocence is the only question. If the defendant is found guilty there will be a second stage or sentencing hearing. At the conclusion of the sentencing hearing the jury decides between life and death. The jury's decision is final. In this state the death penalty is authorized in particularly aggravated circumstances. The death penalty can be imposed on more serious, more severe murders. Aggravating circumstances means more than being guilty of murder. But if the jury finds aggravating

circumstances it is not required to impose the death penalty. Imposition of
the death penalty is never mandatory. The defense is permitted to present
mitigating circumstances, that is, anything in mercy and fairness having to
do with the defendant or his background. Imposition of the death penalty
is never mandatory. Finally, I would instruct you that you are to draw no
inferences about the guilt or innocence of the defendant from the fact I have
given you these instructions.

These instructions introduce potential jurors to the prospect of imposing a death sentence before they have been empaneled and heard any
evidence. Because the death penalty is never mandatory, the potential
jurors at the outset would have to face the question of whether they
could, should circumstances warrant, impose death as a punishment. As
part of what is called the process of "death qualification," Lawson asked
each of the jurors, "Are you conscientiously opposed to the death penalty?" "If the state seeks the death penalty and you felt the death penalty
was justified would you be able to vote to impose it?"

36. As Garfinkel puts it, in a successful degradation ceremony "the
denounced person must be ritually separated from a place in the legitimate order. . . . He must be placed 'outside,' he must be made 'strange.'
The denouncer must arrange to be invested with the right to speak in
the name of those ultimate values. . . . The denouncer must get himself
so defined by the witnesses that they locate him as a supporter of those
values. Not only must the denouncer fix his own distance from the person being denounced, but the witnesses must be made to experience
their distance from him also." See Garfinkel, "Conditions of Successful
Degradation Ceremonies," 423.

37. When I later asked Brooks's defense lawyer to explain the verdict,
Bright suggested that "No jury is just going to let a guy walk away free
when he's responsible for another person dying. . . . But this is the kind
of thing that would cause a jury to compromise upon a penalty verdict.
I don't think they were sure that he [Brooks] really maliciously intended
this, but they could go and convict him of murder and then give him a
life sentence as a compromise." For an analysis of the jury deliberations
that led to this life sentence, see McFeely, *Proximity to Death*, 169–75.

38. Weisberg, "Deregulating Death," 361. Also Doyle, "The Lawyers'
Art."

39. Robert Weisberg, "Private Violence as Moral Action: The Law as
Inspiration and Example," in *Law's Violence*, ed. Austin Sarat and

Thomas R. Kearns (Ann Arbor: University of Michigan Press, 1992) 175–76.

40. Benjamin, "Critique of Violence," 286.

41. Dominick LaCapra, "Violence, Justice, and the Force of Law," *Cardozo Law Review* 11 (1990): 1065.

42. *McCleskey v. Kemp*, 481 U.S. 279, 313 (1987).

CHAPTER 5
THE RULE OF THE JURY IN STATE KILLING

1. For a discussion of contemporary controversies surrounding the jury, see Jeffrey Abramson, *We, The Jury: the Jury System and the Ideal of Democracy* (New York: Basic Books, 1994).

2. See *Spaziano v. Florida*, 468 U.S. 447, 490, 489 (1984).

3. As Justice Stewart said in *Woodson v. North Carolina*, 428 U.S. 280, 303–4 (1976), "death is a punishment different from all other sanctions in kind rather than degree."

4. Supreme Court decisions that have retreated significantly from this effort include *Blystone v. Pennsylvania*, 494 U.S. 299 (1990), and *Walton v. Arizona*, 497 U.S. 639 (1990).

5. Robert Weisberg, "Deregulating Death," *Supreme Court Review* (1983): 361.

6. Patrick Higginbotham "Juries and the Death Penalty," *Case Western Reserve Law Review* 41 (1991): 1048–49. Justice Stevens in *Spaziano* argues that "The authors of our federal and state constitutional guarantees recognized the special function of the jury in any exercise of plenary power over the life and liberty of the citizen" (490). See also Stephen Gillers, "Deciding Who Dies," *University of Pennsylvania Law Review* 129 (1980): 1.

7. Higginbotham "Juries and the Death Penalty," 1048–49.

8. Justice Stevens, dissenting in *Spaziano*, argued that because of the uniqueness of the death penalty "it is the one punishment that cannot be prescribed by a rule of law as judges normally understand such rules" (469). Agamben suggests that this capacity to be both inside and outside the law is a defining characteristic of sovereignty itself. See Giorgio Agamben, *Homo Sacer: Sovereign Power and Bare Life*, trans. Daniel Heller-Roazen (Stanford: Stanford University Press, 1998), 15.

9. See *Spaziano*, 480, 490.

10. In *Spaziano* the Court rejected a due process claim that defendants were constitutionally entitled to have a jury make sentencing determinations in capital cases. However, thirty of thirty-eight states with capital punishment now leave the life or death decision exclusively to the jury. See Vivian Berger, "'Black Box Decisions' on Life or Death—If They're Arbitrary, Don't Blame the Jury: A Reply to Judge Patrick Higginbotham," *Case Western Reserve Law Review* 41 (1991): 1067.

11. See *McGautha v. California*, 402 U.S. 183 (1970).

12. See Ibid., 185.

13. These two different responses have been a persistent feature of the Supreme Court's death penalty decision. For a critique of the Court's inability to choose definitively between them see Justice Scalia's concurrence in *Walton*, 497 U.S. 657–59.

14. See *McGautha*, 204.

15. Alexis de Tocqueville, *Democracy in America*, trans. Henry Reeve (Boston: John Allyn, 1876), 364.

16. *McGautha*, 208.

17. Ibid., 271.

18. Ibid., 248, 249. Brennan was, I think, prophetic in framing the debate about capital punishment as a debate about the rule of law itself. For an elaboration of his prophesy, see Justice Marshall's dissent in *Payne v. Tennessee*. See 501 U.S. 809, 844 (1991).

19. *Furman v. Georgia*, 408 U.S. 238, 245, 253 (1972).

20. Ibid., 402, 388.

21. See *Gregg v. Georgia* 428 U.S. 153, 189, 206 (1976).

22. Ibid., 193, 192, 198.

23. See, for example, *Pulley v. Harris*, 465 U.S. 37 (1984). Bowers, Sandys, and Steiner note that, "Instead of giving shape and force to these specific requirements, the Court has articulated broader, more amorphous constitutional standards." William Bowers, Marla Sandys, and Benjamin Steiner, "Foreclosed Impartiality in Capital Sentencing: Jurors' Predispositions, Guilt-Trial Experience, and Premature Decision-Making," *Cornell Law Review* 83 (1998): 1481.

24. See *McCleskey v. Kemp*, 481 U.S. 311 (1987).

25. Robert Cover, "Violence and the Word," *Yale Law Journal* 95 (1986): 1622.

26. Ibid., 1613, 1614.

27. Ibid., 1626.

28. Ibid., 1615.

29. See Joseph Hoffmann, "Where's the Buck? Juror Misperception of Sentencing Responsibility in Death Penalty Cases," *Indiana Law Journal* 70 (1995): 1156.

30. *Caldwell v. Mississippi*, 472 U.S. 320 (1985).

31. But in *Sawyer v. Smith*, 497 U.S. 227 (1990), the Court upheld a death sentence, although the jury had been told explicitly that it was not ultimately responsible for the sentence it imposed.

32. *Caldwell*, 330.

33. Ibid., 333.

34. Ibid., 331.

35. This is a pseudonym. In order to protect my respondents's confidentiality I have also used a pseudonym for the case I describe and for the jurors whose views I discuss.

36. One of the jurors in the Connors case explained how the police were able to link the money to the defendant. "In convenience stores they have several different kinds of detection devices that let them know that they're being robbed or going to be robbed or are in the process of being robbed. They have . . . I call it a panic button, a red button. You mash it and all these sirens go off. Some of them are silent, some of them send a signal directly to the police. In some they have the cash drawer arranged with ones, fives, tens, and they have a spot for what they call, not fake money, but mad money. They reach in and may grab this mad money. It is marked so they know when it is recovered. It's got a little sensor on the bottom and when the mad money is taken it goes off automatically signaling the police."

37. The Connors case was one of thirty Georgia cases I studied as part of a national study of jurors and the death penalty. One object of that study was to understand how jurors understand their role in capital trials and how they come to be enlisted as agents of state killing. In each of the Georgia cases four jurors were randomly selected and interviewed about the case; interviews lasted between two and five hours. See William Bowers and Benjamin Steiner, "Death by Default: An Empirical Demonstration of False and Forced Choices in Capital Sentencing," *Texas Law Review* 77 (1999): 643, for further details of the study from which these data are taken.

38. See Case No. 95, 973, Corrected Opinion (September 24, 1999), Supreme Court of Florida, Justice Shaw dissenting.

39. Luc Sante, *Evidence* (New York: Farrar, Straus, and Giroux, 1992), 60.

40. See *Garrett v. Estelle*, 556 F. 2d 1274 (5th Cir. 1974), cert. denied, 438 U.S. 914 (1978). Also *KQED v. Vasquez*, No. C-90–1383 RHS, 1991 U.S. Dist. LEXIS 19791 (N.D. Ca. 1991).

41. So pervasive and powerful is the attraction of victim talk that even those whose responsibility it is to respond to the victimization of others use it.

42. Sante, *Evidence*, 60. Kristin Bumiller has argued, referring to similar evidence in a rape trial, that the principle that ensures that the images of violence have such an effect is one of "maximum visibility." This principle "is applied by using the techniques of close-ups and editing made possible by staged film production to orient the spectator in the most ideal position for viewing pleasure. In the courtroom, the prosecutor and expert master . . . [the] body as technique rather than art; they make use of photographs . . . to stage repetitive viewings of parts of . . . [the] body. This technique fetishizes the wound." See Kristin Bumiller, "Real Violence/Body Fictions" (unpublished manuscript, Amherst College, Amherst, Mass., 1991), 9.

43. See Robin West, "Narrative, Responsibility and Death: A Comment on the Death Penalty Cases from the 1989 Term," *Maryland Journal of Contemporary Legal Issues* 1 (1990): 1, 11.

44. Ibid., 12.

45. Ibid.

46. Robin West, "Taking Freedom Seriously," *Harvard Law Review* 104 (1990): 91.

47. See Herbert Morris, "Persons and Punishment," in *Human Rights*, ed. A. I. Meldren (Belmont, Caif.: Wadsworth, 1970).

48. Cover, "Violence and the Word," 1628.

49. Benjamin Steiner, William Bowers, and Austin Sarat, "Folk Knowledge as Legal Action: Death Penalty Judgments and the Tenet of Early Release in a Culture of Mistrust and Punitiveness," *Law & Society Review* 33 (1999): 461.

50. See Stuart Scheingold, *The Politics of Law and Order: Street Crime and Public Policy* (New York: Basic Books, 1984), 64.

51. John M. Sloop has shown how this tendency has been reinforced in the public mind through accounts and portrayals of crime in the popular media over the past several decades. See *The Cultural Prison: Discourse, Prisoners, and Punishment* (Tuscaloosa: University of Alabama Press, 1998).

52. See Stuart Scheingold, "Criminology and the Politicization of Crime and Punishment," in *Politics, Crime Control, and Culture*, ed., Gerald Mars and David Nelken (Aldershot: Dartmouth/Ashgate, 1998), 8.

53. More than three decades of research demonstrates that the public sees courts as too lenient. See Julian Roberts, "Public Opinion, Crime, and Criminal Justice," in *Crime and Justice: A Review of Research*, ed. Michael Tonry (Chicago: University of Chicago Press, 1992), 31–57.

54. In Georgia, the Georgia State Board of Pardons and Paroles indicated that fifteen years is the minimum before parole consideration for murder I (offenders convicted of capital murder but not given the death penalty); offenders sentenced to life for other crimes may be paroled in seven years, but only 1 percent actually are, and murderers are underrepresented among that 1 percent. Anthony Paduano and Clive Stafford-Smith, "Deathly Errors: Juror Misperceptions Concerning Parole in the Imposition of the Death Penalty," *Columbia Human Rights Law Review* 18 (1987): 211.

55. The Parole Board's annual report for fiscal year 1985 indicated that only 1 percent (12 out of 949) of all life-sentenced inmates were released upon their first application after seven years, that class II (noncapital) murderers were less likely than other lifers to be paroled, and that none of those paroled were class I (capital) murderers. Paduano and Stafford-Smith, "Deathly Errors," 229.

56. Ga. Code Ann S 17–10–31.1.

57. The extent to which issues of crime and punishment are solidly anchored in cultural common sense or are politicized from above is an open question. Beckett argues that issues of crime and punishment get politicized from above. Katherine Beckett, *Making Crime Pay: Law and Order in Contemporary American Politics* (New York: Oxford University Press, 1997). For a similar view see Friedman. As he puts it, "From TV, and from the political pulpit, come messages that somehow play into the public lust for more and tougher punishment." Lawrence Friedman, "On Stage: Some Historical Notes about Criminal Justice," in *Social Science, Social Policy and the Law*, ed. Patricia Ewick, Robert Kagan, and Austin Sarat (New York: Russell Sage Foundation, 1999), 69.

58. The Horton advertisements blamed Dukakis for the occurrence of senseless, brutal crimes because of his alleged policy of letting serious violent offenders back into society far too soon. Kathleen Hall Jamieson demonstrated the substantial effect of these ads on the public's con-

sciousness of crime and punishment. Katherine Hall Jamieson, *Dirty Politics* (New York: Oxford University Press, 1992).

59. The Horton narrative provides both the underpinnings for a punitive response to social change and disorder, and the rationale for stereotyping and scapegoating categories or classes of people as the "criminal element." See Scheingold, *The Politics of Law and Order*, 226.

60. Jamieson, *Dirty Politics*, 134.

61. Such a claim also was recently recognized by Georgia's highest judicial authorities to be the prevailing cultural common sense. Georgia Supreme Court judge Charles Weltner is quoted as having said, "Everybody believes that a person sentenced to life for murder will be walking the streets in seven years." Apparently of little avail was State Parole Board chairman James T. Morris's response, "That's the greatest myth that's been perpetrated on the Georgia people, I blame the district attorneys and the judges of the state for putting it out." Mark Silk, "Juries Prefer Alternative to Death Penalty," *Atlanta Journal and Constitution*, July 3, 1996, B1.

62. See *California v. Brown*, 479 U.S. 538 (1987), *Franklin v. Lynaugh*, 487 U.S. 164 (1988), and *Penry v. Lynaugh*, 492 U.S. 302 (1989). For a detailed discussion of the Supreme Court's articulation of "reasoned moral choice" as one grounded foremost in retributive purposes of punishment, see Bowers and Steiner, "Death by Default," 622–27.

63. See Bowers, Sandys, and Steiner, "Foreclosed Impartiality."

64. Friedman, "On Stage," 81.

65. *Simmons v. South Carolina*, 512 U.S. 154 (1994).

66. The Court restricted the circumstances in which this is required to cases where the alternative was life with no chance of parole and the defendant was alleged to be dangerous in the future. In opposition to these restrictions, Justice Souter concurring in *Simmons*, wrote that the Eighth Amendment requirement of a heightened standard of reliability in capital sentencing requires that the judge unambiguously inform the jurors of the alternative to the death penalty whether or not future dangerousness is alleged and whether or not the alternative is life with no chance of parole.

67. See Lynn Chancer and Pamela Donavan, "A Mass Psychology of Punishment: Crime and the Futility of Rationally Based Approaches," *Social Justice* 21 (1994): 50. Thus, despite being told that a life sentence means life without parole by trial judges in California, only 18.4 percent of 152 capital jurors interviewed in California indicated that they believed capital murderers given a life sentence would usually spend

the rest of their lives in prison. See Bowers and Steiner, "Death by Default," 653, n. 20. As one of these jurors recounted, "the judge explained to me that if [the defendant] gets a life sentence there was absolutely no chance that he would get out. I thought he might get out. I don't trust anybody about it. You can do anything you want to if you're crooked enough or whatever." Ibid., 698. The tenaciousness of folk beliefs in early release is also evident in one of Jamieson's focus group members who reacted to information contradicting the Horton narrative with the quip, "Crime's not statistics, honey." Jamieson, *Dirty Politics*, 31–32.

CHAPTER 6
NARRATIVE STRATEGY AND DEATH PENALTY ADVOCACY

1. See Austin Sarat, "Between (the Presence of) Violence and (the Possibility of) Justice: Lawyering against Capital Punishment," in *Cause Lawyering: Political Commitments and Professional Responsibilities*, ed. Austin Sarat and Stuart Scheingold (New York: Oxford University Press, 1998), 317–48.

2. Interviews were conducted in ten states. One of those states is in the East; three are in the Midwest; four are in the South or Southwest, and two are in the West. Some of the lawyers I interviewed practiced in private firms or in public interest settings, but most were at the time of the interviews employed in federally funded Capital Defense Resource Centers. Interviews were from one to three hours in length. In order to protect the confidentiality of my sources I provide only minimal descriptive information about the people with whom I talked.

3. Jeremiah Donovan, "Some Off-the-Cuff Remarks about Lawyers as Storytellers," *Vermont Law Review* 18 (1994): 751.

4. See Robert Cover, "Violence and the Word," *Yale Law Journal* 95 (1986): 1604.

5. Robert Cover, "The Supreme Court, 1982 Term-Foreword: Nomos and Narrative," *Harvard Law Review* 97 (1983): 34.

6. Drucilla Cornell, "From the Lighthouse: The Promise of Redemption and the Possibility of Legal Interpretation," *Cardozo Law Review* 11 (1990): 1697. David Luban points to social protest movements as particularly important in this regard. "It is the narrative of social protest and moments of 'creative tension' that remind us of unkept promises

and of the moral emergency in which we live." See "Difference Made Legal: The Court and Dr. King," *Michigan Law Review* 87 (1989): 2224.

7. For a look at the work done by these lawyers and their vision of the future, see William McFeely, *Proximity to Death* (New York: Norton, 1999).

8. On the opposition between political and traditional lawyering, see Daniel Bell, "Serving Two Masters: Integration Ideals and Client Interests in School Desegregation Litigation," *Yale Law Journal* 85 (1976): 470. Also David Luban, *Lawyers and Justice: An Ethical Study* (Princeton: Princeton University Press, 1988), chap. 6.

9. Michael Meltsner, *Cruel and Unusual: The Supreme Court and Capital Punishment* (New York: Random House, 1973).

10. See Welch White, *The Death Penalty in the Nineties* (Ann Arbor: University of Michigan Press, 1992).

11. *Furman v. Georgia*, 408 U.S. 238 (1972).

12. Philip Kurland, "1971 Term: The Year of the Stewart-White Court," *Supreme Court Review* (1972): 296–97.

13. Quoted in Meltsner, *Cruel and Unusual*, 291.

14. Franklin Zimring and Gordon Hawkins, *Capital Punishment and the American Agenda* (Cambridge: Cambridge University Press, 1986), chap. 1, 2; quotation from p. 42.

15. See *Gregg v. Georgia* 428 U.S. 153, 179, 169 (1976).

16. See Michel Foucault, *Discipline and Punish: The Birth of the Prison*, trans. Alan Sheridan (New York: Vintage Books, 1977). Foucault writes that "Besides its immediate victim, the crime attacks the sovereign: it attacks him personally, since the law represents the will of the sovereign; it attacks him physically, since the force of the law is the force of the prince. . . . Punishment, therefore, cannot be identified with or even measured by the redress of injury; in punishment, there must always be a portion that belongs to the prince, and, even when it is combined with the redress laid down, it constitutes the most important element in the penal liquidation of the crime" (47–48).

17. See *State v. T Makwanyane and M Mchunu*, Constitutional Court of the Republic of South Africa, Case No. CCT/3/94 (1995).

18. United Nations Commission on Human Rights, United Nations Document CCPR/c/79, Add 50 (1995), para. 14.

19. See *State v. Moore*, Case No. 77CR-8676, Transcript of Motions Proceedings, Superior Court of Monroe County, McDonough, Georgia, September 28, 1995, 224. "And more recently, Your Honor, the Constitutional Court of South Africa—which I realize is not binding, obviously

on this Court, but is nevertheless persuasive authority from a highly respected court—unanimously agreed that the death penalty was unconstitutional under the South African Constitution." Also Supplemental Memorandum in Support of Motions to Bar the Death Penalty Because of Racial Discrimination, September 28, 1995, 29. "South Africa, like Georgia, has had capital punishment as part of its 'harsh legal heritage.' . . . Yet South Africa is moving forward to a new day, while Georgia remains tied to an outdated, racist and discredited form of punishment."

20. See Robert Weisberg, "Deregulating Death," *Supreme Court Review* (1983): 305. Also Anthony Amsterdam, "*In Favorem Mortis*: The Supreme Court and Capital Punishment," *Human Rights* 14 (1987): 14.

21. See *Teague v. Lane*, 489 U.S. 288 (1989), and *Penry v. Lynaugh*, 492 U.S. 302 (1989).

22. *Butler v. McKellar*, 494 U.S. 407 (1990).

23. See *Stringer v. Black*, 503 U.S. 334 (1992).

24. James Liebman, "More Than 'Slightly Retro': The Rehnquist Court's Rout of Habeas Corpus Jurisdiction in *Teague v. Lane*," *NYU Review of Law & Social Change* 18 (1990–91): 357; Steven Goldstein, "Chipping Away at the Great Writ: Will Death Sentenced Federal Habeas Corpus Petitioners Be Able to Seek and Utilize Changes in the Law?" *NYU Review of Law & Social Change* 18 (1990–91): 357.

25. Evan Caminker and Erwin Chemrinsky, "The Lawless Execution of Robert Alton Harris," *Yale Law Journal* 102 (1992): 226.

26. Michael Oreskes, "The Political Stampede on Execution," *New York Times*, April 4, 1990, A16. There are, of course, occasionally visible and sometimes successful campaigns to prevent an execution. One example is the effort on behalf of Mumia Abu-Jamal who is under death sentence in Pennsylvania. However, such campaigns serve as triage rather than as a sustained abolitionist movement.

27. Interpreting the Anti-Terrorism and Effective Death Penalty Act in a pair of cases with the same name (*Williams v. Taylor*, 120 S.Ct. 1479 [2000] and *William v. Taylor*, 120 S.Ct. 1495 [2000]), the Supreme Court decided that federal judges should intervene in state cases only when "clearly established" constitutional rights have been ignored. As one commentator observed, "The pair of rulings announced Tuesday set a moderately conservative standard for reviewing death penalty cases in federal courts. . . . With Justice Sandra Day O'Connor taking the lead, the high court [held that] the 1996 law 'places a new constraint' on the power of federal courts to take up appeals from state inmates. However, it does not close the door entirely. Federal judges should take up appeals

when they see state cases that 'involve an unreasonable application . . . of clearly established' constitutional standards." See David Savage, "Appeals Wrongly Denied in 2 Death Cases, Justices Say," *Los Angeles Times*, April 19, 2000, A20.

28. See *Gomez v. United States*, 503 U.S. 653 (1992) (castigating legal tactics of defense in death penalty appeals). For an important response, see Charles Sevilla and Michael Laurence, "Thoughts on the Cause of the Present Discontents: The Death Penalty Case of Robert Alton Harris," *UCLA Law Review* 40 (1992): 345.

29. This image is developed by Michael Mello, "Facing Death Alone: The Post-Conviction Attorney Crisis on Death Row," *American University Law Review* 37 (1988): 513.

30. As I noted earlier, Harris was the first person executed in California in the post-*Furman* era.

31. See *Gomez*, 654. For an important response, see Sevilla and Laurence, "Thoughts on the Cause of the Present Discontents," 345.

32. See Richard Abel, "Speaking Law to Power: Occasions for Cause Lawyering," in *Cause Lawyering: Political Commitments and Professional Responsibilities*, ed. Austin Sarat and Stuart Scheingold (New York: Oxford University Press, 1998), 69–117. Also Ronen Shamir, "Litigation as Consummatory Action: The Instrumental Paradigm Reconsidered," *Studies in Law, Politics and Society* 11 (1991): 41.

33. See *The Arabian Nights*, trans. Husain Haddawy (New York: Alfred A. Knopf, 1990).

34. "When I go to the king," Scheherazade told her sister, "I will send for you, and when you come and see that the king has finished with me, say, 'Sister, if you are not sleepy, tell us a story.' Then I will begin to tell a story, and it will cause the king to stop his practice (execution), save myself, and deliver the people." Ibid., 16.

35. For a discussion of realism, see Hayden White, *The Content of the Form: Narrative Discourse and Historical Representation* (Baltimore: Johns Hopkins University Press, 1987), 101–2. Also Robert Scholes and Robert Kellogg, *The Nature of Narrative* (New York: Oxford University Press, 1966), 85.

36. Scholes and Kellogg, *The Nature of Narrative*, 250.

37. Death penalty lawyers provide "the testimonial *bridge* which, mediating between narrative and history, guarantees their correspondence and adherence to each other. This bridging between narrative and history is possible since the narrator is both an *informed* and an *honest* witness. . . . All the witness has to do is to *efface himself*, and let the

literality of events voice its own *self-evidence*. 'His business is only to say: *this is what happened*, when he knows that it actually did happen.' " As Feldman argues, "To testify before a court of law or before the court of history and of the future. . . is more than simply to report a fact or an event or to relate what has been lived, recorded and remembered. Memory is conjured here essentially in order to address another, to impress upon a listener, to *appeal* to a community." Ibid., 204. See Shoshana Feldman and Dori Laub, *Testimony: Crises of Witnessing in Literature, Psychoanalysis, and History* (New York: Routledge, 1992), 101, 204.

38. Pierre Nora, "Between Memory and History: *Les lieux de memoire,"Representations* 26 (1989): 7. As Nora argues, "Modern memory is, above all, archival. It relies entirely on the materiality of the trace, the immediacy of the recording, the visibility of the image" (15).

39. See Bernard Jackson, "Narrative Models in Legal Proof," in *Narrative and the Legal Discourse: A Reader in Storytelling and the Law*, ed. David Papke (Liverpool: Deborah Charles Publications, 1991), 163.

40. Jim Thomas, "Prisoner Cases as Narrative," in *Narrative and the Legal Discourse*, ed. David Papke (Liverpool: Deborah Charles Publications, 1991), 243–44.

41. Scholes and Kellogg, *The Nature of Narrative*, 13.

42. Ibid. See also White, *The Content of the Form*, 20.

43. "Effective lawyering," Richard Sherwin argues,"requires sound narrative analysis. Examples include choice of imagery, and the associations that one's images conjure; choice of genre, and the narrative expectations that genre produces; choice of role for one's audience. . . . these and other strategic narrative considerations are hardly self-evident." See "The Narrative Construction of Legal Reality," *Vermont Law Review* 18 (1994): 681.

44. Welsh White,"Effective Assistance of Counsel in Capital Cases: The Evolving Standard of Care," *University of Illinois Law Forum* (1993): 361. Also James Doyle, "The Lawyers' Art: 'Representation' in Capital Cases," *Yale Journal of Law & the Humanities* 8 (1996): 426.

45. The emphasis on fact-intensive investigation is typically greatest in the context of efforts to obtain habeas corpus relief. Only by arguing that the mitigation stage was constitutionally deficient can death penalty lawyers assert the relevance of the new facts that their factual investigations so frequently turn up. They retell the story of the client to show the inadequacies of the story as it was originally presented to the sentencing jury.

46. One difficulty for death penalty lawyers is that in telling their clients' stories they must be careful to walk a fine line such that those clients are not made to appear so damaged as to seem beyond help or hope.

47. Here there are striking resemblances between appellate and post-conviction work and the lawyering that goes on in the penalty phase of capital trials. Many death penalty lawyers describe the crucial part of their work as coming after direct appeals have been exhausted in the process of relitigating the case in habeas review. They note that in making habeas claims under ineffective assistance claims they must reinvestigate the entire case to find what the trial counsel did not and to show its material connection to the result at trial. For them, the process of making a convincing argument for habeas relief is not unlike trying a case, with its attention to the vivid details of lives lived and choices made. See Robert Weisberg, "Deregulating Death," *Supreme Court Review* (1983): 361. In the penalty phase of the capital trial the "overall goal of the defense is to present a human narrative, an explanation of the defendant's apparently malignant violence as in some way rooted in understandable aspects of the human condition."

48. On the history of sentimentality as a narrative device, see Louis Bredvold, *The Natural History of Sensibility* (Detroit: Wayne State University Press, 1962), and Barbara Benedict, *Framing Feeling: Sentiment and Style in English Prose Fiction, 1745–1800* (New York: AMS Press, 1994). The capacity to effect the genre shift from horror to sentiment is, of course, deeply influenced by racial and gender considerations in the stories they tell. For example, the young black man raping an "innocent" white woman (see chapter 4 in this book) does not easily fit into the genre of sentimentality. Shirley Samuel, ed., *The Culture of Sentiment: Race, Gender, and Sentimentality* (New York: Oxford University Press, 1992).

49. Robert Gordon indicates that lawyers may frame the injustices they seek to record in one of three narrative styles. See "Undoing Historical Injustice," in *Justice and Injustice in Law and Legal Theory*, ed. Austin Sarat and Thomas R. Kearns (Ann Arbor: University of Michigan Press, 1996), 36. The first style Gordon calls "legalist." This narrative treats the injustices of the present as wrongs "done by specific perpetrators to specific victims." It stays within the frame of liberal legalism and describes present injustice in terms of the remedies that law itself, should it be willing, could easily supply. The second narrative also stays within the legalist mode though it involves what Gordon calls "broad

agency." In this narrative the history of injustice is a history of collective action taken by one *group* against another. The third narrative attributes injustice to "bad structures rather than bad agents. . . . This historical enterprise takes the form of a search for explanations rather than a search for villainous agents and attribution of blame" (37). In this third narrative, lawyers broaden the scope of inquiry by linking the particular injustices to which they are opposed with broader patterns of injustice and institutional practice.

50. See Louis Mink, "The Autonomy of Historical Understanding," *History and Theory* 5 (1966): 24.

51. Kim Lanc Scheppele, "Foreword: Telling Stories," *Michigan Law Review* 87 (1989): 2083–84.

52. Barbara Hernstein-Smith, "Narrative Versions, Narrative Theories," *Critical Inquiry* 7 (1980): 232, 234.

53. Hayden White, "The Narrativization of Real Events," *Critical Inquiry* 7 (1981): 794.

54. White, *The Content of the Form*, 20.

55. I am grateful to Lawrence Douglas for suggesting this way of thinking about the narrative strategy of death penalty lawyers.

56. Luhan, "Difference Made Legal," 2152.

57. As one relatively inexperienced death penalty lawyer said, "What I do is sort of making a narrative. I'm telling a story with page after page of facts which are put together to show the richness and complexity of my client's life, of the crime, and of the injustices of his trial. . . . This is the best way to win in court, and it is the best way to make sure that the story is not just pushed aside and forgotten. And if enough of these narratives get produced then maybe they won't be ignored when, say fifty years from now, people try to figure out why we were executing the people we were executing in the way we were doing it."

58. Yet McFeely suggests that this emphasis on the future as a way of understanding the work of death penalty lawyers is misplaced, that the emphasis on the future is available to those who are, "not in daily contact" with state killing, while for those who are, the immediacy of the present task is overwhelming. See McFeely, *Proximity to Death*, 173. As my analysis shows, however, McFeely has missed something crucial in the work of those fighting to end capital punishment.

59. Cover, "Nomos and Narrative," 34, 39.

60. This "democratic optimism" is shared by some students of capital punishment. As McFeely observes, "As overwhelming as seems the dominance of people who disagree with them, who demand and get exe-

cutions, this tiny band finally will not be beaten. . . . Their voices will herald . . . change." See McFeely, *Proximity to Death*, 186.

61. See *Furman*, 361, 363.

62. The reference here is to Justice Blackmun's dissent in *Callins v. Collins*, 510 U.S. 1141, 1143 (1994), one of the many cases in which the Supreme Court has refused to hear a constitutional challenge to state killing.

63. See Paul Ricoeur, "Narrative Time," *Critical Inquiry* 7 (1980): 169: "narrativity and temporality are closely related. . . . Indeed I take temporality to be that structure of existence that reaches language in narrativity and narrativity to be the language structure that has temporality as its ultimate referent."

CHAPTER 7
TO SEE OR NOT TO SEE

1. Wendy Lesser, *Pictures at an Execution: An Inquiry into the Subject of Murder* (Cambridge: Harvard University Press, 1993), 4.

2. Ibid., 57.

3. Michel Foucault, *Discipline and Punish: The Birth of the Prison*, trans. Alan Sheridan (New York: Vintage Books, 1977), 59–60, 63.

4. See John Bessler, *Death in the Dark: Midnight Executions in America* (Boston: Northeastern University Press, 1997), 72–75.

5. Foucault, *Discipline and Punish*, 9.

6. This is one reason why the decision by Justice Shaw (discussed in chapter 3) to publish photographs of the aftermath of the execution of Allen Lee Davis was so unusual.

7. Foucault, *Discipline and Punish*, 9.

8. I am grateful to Tom Dumm for suggesting this association.

9. Lesser, *Pictures at an Execution*, 1.

10. *KQED v. Vasquez*, No. C-90-1383 RHS, 1991 U.S. Dist. LEXIS 19791 (N.D. Cal. 1991).

11. Lesser, *Pictures at an Execution*, 7, 8.

12. Videotape of ABC *Nightline*, January 16, 17, 1995.

13. *Holden v. State of Minnesota*, 137 U.S. 483, 491 (1890).

14. Bessler, *Death in the Dark*, chap. 3. Also Michael Madow, "Forbidden Spectacle: Executions, the Public and the Press in Nineteenth Century New York," *Buffalo Law Review* 43 (1995): 461.

15. Warden Vasquez specifically addressed this issue when he said that he wanted the Harris execution to "be carried out with tactfulness and precision." See Lesser, *Pictures at An Execution*, 203. Also Mona Lynch, "The Disposal of Inmate #85271: Notes on a Routine Execution," *Studies in Law, Politics, and Society* 20 (2000): 3.

16. Susan Blaustein, "Witness to Another Execution," *Harper's*, May 1994, 53, 60–61.

17. See Roger Caillois, "The Sociology of the Executioner," in *The College of Sociology* (1937–39), ed. Denis Hollier, (Minneapolis: University of Minnesota Press, 1988), 234.

18. Richard Johnson, *Death Work: A Study of the Modern Execution Process* (Pacific Grove, Calif.: Brooks/Cole, 1990). As Blaustein notes about death by lethal injection, within a few minutes, "the show was over; the passage from life to death was horrifyingly invisible, a silent and efficient erasure." Blaustein "Witness to Another Execution," 61.

19. Ibid., 32.

20. See Gary Howells, Kelly Flanagan, and Vivian Hagan, "Does Viewing a Televised Execution Affect Attitudes toward Capital Punishment?" *Criminal Justice & Behavior* 22 (1995): 411.

21. *Garrett v. Estelle*, 556 F. 2d 1274, 1277 (5th cir. 1977).

22. Ibid., 1278.

23. Ibid.

24. Lesser, *Pictures at an Execution*, 39.

25. *Garrett*, 1278.

26. Ibid., 1279.

27. Of course not everyone agrees with this position. As Michael Schwartz, news director for KQED, put it, "I think a camera alone can provide a true and clear and complete and accurate picture that is unmediated by an individual's personal interpretation of the event." Quoted in Seth Rosenfeld, "Warden Afraid of Revenge on Guards If Execution on TV," *San Francisco Examiner*, March 28, 1991, A5.

28. It is almost as if Ainsworth were enacting a parody of a postmodern understanding in which signs and referents float free of one another.

29. *Garrett*, 1279–80.

30. Lesser, *Pictures at an Execution*, 170.

31. Foucault, *Discipline and Punish*, 59.

32. Lesser, *Pictures at an Execution*, 141.

33. Ibid., 139.

34. Ibid., 142.

35. Ibid., 17, 18. Real-life murder tales, for Lesser, seem inadequate compared with fiction, for they fail to provide a sense of closure. More important, however, they often fail to pay the proper homage to their subject.

36. Here she replays the objections to public executions of reformers in the nineteenth century. See Lewis Mazur, *Rites of Execution: Capital Punishment and the Transformation of American Culture, 1776–1865* (New York: Oxford University Press, 1989), chap. 5.

37. The question of whether mediated representation of execution allows vision without involvement is the subject of the film, *Somebody Has to Shoot the Picture.* In this film a photojournalist who is asked to photograph an execution becomes caught up in last-minute efforts to save the condemned. *Somebody Has to Shoot the Picture,* MCA Universal, Frank Pierson, director, 1990.

38. Lesser, *Pictures at an Execution,* 141.

39. See Bessler, *Death in the Dark,* 175. In the end, in neither case was the execution televised. Courts more typically refuse requests to televise executions. See, for example, *Philadelphia Newspapers, Inc. v. Jerome,* 387 2d 425 (Pa. 1978), appeal dismissed for want of a federal question, 443 U.S. 913 (1979); *Halquist v. Department of Corrections,* 783 P. 2d 1065 (Wash. 1989); *Lawson v. Dixon,* 25 F. 3d 1040 (4th Cir. 1994).

40. *Houchins v. KQED,* 438 U.S. 1, 17 (1977).

41. Moreover, Justice Stevens in his *Houchins* dissent, 36, noted that "While prison officials have an interest in the time and manner of public acquisition of information about the institutions they administer, there is no legitimate penological justification for concealing from citizens the conditions in which their fellow citizens are being confined. The reasons which militate in favor of providing special protection to the flow of information to the public about prisons relate to the unique function they perform in a democratic society."

42. *Cable News Network v. American Broadcast Cos.,* 518 F. Supp. 1238, 1245 (N.D. Ga. 1981).

43. See *Zacchini v. Scripps-Howard Broadcasting,* 433 U.S. 562, 581 (1977).

44. Quoted in Jef Richards and R. Bruce Easter, "Televising Executions: The High-Tech Alternative to Public Hangings," *UCLA Law Review* 40 (1992): 391. When Patel eventually made her decision on the merits of the constitutional challenge to the use of gas as a method of

execution, she made no reference at all to the videotape of the Harris execution. See *Fierro v. Gomez*, 865 F. Supp. 1387 (1994).

45. *In re Thomas*, 155 F.R.D. 124, 125 (D. Md. 1994).

46. Ibid., 126, 127.

47. For a general examination of the power of visual images see Robert Schwartz, "The Power of Pictures," *Journal of Philosophy* 82 (1985): 711. William Turner and Beth Brinkmann argue that, "In the reporting of state executions, television is indispensable in allowing the public to see and hear, for themselves, what a witness sees and hears, as opposed to having the information filtered through a reporter who may or may not be able to convey, in words, a sense of what the execution looked and sounded like." William Turner and Beth Brinkmann, "Televising Executions: The First Amendment Issues," *Santa Clara Law Review* 32 (1992): 1135, 1153.

48. See Stanley Cavell, *Themes Out of School: Effects and Causes* (San Francisco: North Point, 1984), and Todd Gitlin, ed., *Watching Television* (New York: Pantheon, 1986).

49. Avital Ronell, *Finitude's Score: Essays for the End of the Millennium* (Lincoln: University of Nebraska Press, 1994), 317–27.

50. Lesser, *Pictures at an Execution*, 211, 38, 39.

51. See Tom Dumm, *united states* (Ithaca: Cornell University Press, 1994), 178.

52. Ibid., 182–83.

53. Ronell, *Finitude's Score*, 308.

54. Lesser, *Pictures at an Execution*, 100.

55. V.A.C. Gatrell, *The Hanging Tree: Execution and the English People, 1770–1868* (New York: Oxford University Press, 1994), 601.

56. Lesser, *Pictures at an Execution*, 134.

57. Ibid., 10, 42.

58. See Lesser, *Pictures at an Execution*, chap. 2.

59. See Foucault, *Discipline and Punish*, 50.

60. Bessler, *Death in the Dark*, 207.

61. See Michel Foucault, *The History of Sexuality*, vol. 1, trans. Robert Hurley (New York: Vintage Books, 1980), 133–59.

62. Ibid., 138.

63. Roland Barthes, *Camera Lucida: Reflections on Photography*, trans. Richard Howard (New York: Hill and Wang, 1981), 79, 80.

64. Kate Millett, *The Politics of Cruelty: An Essay on the Literature of Political Imprisonment* (New York: W. W. Norton, 1994), 153.

65. See Richards and Easter, "Televising Executions" 417.

66. Is the executioner—even a state employee—a member of the public whom the state permits to manifest a dark wish to see another person die?" See "Public Executions," *Hastings Constitutional Law Quarterly* 19 (1992): 413, 455.

67. Foucault, *Discipline and Punish*, 10.

CHAPTER 8
STATE KILLING IN POPULAR CULTURE

1. Friedrich Nietzsche, *The Birth of Tragedy and the Genealogy of Morals*, trans. Francis Golffing (Garden City, N.Y.: Doubleday, 1956), 211–16, 189.

2. For a useful discussion of the significance of these moral tenets and legal doctrines, see Jennifer Culbert, "Beyond Intention: A Critique of 'Normal' Criminal Agency, Responsibility, and Punishment in American Death Penalty Jurisprudence," in *The Killing State: Capital Punishment in Law, Politics, and Culture*, ed. Austin Sarat (New York: Oxford University Press, 1999), 206–25.

3. H.L.A. Hart, *Punishment and Responsibility: Essays in the Philosophy of Law* (Oxford: Clarendon Press, 1968). Hart claims that "all civilized penal systems make liability to punishment for . . . serious crime dependent not merely on the fact that the person to be punished has done the outward act of a crime, but on his having done it in a certain state or frame of mind or will" (114).

4. Sir William Blackstone, *Commentaries on the Laws of England*, vol. 2, ed. William Carey Jones (Baton Rouge, La.: Claitor's Publishing, 1976), 2175. Also Aristotle, *Nicomachean Ethics*, trans. W. D. Ross, (Oxford: Clarendon, 1925), book v, chap. 8. In the modern law of criminal responsibility the language of vicious will or depraved state of mind has receded. More often, criminal intent is framed as a question of fact, the relevant issue being whether the defendant had knowledge of the likely consequences of the prohibited nature of his act. See George Fletcher, *Rethinking the Criminal Law* (Boston: Little, Brown, 1978), 397.

5. William Connolly, "The Will, Capital Punishment, and Cultural War," in *The Killing State: Capital Punishment in Law, Politics, and Culture*, ed. Austin Sarat (New York: Oxford University Press, 1999), 7.

6. Lawrence Friedman, *Crime and Punishment in American History* (New York: Basic Books, 1993), 445.

7. I make no claims here about the representativeness of these films. My purpose is to read them as cultural productions. Yet it might be worth noting that two of the films (*Last Dance*, Touchstone Pictures. Bruce Beresford, director, 1996; and *Dead Man Walking*, Polygram Filmed Entertainment, Tim Robbins, director, 1996) are examples of one type of death penalty film that I label the sentimental tale. These films focus on a biographical or autobiographical reconstruction of the condemned, raising questions of responsibility, and repentance. The other (*The Green Mile*, Warner Brother, Frank Darabout, director, 1999) is what I label an injustice tale, taking as its central thematic the question of whether the condemned is really guilty, that is, whether an innocent person will be executed. (The classic of this genre is *I Want to Live*.)

8. See, for example, Michael Tonry, *Malign Neglect: Race, Crime, and Punishment in America* (New York: Oxford University Press, 1995).

9. Connolly, "The Will, Capital Punishment, and Culture War." See also Wendy Brown, *States of Injury: Power and Freedom in Late Modernity* (Princeton: Princeton University Press, 1995) and Homi Bhabha, "Anxiety in the Midst of Difference," *Critical Inquiry* 3 (1997): 1–29.

10. The very title of the film *Dead Man Walking* invites the viewer to imagine the impossible—a dead man walking—and conveys the undecidability of death in the sense that death row inmates are described as dead men before they are actually put to death. I am grateful to Susan Schmeiser for pointing this out to me.

11. Wendy Lesser, *Pictures at an Execution: An Inquiry into the Subject of Murder* (Cambridge: Harvard University Press, 1993).

12. As I argued in chapter 7, the public has a right to see state killing. While sight may inspire resistance and help transfer the locus of control, the viewer should not be taken in by the apparent transparency of any set of representations of state killing.

13. Others have pointed toward such a reading of *Dead Man Walking*. "The movie *Dead Man Walking* . . . fails to deliver the same unequivocal abolitionist punch as the book. . . . viewers are torn about whether or not this is even a film with an anti-capital punishment point of view." See Carole Shapiro, "Do or Die: Does *Dead Man Walking* Run?" *University of San Francisco Law Review* 30 (1996): 1144.

14. Shapiro contends that *Dead Man Walking* "leaves the audience clueless about the systematic inequities and arbitrariness" of the death penalty. See Shapiro, "Do or Die," 1145.

15. Stuart Scheingold, *The Politics of Law and Order: Street Crime and Public Policy* (New York: Longman, 1984), 66. Also Friedman, *Crime and Punishment in American History*.

16. See *Morisette v. United States*, 342 U.S. 246, 250 (1952).

17. Stephen Carter, "When Victims Happen to Be Black," *Yale Law Journal* 97 (1988): 421.

18. Ibid., 426.

19. Robert Gordon, "Undoing Historical Injustice," in *Justice and Injustice in Law and Legal Theory*, ed. Austin Sarat and Thomas R. Kearns (Ann Arbor: University of Michigan Press, 1996), 38.

20. Such stories are precisely the kind that defense lawyers in capital cases typically deploy in the penalty phase. See James Doyle, "The Lawyer's Art: 'Representation' in Capital Cases," *Yale Journal of Law & the Humanities* 8 (1996): 428–34.

21. Many death penalty films are structured around the relationship of the condemned and another person who befriends him or takes up his cause. In these films we are invited to see the condemned through that person. Harding contends that "these secondary characters are pivotal" in that they are often able to see the human face behind the monstrous deed that brings someone to death row. See Roberta Harding, "Celluloid Death: Cinematic Depictions of Capital Punishment," *University of San Francisco Law Review* 30 (1996): 1172.

22. See Alison Young, "Murder in the Eyes of the Law," *Studies in Law, Politics, and Society* 17 (1997): 44–45.

23. See Philip Fisher, *Hard Facts: Setting and Form in the American Novel* (New York: Oxford University Press, 1985), 108.

24. This moment is a reminder of the stark fact that when law runs out, sitting just beyond law is the power to pardon, a plenary power of the executive. See Kathleen Dean Moore, *Pardons: Justice, Mercy, and the Public Interest* (New York: Oxford University Press, 1989). The haunting specter of executive clemency depends on the will of a single person, who sits as an omnipotent force with the power to grant, or save, life. To enlist this power, as Davis reminds us, requires the fashioning of persuasive narratives, narratives of the kind that Rick tries to provide for the governor. See Natalie Zemon Davis, *Fiction in the Archives: Pardon Tales and Their Tellers in Sixteenth Century France* (Stanford: Stanford University Press, 1987). Yet, as *Last Dance* so vividly demonstrates, no narrative can guarantee clemency.

25. This is, of course, the classic anti–capital punishment argument made by Albert Camus, "Reflections on the Guillotine," in Albert

Camus and Arthur Koestler, *Reflections on Capital Punishment* (Paris: Calmann-Levy, 1957) 127–238.

26. A truth is revealed to the film's viewers that was not available at her trial since evidence of her use of crack before the crime was suppressed by an incompetent judge during the penalty phase of her trial.

27. On the transformation of Karla Faye Tucker, see Beverly Lowry, "The Good Bad Girl," *New Yorker*, February 9, 1998.

28. In so doing Cindy plays out a powerful theme in contemporary legality. The more law is challenged by theories that question prevailing conceptions of responsibility (for one example, see Thomas Dumm, *Democracy and Punishment: Disciplinary Origins of the United States* [Madison: University of Wisconsin Press, 1987], 7–11), the more it seeks to affirm "that an individual is completely responsible for his actions. . . . [Law] needs an autonomous, rational, self-determining individual to assume the position of the cause of events that disrupt the pattern of everyday life in an ordered society. And, it must affirm this figure without skepticism." Culbert, "Beyond Intention," 29.

29. Peter Brooks, "Storytelling without Fear? Confession in Law and Literature," in *Law's Stories: Narrative and Rhetoric in the Law*, ed. Peter Brooks and Paul Gewirtz (New Haven: Yale University Press, 1996), 115.

30. As Shapiro contends, "the confession is, in fact, the pivot on which the movie balances. . . . It might also be said that without the confession, *Dead Man Walking* would give viewers little reason for opposing the execution since this sympathy is largely dependent upon the defendant's act of contrition." Shapiro, "Do or Die," 1153.

31. The film presents a transposition from the verbal to the visual where the verbal is at least initially given priority as an accurate rendition of events. On the significance of such transpositions, see Carol Emerson, *Boris Godunov: Transpositions of a Russian Theme* (Bloomington: Indiana University Press, 1986), chap. 1.

32. Fisher notes that "The tears that are so important a part of sentimentality are best understood in this context. Weeping is a sign of powerlessness. Tears represent the fact that only a witness who cannot effect action will experience suffering as deeply as the victim." Fisher, *Hard Facts*, 108.

33. William Connolly, *The Ethos of Pluralization* (Minneapolis: University of Minnesota Press, 1995), 47.

34. Ibid., 45.

35. For a different reading of this scene see Jennifer Culbert, "America's Affair with Capital Punishment: Love, Sex, and Redemption in 'Dead Man Walking'" (unpublished manuscript, Amherst College, Amherst, Mass., 1999).

36. Fisher, *Hard Facts*, 93.

37. Laura Hanft Korobkin, "The Maintenance of Mutual Confidence: Sentimental Strategies at the Adultery Trial of Henry Ward Beecher," *Yale Journal of Law & the Humanities* 7 (1995): 45.

38. Peter Fitzpatrick, "'Always More to Do': Capital Punishment and the (De)Composition of Law," in *The Killing State: Capital Punishment in Law, Politics, and Culture*, ed. Austin Sarat (New York: Oxford University Press, 1999), 12.

39. Peter Brooks, "The Overborne Will," *Representations* 64 (1998): 10, 12.

40. Harding suggests that "By alternating shots between the dying Matthew and the victims the film maker poses many questions to the audience. The physical position of Matthew's body resembles that of his victims. Does that mean that Matthew is also a victim? Is it done to tell us that this penalty is acceptable by reminding us of the victims as their killer is dying? Or, does it mean that the death penalty is futile because all that has been accomplished is the taking of three lives instead of two?" See "Celluloid Death," 1176. In addition, Shapiro argues that "the movie indicates that Poncelet confesses and is redeemed only *because* of his death sentence." See "Do or Die," 1153.

41. Polly Klaas was twelve years old when she was kidnaped at knife point from her bedroom slumber party on October 1, 1993, in the small town of Petaluma, California. On July 29, 1994, Megan Kanka, a seven-year-old child, was abducted, raped, and murdered near her home. The man who confessed to Megan's murder lived in a house across the street from the Kanka family and had twice been convicted of sex offenses involving young girls. Megan, her parents, local police, and the members of the community were unaware of the accused murderer's history; nor did they know that he shared his house with two other men who also had been convicted of sex offenses.

42. For another example of this phenomena in film, see *Somebody Has to Shoot the Picture*, MCA Universal, Frank Pierson, director, 1990, in which the question of whether an execution can be photographed provides the backdrop for the story.

43. Colin McCabe, "Theory and Film; Principles of Realism and Pleasure," in *Narrative, Apparatus, Ideology: A Film Theory Reader*, ed. Philip Rosen (New York: Columbia University Press, 1986), 180.

44. Ron Steffey, "Witness for the Condemned," *Virginia Quarterly Review* 69 (1993): 607. Also Susan Blaustein, "Witness to Another Execution," *Harper's*, May 1994, 53.

45. But perhaps the distinction between witness and viewer is less stark than it might at first seem. As Steffey says about his own witnessing of an actual electrocution, "This has to be a Charles Bronson movie. . . . My thoughts even have trouble distinguishing whether tonight was another Bronson movie or reality." Steffey, "Witness for the Condemned," 614, 618.

46. Catherine Russell, *Narrative Mortality: Death, Closure, and New Wave Cinemas* (Minneapolis: University of Minnesota Press, 1995), 7–8. Russell suggests that, "As a symbolic act, the representation of death in film upholds the law of the text: the believability of the image. Insofar as this belief depends on the denial of the film's celluloid status, its twenty-four-frames-a-second 'mortal' state, the illusion of reality sustains itself through a strict censorship of this reminder."

47. Fitzpatrick, "'Always More to Do,'" 5–6.

48. This effort may also explain Justice Shaw's use of photographs in his *Provenzano* opinion.

49. Robert Cover, "Violence and the Word," *Yale Law Journal* 95 (1986): 1623.

50. For an interesting analysis of this public outrage and its translation into judicial opinions, see Anthony Amsterdam, "Selling a Quick Fix for Boot Hill: The Myth of Justice Delayed in Death Cases," in *The Killing State: Capital Punishment in Law, Politics, and Culture*, ed. Austin Sarat (New York: Oxford University Press, 1999), 148–86.

51. Laura Mulvey, "Visual Pleasure and Narrative Cinema," in *Narrative, Apparatus, Ideology: A Film Theory Reader*, ed. Philip Rosen (New York: Columbia University Press, 1986), 201.

52. Cindy Liggitt dies with a single gasp, her face reflected in the glass through which Rick and we see her death. She dies in his eyes and through him in ours. Death is given its meaning, death redeemed, through acts of viewing. However, unlike Rick, whose presence is crucial to Cindy, the audience to the film of an execution "becomes . . . a non-existent presence, an invisible crowd of spectators who yield up

nothing on behalf of the performer." Lesser, *Pictures at an Execution*, 205.

53. Ibid., 60.

54. Fitzpatrick, " 'Always More to Do,' " 3.

55. Russell, *Narrative Mortality*, 48.

56. As Carol Clover notes, "Anglo-American movies are already trial like to begin with. . . . the plot structures and narrative procedures . . . of a broad stripe of American popular culture are derived from the structure and procedures of the Anglo-American trial, . . . this structure and these procedures are so deeply embedded in our narrative tradition that they shape plots that never step into a courtroom." Carol Clover, "Law and the Order of Popular Culture," in *Law in the Domains of Culture*, ed. Austin Sarat and Thomas Kearns (Ann Arbor: University of Michigan Press, 1998), 99.

57. The shouting of the demonstrators is contrasted with the cool dispassion of the death squad that manages Cindy during her execution. In addition, a close-up of two nuns carrying signs that say "Thou Shalt Not Kill" suggests the ironic indeterminacy of a message that could apply with equal force either to Liggitt or to the state that is about to kill her.

58. Connolly, "The Will, Capital Punishment, and Culture War," 16.

59. Yet there are at least two suggestions to the contrary that call into question the realism on which the films depend. First, as I have already noted, is the juxtaposition of the past and present, the embodied and the spectral in the execution scenes of *Dead Man Walking*. Second is the description that Poncelet provides to Sister Helen of the way lethal injection works, with the first chemical designed to tranquilize such that the horrible physical effects of the remaining chemicals are not registered on the body of the condemned.

In this description we are reminded that the visual field of the modern execution, the fact that there is "nothing to see," depends on a technologically induced condition. Yet it is another such condition, film itself, with its angles, pans, and close-ups, that produces the illusion that seeing is knowing, that to see an execution enacted in film is to know the meaning of death at the hands of the state. See Stephen Heath, "Narrative Space," in *Narrative, Apparatus, Ideology: A Film Theory Reader*, ed. Philip Rosen (New York: Columbia University Press, 1986), 379–420.

60. Russell, *Narrative Mortality*, 23. The "violent deaths" to which Russell refers apply both to the death of the victims and to the executions in *Last Dance* and *Dead Man Walking*.

CHAPTER 9
CONCLUSION

1. Punitive responses to crime are themselves symptomatic of "a post-liberal state unable to maintain the economic and social conditions that minimize crime and maximize the well being of the society as a whole. Incapable of building a truly inclusive society and thus being vulnerable to various kinds of disorder, the state turns to punishment, exclusion, and the 'new penology' to maintain its grip on power." See William Lyons and Stuart Scheingold, "The Politics of Crime and Punishment" (unpublished manuscript, University of Washington, Seattle, 1999), 17.

2. As Minow notes, "Talk of victims tends to divide the world into only two categories: victims and victimizers. No one wants to be a victimizer, so potential victimizers try to recast themselves as victims. It becomes a world of only two identities, which essentially reduce to one characteristic, that of helpless victim." See Martha Minow, "Surviving Victim Talk," UCLA Law Review 40 (1993): 1433.

3. William Connolly, "The Will, Capital Punishment, and Cultural War," in The Killing State. Capital Punishment in Law, Politics, and Culture, ed. Austin Sarat (New York: Oxford University Press, 1999), 200.

4. Ibid.

5. Eric Zorn argues that "Proponents of the death penalty have successfully turned the very weakness of their position into its primary strength—that is to say that, with only emotion on their side, they have managed to make this an almost exclusively emotional issue. . . . There needs to be thunder in the voices of the opposition; the arguments must be made louder and longer—they must be attacks, not defenses. It's absurd that those who oppose this extraordinary and useless practice are playing defense instead of offense." "How to Win the Death Penalty Argument," speech before the Illinois Coalition against the Death Penalty (November 1994), 1–2.

6. Connolly, "The Will," 200–201.

7. See Albert Camus and Arthur Koestler, Reflections on Capital Punishment (Paris: Calmann–Levy, 1957).

8. Hugo Adam Bedau, Death Is Different: Studies in the Morality, Law, and Politics of Capital Punishment (Boston: Northeastern University Press, 1987).

9. See *Furman v. Georgia*, 408 U.S. 405, 290 (1972), Justice Brennan concurring.

10. George Kateb, *The Inner Ocean: Individualism and Democratic Culture* (Ithaca: Cornell University Press, 1992) 191–92.

11. Bedau, *Death Is Different.*

12. For one example of the retributivist rationale, see Walter Berns, *For Capital Punishment: Crime and the Morality of the Death Penalty* (New York: Basic Books, 1979).

13. The catalog immediately drew its share of criticism. Victims' advocates protested that it glamorized killers and ignored their crimes. Sears, Roebuck & Co. terminated an agreement to sell a line of Benetton clothes, saying that *We, on Death Row* was "terribly insensitive." The attorney general of Missouri, one of the states where Benetton was given permission to photograph, sued the company for fraud, alleging that it misrepresented its intentions and is using the catalog for commercial purposes. While Benetton's effort deserves to be criticized on all these counts, it is also a step backward for the cause it seeks to advance. It asks its readers to identify, or at least sympathize, with those on death row, reminding us that whatever they have done they have the capacity to love and be loved, to hope and fear, to laugh, and to repent. There is no reason to think that another such effort, no matter how glamorous or powerful its sponsor, will succeed. Indeed, there is reason to fear that it will distract attention from the issues that today may be changing attitudes toward the death penalty.

14. See Lyons and Scheingold, "The Politics of Crime and Punishment," 1.

15. See *Callins v. Collins*, 510 U.S. 1141, 1145 (1994).

16. *Furman, 410.*

17. *See Jeffrey King, "Now Turn to the Left: The Changing Ideology of Justice Harry A. Blackmun," Houston Law Review* 33 (1996): 297, 296. Also Randall Coyne, "Marking the Progress of a Humane Justice: Harry Blackmun's Death Penalty Epiphany," *University of Kansas Law Review* 43 (1995): 367.

18. See Carol Steiker and Jordan Steiker, "Sober Second Thoughts: Reflections on Two Decades of Constitutional Regulation of Capital Punishment," *Harvard Law Review* 109 (1995): 355.

19. *Callins,* 1144.

20. Ibid., 1157.

21. Ibid., 1145.

22. Recommendation 107, ABA House of Delegates, February 3, 1997. In May 2000, the president of the American Bar Association called on President Clinton to declare a moratorium on the federal death penalty and urged a "comprehensive examination of the federal death penalty that would not be limited to the question of racial discrimination." See Raymond Bonner, "Charges of Bias Challenge U.S. Death Penalty," *New York Times*, June 24, 2000, A1, A7.

23. Ibid.

24. Stephen Bright, "Counsel for the Poor: The Death Sentence Not for the Worst Crime, But for the Worst Lawyer," *Yale Law Journal* 103 (1994): 1835.

25. Charlotte Holdman, "Is There Any *Habeas* Left in This *Corpus*?" *Loyola University of Chicago Law Journal* 27 (1996): 524.

26. Report of the ABA. Submitted with Recommendation 107, 5.

27. Ibid., 11.

28. See Michael Radelet, Hugo Adam Bedau, and Constance Putnam, *In Spite of Innocence: Erroneous Convictions in Capital Cases* (Boston: Northeastern University Press, 1992).

29. See *Herrera v. Collins*, 506 U.S. 390, 399 (1993).

30. Ibid., 417.

31. Report of the ABA, 13.

32. David Baldus, George Woodworth, and Charles Pulaski, *Equal Justice and the Death Penalty: A Legal and Empirical Analysis* (Boston: Northeastern University Press, 1990).

33. See Samuel Gross and Robert Mauro, *Death and Discrimination: Racial Disparities in Capital Sentences* (Boston: Northeastern University Press, 1989).

34. Report of the ABA, 14.

35. *Callins*, 1154–55.

36. See "The Death Penalty on Trial," *Newsweek*, June 12, 2000, 26.

37. "The New Death Penalty Politics," *New York Times*, June 7, 2000, A22.

38. These developments are discussed in Barry Scheck, Peter Neufeld, and Jim Dwyer, *Actual Innocence* (New York: Random House, 2000).

39. Dirk Johnson, "Illinois, Citing Faulty Verdicts, Bars Executions," *New York Times*, February 1, 2000, A1.

40. Dirk Johnson, "No Executions in Illinois until System Is Repaired," *New York Times*, May 21, 2000, A12.

41. "New Looks at the Death Penalty," *New York Times*, February 19, 2000, A21.

42. The Innocence Protection Act of 2000 (S.2073) was introduced in the Senate by Senator Leahy of Vermont on February 10, 2000.

43. The National Death Penalty Moratorium Act of 2000 (S. 2463) was introduced by Senators Feingold of Wisconsin and Levin of Michigan on April 26, 2000.

44. Rachel Collins, "N.H. Senate OK's Death Penalty Ban," *Boston Globe*, May 19, 2000, B1,

45. John Kifner, "A State Votes to End Its Death Penalty," *New York Times*, May 19, 2000, A8.

46. See, for example, "The Death Penalty on Trial," 28.

47. Statement by Senator Russell Feingold introducing the Federal Death Penalty Abolition Act of 1999, November 10, 1999 <http://www.senate.gov/%7Efeingold/feddp.html>.

INDEX